D0258075

UNIVERSITY OF MICHIGAN EDUCATION MONOGRAPHS, NUMBER 3

COMMUNITY WORKSHOPS FOR TEACHERS IN THE

MICHIGAN COMMUNITY HEALTH PROJECT

# COMMUNITY WORKSHOPS

## FOR TEACHERS IN THE

## MICHIGAN COMMUNITY HEALTH PROJECT

BY

### HENRY J. OTTO
*Graduate Professor of Elementary Administration and Curriculum
University of Texas*

### J. DARRELL BARNARD
*Professor of Secondary Education, Colorado State College
of Education*

### VIVIAN V. DRENCKHAHN
*Lecturer in Education, University of Michigan*

### FRED A. MILLER
*Instructor in Education, University of Chicago*

### WILLIAM G. WOODS
*Assistant Dean of Men, North Texas State Teachers College*

### UNIVERSITY OF MICHIGAN PRESS
### ANN ARBOR, MICHIGAN

COPYRIGHT 1942 BY THE

UNIVERSITY OF MICHIGAN PRESS

*Composed and Printed in the United States of America*

G.14577

# FOREWORD

Recently, discussions in educational circles have increasingly emphasized the importance of more generous use of community resources in the total program of education for children, youth, and adults. Although some highly instructive demonstrations of ways to use such resources have been made, more are necessary, before the idea of the community-centered school is widely accepted. This monograph presents an account of four summer workshops in which the use of community resources was given major emphasis. These workshops were provided during the summer of 1941 for teachers in the seven counties of Western Michigan that constitute the area of the Michigan Community Health Project. Two of the workshops were under the direction of the University of Chicago, and two were directed by the University of Michigan. Their organization, however, was largely due to the efforts of county committees of teachers. Most of the students were holders of tuition scholarships granted by these county committees from funds provided by the W. K. Kellogg Foundation.

The four workshops had several characteristics in common. Each was located in a relatively small center of population and in a community favorable to the experimental use of its available resources. Each was conducted by a director who was familiar with the community and was acquainted with many of the schools in which the members had served as teachers during the preceding year. All the workshops, of course, required much preliminary planning by teacher committees, staffs, and directors. Emphasis was placed on relating theory to the actual problems of the schools represented in the workshops. Each workshop had a small staff of experts in such fields as health education, curriculum construction, and sociology. Each had its own laboratory school for the study and demonstration of good practices, especially those involving the use of community resources. In each workshop, community resources were studied and plans were made by the teachers to use these resources in enriching and vitalizing their own teaching.

Much of the success of the four workshops was due to their location in the area of the Michigan Community Health Project, which consists of Allegan, Barry, Branch, Calhoun, Eaton, Hillsdale, and Van Buren counties. A program concerned with the improvement of

rural life has been inaugurated in this area, a program which illustrates
the child-centered approach to the improvement of community life
and which envisions the "whole child" in the "total community."
This program has been subsidized since 1931 by the W. K. Kellogg
Foundation.

The immediate concern which led to the establishment of the workshops was the improvement of school curriculums and teaching procedures in the schools of the area. This effort called not only for the
continuation of in-service training of teachers, but also for the development and effective application of new techniques in teacher
education. Closely allied problems with respect to which teachers
needed help were the problems of lay education, home and school
relationships, and community organization.

In view of the experimental spirit that has been encouraged in the
seven counties it is not surprising that the possible values of workshops as a means for in-service education of teachers should be explored. The education of teachers in workshops is a relatively new
venture. The workshop is a professional seminar, providing for a
larger measure of self-expression and constructive criticism than is
offered in some of the older forms of class instruction. Some of the
features of the panel and forum methods of discussion and the individual conference and work periods are used, and much opportunity
is afforded for varied participation by all. The workshop offers a
laboratory setting and develops an atmosphere favoring cooperative
work on the part of its members. The instructor in the workshop is
a resource person and serves as a friendly guide in the inquiries carried
forward by the participants.

It must be granted that there are some active critics of workshops,
because the program of instruction is not organized in terms of logical
outlines. The informality of the workshop also creates in some
visitors the impression that students are playing at learning rather
than working in the usual ways of the real student. To those who
believe in more traditional theories of education, the enthusiasm of
the students in a workshop may arouse the suspicion that something
is wrong.

The instruction in the workshops was not planned to enable
teachers to meet the specific requirements for degrees or certificates,
but was designed rather to help teachers increase their own effectiveness in meeting the problems of their school in its community setting.
While it is true that many of the enrolled teachers were able to

secure credit toward degrees, the directors made it clear from the beginning that those who were only seeking credit were not wanted.

Many of the basic ideals in the workshop were contributed by Dr. Henry J. Otto, who served as educational director of the W. K. Kellogg Foundation for the seven-year period ending January, 1942. It was his initiative and planning that made this monograph possible, and it was his interest that led the Foundation to make a grant to the University of Michigan for the publication of the monograph.

The first chapter and the last were written by Dr. Otto, The other chapters were prepared by the directors of the workshops that are described in these chapters: Chapter II, Miss Drenckhahn; Chapter III, Mr. Darrell Barnard; Chapter IV, Mr. William G. Woods; Chapter V, Mr. Fred Miller. The first draft of these chapters was prepared at the close of the workshop sessions. Frequent meetings of the directors were held for a discussion of plans for chapter organization and related matters. However, there was no effort to insure a standardized method of presentation.

As representatives of the two sponsoring universities, we express our thanks to the cities of Allegan, Grand Ledge, Hastings, Hillsdale, and Marshall for housing the workshops and for providing so many helpful kinds of community services. We are indebted to the workshop staffs for their initiative, enthusiasm, and constructive work, as well as for their experimental attitude toward the whole undertaking. We are also indebted to Mr. Warren R. Good of the University of Michigan for editorial assistance.

On the basis of the evidence secured in the four workshops we are convinced that a workshop in a community setting can be made a real success, provided that much time is devoted to the necessary preliminary planning, and provided that an expert staff of sufficient size is engaged. It is our judgment, however, that the task of establishing and operating a successful workshop is a more difficult undertaking in the field than on a university campus. But it is also more expensive. The actual expenditure per student for instructional service in the four workshops was much higher than for comparable courses on the campuses of the two universities.

It is our hope that this monograph will prove helpful to students of the purposes, the organization, and the techniques of workshops, as well as to students of problems involved in relating the school to its community resources.

J. B. EDMONSON
RALPH W. TYLER

# CONTENTS

# CHAPTER I

# THE BACKGROUND FOR THE 1941 WORKSHOPS[1]

The Michigan Community Health Project is conducted in seven rural counties in southwestern Michigan which for a period of years have been receiving financial aid from the W. K. Kellogg Foundation for a comprehensive program for the improvement of rural life, with special emphasis on the improvement of the health, happiness, and well-being of children.[2] It is a project of the men and women in the area. The program is not designed to promote any preconceived plan but to bring to the communities, through their own leaders, the more promising of current ideas on community betterment in order that those directly concerned with the problems can work out their own answers.

Some of the assumptions underlying the methodology of the program are: (*a*) that rural areas have a variety of resources, human and physical, which, with appropriate stimulation and assistance, can be developed into effective forces for human betterment; (*b*) that the strength and permanence of a program depend largely on the development of local resources rather than on the implantation of extraneous and frequently temporary services or facilities; (*c*) that steady and more lasting progress can be made if all of the component elements in a community are moving forward at the same time and are coordinating their efforts toward a common goal; (*d*) that the most lasting contribution of assistance from an outside agency is the education of the people in the area; and (*e*) that the program develops from, with, and for the people of the area.

The manner in which the program is conceived and moves forward implies much emphasis on the in-service training of the local professional groups and lay leaders. It also suggests the importance of democratic processes in identifying local problems and in methods of attack on them. In a very real sense efforts are made to improve the

[1] This chapter was prepared by Dr. Henry J. Otto, who was Consultant in Education to the W. K. Kellogg Foundation from 1935 to 1942. Dr. Otto resigned his position to accept a graduate professorship in the School of Education at the University of Texas with duties beginning in February, 1942.

[2] Financial aid from the W. K. Kellogg Foundation began in each of these counties at the time the county established an official county health department. The dates are: Barry Co., September 1931; Allegan Co., April 1932; Eaton Co., March 1933; Van Buren Co., July 1934; Hillsdale Co., September 1934; Calhoun Co., June 1935; Branch Co., September 1935.

practical functioning of democracy in local communities. The challenge is to see whether local leadership so stimulated can develop really effective methods to meet community needs and thus advance the cause of child health, education, and welfare over many fronts— local, state, and national.

### THE PLACE OF TEACHER EDUCATION IN A COMMUNITY IMPROVEMENT PROGRAM

America has given an important place to its public elementary and secondary schools. The ideal of free public schooling through the twelve years of the elementary and secondary school for all children of all the people is deeply imbedded in American thought and is fundamental to the maintenance of a democratic, self-governing society. Next to the home, the school is the most important social institution in this country. It is society's agent for the organized schooling of its young. Whatever is done to improve the quality and adequacy of the school program gives added strength to this cherished resource of the community.

Schools have been one of civilization's major instruments for social progress, and social progress is facilitated if the school concerns itself with the education of the adults as well as the children of the community. In fact, the school renders its greatest service if the educational work with young and old deals with the practical problems of everyday living. To say that a good school concerns itself with community education sounds as if schools had in addition some other field of operation. If a school really carries on dynamic community education, it makes its greatest contribution toward social improvement.

For schools to make such a contribution to a community requires knowledge, leadership, and talents which have not been common among American teachers. They need to know how to identify themselves with the community in such a way as to recognize and to understand the problems of the people. They need to know how education may be helpful to people in arriving at more satisfactory ways of dealing with their problems. Teachers need to know the resources that may be utilized in solving problems and the techniques by which the people of a community may cooperate democratically in doing better for themselves and their children. Teachers need to know ways in which children can learn real citizenship by contributing their share toward community service and improvement. Teachers need to be real educators; otherwise the school cannot contribute that which the people might legitimately expect of it.

But most persons who become teachers in public schools are not born with the qualities required to be real educators. Nor can very many of these abilities be acquired in the brief pre-service training demanded by present certification standards in the United States. It is possible that some of the most fundamental skills cannot be learned until one finds himself in a real teaching position in some community. Among other things, teachers need to learn how the members of the profession can function democratically in providing real educational leadership, and how that leadership may be exerted in terms of the educational needs of the community.

Anyone who understands the function of the school in community education must see very clearly the part which the school has to play in any program of community improvement and the place of teacher education in a comprehensive program for the improvement of the health, happiness, and well-being of rural children.

### SCHOOLS AND TEACHERS IN THE SEVEN-COUNTY AREA

In the seven counties comprising the Michigan Community Health Project there are 864 rural schools (mostly one-teacher schools) and fifty-eight twelve-grade schools, most of which are located in the villages and small cities. These schools are staffed by approximately 2,000 teachers. The majority of the persons who teach in the twelve-grade schools hold the bachelor's degree and a small percentage, mostly the administrators, have the master's degree. The average amount of training for those teaching in the one-teacher schools is just a little more than two years beyond high school graduation. Michigan still grants a temporary certificate for one year's training beyond high school.

### TEACHER DEVELOPMENT PRIOR TO 1941

*The State Program.*—In Michigan, as elsewhere, teachers have been availing themselves regularly of extension and summer courses and the other usual channels for in-service training. The rate at which school programs were changed and improved was probably about the same as in other states with similar conditions and resources. That there was a distinct lag between current practices in schools and modern concepts of education will be denied by few. With teachers, as with most professional groups, the constant effort is to keep as nearly abreast of the times as conditions will permit. It is no secret that the problem of keeping school programs up-to-date is a tough assignment. To assist with this problem Michigan (as did many other states) inaugurated a state-wide program for curriculum improvement in which most of the state agencies and teacher training institutions participated. For some phases of the curriculum program, outside assistance was obtained.

The counties in the Michigan Community Health Project, like the other counties of the state, needed stimulation to increase the rate of school improvement. Schools in the seven counties, however, had an additional problem; namely, that of developing programs which would not only keep up with broad programs for general community improvement that were under way, but would also contribute to these broad programs. Teachers had to re-orient themselves and to redefine their functions in communities in which new approaches were being made to health, medical and dental care, hospital and clinical and x-ray laboratory services, library services, environmental sanitation, recreation, modernization of school facilities, camping, agricultural and home-making education, youth problems, and parent education. Communities provide dynamic environments for teachers and school administrators when representatives of many services—physicians, dentists, court officials, law enforcement officers, school board members, parents, library trustees, librarians, hospital administrators, nurses, hospital trustees, members of the county board of supervisors, milk pasteurizing plant operators, leaders of youth organizations, ministers, and a number of other groups—are participating regularly in in-service training activities to focus their efforts on improving the care and training of children and general community betterment. Financial aid for in-service training has been made available to each of these groups by the W. K. Kellogg Foundation.

*Purposes of Foundation Aid.*—It was to help teachers and school administrators give appropriate leadership in the community-wide program for improving the health, happiness, and well-being of children and in the development of significant programs of community education that the W. K. Kellogg Foundation made available funds for supplementing the usual channels of in-service training of teachers. The Foundation's contribution to teacher education was similar to the contributions made for the education of the other groups previously named. The methods used in teacher education and school improvement differ from those used in some of the other fields, but the basic principles were the same.

Funds provided by the Foundation have been used to give teachers and administrators a clearer understanding of the philosophy, psychology, and procedures involved in the newer concepts of education; to give teachers the added skills and techniques necessary to work with community groups in inaugurating changes in the school program; to give teachers assistance in putting new practices into operation in their own schools; to give teachers the skills and competence needed to work cooperatively with each other in studying problems, making plans, and utilizing available resources; and to give colleges and universities opportunities to experiment with improved techniques in teacher education. Professionalization of the teachers and the development of machinery through which teachers could function cooperatively was a major problem. That considerable progress in school improvement has been made is evidenced by certain published materials.[1]

*Activities in Teacher Education.*—Activities in teacher education included extension courses offered for credit by nearby institutions, week-end gatherings of large groups of teachers at the Foundation's camps, regular meetings (usually monthly) of teachers clubs[2] and the county educational council, group meetings of teachers with similar problems and interests, committee work on problems of county-wide interest, consultative service by qualified staff members from nearby universities, inter-visitation, specially planned summer courses offered at various colleges and universities, the on-campus curriculum workshop, and the off-campus community workshop.

In seven years from September, 1934, the registration for credit in special field courses totaled more than 2,700; this was in addition to the extension work normally taken by teachers. Registration in

[1] Henry J. Otto, *Meeting Administrative Problems Growing Out of Changes in Classroom Teaching in 1936–1937 in Graded Elementary Schools in the Area of the Michigan Community Health Project*, 1938, pp. iv+124; *Changes in Classroom Teaching Made during 1938–1939 in Graded Elementary Schools in the Area of the Michigan Community Health Project*, 1940, pp. 124; *Changes in Classroom Teaching Made during 1937–1939 in One-Room Rural Schools in the Area of the Michigan Community Health Project*, 1940, pp. 209. Battle Creek: W. K. Kellogg Foundation (mimeographed reports).

[2] Henry J. Otto and Vivian V. Drenckhahn, "Helping Each Other Professionally," *Educational Method*, XIX (February, 1940), 276–81.

specially planned summer courses numbered 2,011 (exclusive of the summer of 1941). The institutions at which teachers attended specially planned courses were Northwestern, Michigan, Ohio State, Chicago, Minnesota, Harvard, New Hampshire, Syracuse, and New York universities, the Massachusetts Institute of Technology, and the state teachers colleges at Greeley, Colorado; Mankato, Minnesota; and Mt. Pleasant, Ypsilanti, and Kalamazoo, Michigan. Individual teachers attended selected courses at a number of other institutions. The different specially planned summer courses offered by the various institutions covered child growth and development in the elementary school, speech re-education, home hygiene and child care, educational and community leadership, adult education, health education, recreation problems and programs, problems of mental hygiene and social adjustment and the health of adolescents, the off-campus community workshop, and the development of courses offered by instructors resident in summer camps.

After teachers had participated in a number of the extension and summer campus courses they began saying, "We know the theory; what we need now is to have someone help us put the theory into practice." No doubt the teachers themselves would admit that they didn't know all the theory yet, but the implication was quite clear. They wanted practical help in putting theory into practice. This need led to the development of the consultative service through which five full-time persons were provided during 1940–1941. It also led to the summer workshop held in the local community.

*The First Community Workshops.*—During the summer of 1940 four community workshops were held. One of them, a curriculum workshop in elementary education, was sponsored at Coldwater, Michigan, by the Department of Education of the University of Chicago. Another one, emphasizing child development, nutrition, and health education, was sponsored at Plainwell, Michigan, by the Department of Home Economics of the University of Chicago.[1] The third one, emphasizing health education, was conducted at Marshall, Michigan, by the School of Education and the Division of Hygiene and Public Health of the University of Michigan.[2] The fourth one, emphasizing adult education and functionalized teaching in the high school, was conducted at Decatur, Michigan, by the Department of

[1] Maxine Biesenthal, "A Workshop in Health Education," *Forecast*, LVII (March, 1941).

[2] Vivian V. Drenckhahn, "A Summer Course in Health Education," *University of Michigan School of Education Bulletin*, XII (January, 1941), 52–56.

Sociology and the School of Education of the University of Michigan.[1]

These initial efforts at workshops held in local communities verified some of the preliminary assumptions. Teachers received more practical help on their problems because it brought the instructors to the problems instead of abstracting each problem and taking it to some distant college campus. It enabled teachers and instructors to work together in the setting of the problem. It was easier for the faculty to assist teachers in utilizing local resources. Theoretical aspects of teaching could be interpreted in the practical situation. Teachers could see children in their own community respond to improved methods of teaching. Parents, children, and school board members could be included in whatever plans were made for curriculum improvement in the local school. The whole community became such an integral part of the workshop that it became an easier matter for the teachers and the community to make still further progress during the coming year.

Although the community workshops in 1940 were considered very successful, it would be unfair to say that all of the important factors had been thought of in these exploratory efforts. In fact, the workshops in 1940 taught many lessons of commission and omission which were taken into consideration in planning and conducting the 1941 workshops.

### GENERAL PLANNING OF THE 1941 WORKSHOPS

By the fall of 1940 the leadership and interest of teachers had developed to the point where they were taking an active part in analyzing their own training needs in the light of the needs of the schools and communities. In each county the teachers association had appointed a committee on teacher education. In several of the counties this committee made questionnaire and interview studies of the in-service training needs and interests of teachers. Of course there was no hope of meeting all of the individual needs of two thousand teachers, but the data did provide generalizations as to the needs and interests common to large groups of teachers.

After each county committee had drawn some conclusions from its inquiries, the seven committees met in joint session with the university staff members who were giving full time to consultative work

---

[1] H. B. Masters, "A Community Workshop," *University of Michigan School of Education Bulletin*, XII (December, 1940), 42–45.

in the schools. At this meeting ideas were exchanged and agreements reached on the following points:

1. That summer courses should be planned to assist teachers with certificate and degree requirements.
2. That efforts should be made to have those courses offered in such a way as to make them yield more practical value to teachers. Special reference was made to courses in the liberal arts fields, such as English, history, and science.
3. That the workshop was one of the most effective vehicles of teacher education.
4. That the most practical training could be received in workshops held in local communities where special emphasis could be placed on working with parent groups and making use of local resources.

In view of the above agreements and the surveys of teacher needs, the group recommended that five workshops be planned in the Michigan Community Health Project area for the next summer. These five workshops were to have the following emphases:

1. A travel seminar, emphasizing Michigan history, geography, and industry
2. A community workshop to be held in Barry County, emphasizing the physical and biological sciences and perhaps library science
3. A community workshop to be held in Eaton County, emphasizing arts and crafts
4. A community workshop to be held in Calhoun County, emphasizing the biological and health sciences
5. A community workshop to be held in Hillsdale County, emphasizing the social studies, the language arts, and perhaps library science

Further deliberations of the teacher education committees resulted in the following additional recommendations:

1. That these five workshops be considered on a seven-county basis so that any teacher in any county could choose to attend any one of the five workshops.
2. That if the Foundation should offer scholarships for summer study, the scholarship stipend should cover tuition and that each teacher be expected to contribute the cost of board, room, and books.
3. That the selection of applicants to these workshops should be made during the winter or early spring so that each teacher could be given some directions as to the things she ought to do to prepare herself for participation in the workshop.
4. That these proposals and ideas be presented to the administrative authorities of the cooperating universities to determine the extent to which it would be feasible to provide these types of summer training.

These various proposals and ideas were then presented and discussed at a joint session with Dr. J. B. Edmonson of the University of Michigan and Dr. Ralph W. Tyler of the University of Chicago. Within three weeks, after institutional resources had been explored and necessary adjustments made, it was found that the two cooperating institutions could provide types of summer training which would be essentially in harmony with the proposals made by the teacher education committees. A printed brochure describing the proposed courses was then circulated to all teachers early in February. Each teacher who was interested was asked to fill out an application blank. This census of teacher interest provided the basis on which final plans were carried forward.

It was found later that the travel seminar and the workshop in arts and crafts could not be provided. In their stead was planned a workshop which would stress child development, the health sciences, and the social studies. The administrative officers of the two universities then made the necessary arrangements for the four community workshops. Four of the full-time consultants in the area were appointed directors of the four workshops, thus facilitating the relationships and arrangements between the universities and the local communities in which the workshops were to be held. The fact that the four workshop directors were already working in the area as consultants to schools gave them an invaluable background and acquaintanceship with local persons and problems, permitted cooperative planning by the four directors, and enabled them to make personal contacts with all prospective teacher participants, thus carrying out one of the recommendations of the teacher education committees.

### SPECIFIC PLANNING BY WORKSHOP DIRECTORS

As soon as the decision had been reached that these community workshops were to be sponsored as indicated, the four directors of the workshops began intensive planning on the specific problems to be encountered. This specific planning began in February and was continued until the workshops opened on June 23. The four directors met at least once a week in specific planning sessions. Occasionally other resource persons were invited to meet with the directors. Intermittently, during this period, conferences were held or correspondence exchanged with Dr. Edmonson and Dr. Tyler, and selected hypotheses were checked with local communities or the teacher education committees.

*Basic Workshop Techniques.*—One of the first issues to be considered was that of basic workshop techniques. The development of guiding principles on workshop technique was facilitated by the fact that all four directors had had previous experience as staff members in workshops. The principles outlined by Heaton, Camp, and Diederich[1] were very helpful. The way in which these basic principles were applied will be evident in the detailed accounts of succeeding chapters.

*Special Functions of a Community Workshop.*—A second problem involved a thorough consideration of the special values, opportunities, and techniques of an off-campus workshop conducted in a local community. Among the considerations which loomed large were the following:

1. How can the problems which teachers bring to the workshop be given realistic consideration in their natural setting? By what methods can the "university coming out to the problem" assist teachers in making a more effective transfer of theoretical considerations to practical approaches in dealing with the problems? In reality, these two questions constitute the foci for the community workshop; all other issues are largely methods of giving greater significance to this primary function. Specific advantages in relation to this objective are that (a) through preworkshop conferences with the teacher in her own school, the problem can be defined more clearly in terms of its realistic roots, (b) workshop staff members can view the problem realistically by accompanying the teacher to her own school and by conferring with other persons in the community, (c) teachers with similar problems can visit their respective schools in groups and deliberate on the problem under the guidance of one or more staff members, and (d) teachers can more easily deal with the real thing in developing plans to attack the problems.

2. By what methods can maximum use be made of the resources (persons, agencies, and materials) which are actually accessible to the teacher in her local situation? Can these resources be drawn into the discussion of the problem and into laying plans to deal with the problem in such a way as to give new motivation to these resource persons and agencies? Can both the teacher and the resource persons and agencies be led to see new horizons of achievement in the pooling of their energies? What are the unrecognized resources that may be drawn into the picture? The methods of handling these issues will be shown in subsequent chapters.

3. How can a laboratory school make its contribution to a community workshop? How nearly essential is a laboratory demonstration school to the workshop? How can a laboratory-school teacher give genuine application to child development concepts in her work with children and still render a contribution to the varying problems of the workshop participants? Will the natural development of children's activities in the laboratory school illustrate approaches to problems and the use of local resources so as to give other teachers practical leads for their

[1] K. L. Heaton, W. G. Camp, P. B. Diederich, *Professional Education for Experienced Teachers*, pp. 21–43. Chicago: The University of Chicago Press, 1940.

own problems? Must the laboratory school flit about to an unrelated array of isolated "demonstrations" in order to be serviceable to the members of the workshop? By what methods can teachers be helped to gain most from the laboratory school? Again the answers given to these issues are illustrated in the various chapters.

4. How may the members of the boards of education become sufficiently active participants in the plans developed by teachers so that the school boards may give support and encouragement to the improvements in curriculum and teaching which are initiated by the teachers? In one-teacher schools and small communities the teacher feels the closeness of her relationships to the school board much more intensely than do teachers in larger cities. In rural areas the schools, in a very real sense, cannot rise very far above the educational horizons of the school board members.

5. The ideas of parents on educational matters also affect changes desired in the schools. With the parents the problem was to develop methods by which parents could participate in a consideration of problems and in making plans for school improvement so that they too would understand the needs and the plans and would cooperate and participate at whatever points the home, school, and community would need to come together in order to achieve significant progress. The succeeding chapters illustrate some of the methods used in securing the participation of parents whose children were enrolled in the laboratory school, other parents in the same community, and parents in other villages and rural districts in the county.

*Teacher Preparation.*—The third aspect of specific planning deals with the methodology of preparing teachers for effective workshop participation. The teacher education committees had requested that summer programs be crystalized early enough in the school year to permit each prospective participant to engage in some definite preparatory activities. Immediately it became evident that the workshops would begin, not on June 23, but during the spring months when teachers were identifying and clarifying the problems they wished to work on during the six-week summer period. In view of these possibilities the workshop directors developed eight steps or techniques which held promise in assisting teachers during this preparatory period. The first job was the preparation of a mimeographed guide to be discussed with and placed in the hands of each applicant. This guide outlined the conditions for admission to the workshop and to the university sponsoring the project, and suggested a variety of activities in which the teacher might engage to broaden her background for the intensive work during the six-week summer period. The next step consisted of a series of group meetings (one in each county) of those who previously had expressed their interest in the workshops. These meetings were held between

March 31 and April 7.  Each meeting was attended by from forty to fifty teachers.  The purposes of the meetings were:

1. To help the applicants get a better understanding of the purpose of the specific workshop for which they had applied
2. To instruct the teachers concerning the procedure for obtaining admission to the university sponsoring the workshop so that they might receive course credit for their participation
3. To recommend procedures by which each teacher might best prepare herself for workshop activities
4. To discuss any questions which the teachers might have concerning the summer program

It was discovered later that some of these group meetings were not as valuable as had been anticipated.  The lack of free discussion was accounted for by several conditions: (*a*) the physical arrangement of the room was not conducive to free discussion, (*b*) the attendance of three educational consultants caused many of the teachers to hesitate to express themselves, and (*c*) the teachers from the one-room schools were particularly hesitant in the presence of the better-trained village and city teachers.

Since these group meetings had not fully accomplished the purposes for which they had been held, the third technique in teacher preparation became especially valuable.  Each director arranged for individual conferences with the applicants.  These conferences, which began on April 15 and continued through May, were usually held in the teacher's own school.  At the time of this interview the director filled out a specially prepared interview card to which frequent reference could be made before and during the six-week summer period.  The workshop directors were able to have personal interviews with about 90 percent of the applicants.  Others were reached through correspondence.

A number of different kinds of questions were brought out by teachers in the director's interviews with them.  There was a rather common fear, on the part of rural teachers, of working for six weeks with village elementary and high school teachers.  Many of them felt that they would be in direct competition with these teachers, whom they believed to be better prepared.  Most of the teachers were concerned about applying the course credit earned in the workshop toward certificate renewal or degrees.  They were all encouraged to obtain written statements, from the institutions to which they wanted to transfer their workshop credits, that these credits would be accepted.

Very few of the teachers had gone far enough in their thinking with regard to their work to have defined a real teaching problem. Because of the formal college classes to which they had become accustomed, most of them could not comprehend the possibilities of spending six weeks on a particular problem. It should be pointed out here that the directors erred in attempting to give them a picture of the way in which the workshop would operate. They tried to describe a workshop as they conceived it, rather than leaving the

*Teacher-participants were interviewed in their own schools by the director of the workshop before it opened. Here the director (right) and the supervisor of elementary schools in Hastings discuss her problem, "Evaluating the effectiveness of parent-teacher conferences as a means of acquainting parents with the progress of their child in school." During this conference they discussed ways in which this teacher could use the resources of the workshop in attacking her problem.*

teachers with the idea that the general organization of a workshop would depend on the total personnel of the workshop and not on any one person's preconceived idea. This error became evident when certain workshop activities had to be formalized in order to satisfy some members of the staff that the activity was academically respectable.

Although the principal purpose of conducting these interviews with individual teachers was to help them identify the teaching problem or problems they would like to work on during the summer, other matters were discussed, such as special interests of teachers, their college status, future professional plans, and living accommodations for the summer. The problems which teachers decided were important to them were recorded on the card previously prepared for such interviews. Each teacher was encouraged to list her problem on the mimeographed outline which had been given her, and to fill out the blank completely and return it to the director as soon as convenient. The problems which teachers indicated as being important to them are listed later in the separate chapters.

In addition to the mimeographed guide, the interview card, and the individual conferences with teachers, several other procedures were used to help teachers prepare for the workshop. On different occasions a director was invited to attend meetings of rural teachers clubs and the faculty meetings in village schools to discuss the workshop. Since each of the workshop directors had arranged for desk space in the county school commissioner's office six weeks before the opening of the workshops, many additional contacts were made with rural-teacher applicants who regularly called at that office.

In the interviews with teachers it was frequently suggested that they read recommended references, talk with their superintendent or principal about the thing which they were planning to do in the workshop, and discuss the matter with other teachers. There is little evidence that many of them did much reading in preparation for work on their individual problems, although many of them did talk with other teachers, superintendents, or principals, and in some cases with people in the community.

Various members of the teacher education committee, because of their concern that the workshop be a significant experience for the teachers, provided the directors with a great deal of assistance in making these preliminary teacher-contacts effective. On several occasions the director met with members of this committee to discuss the way in which teachers should be approached and ways by which they themselves might help teachers prepare for participation in the workshop program. Since they were nearer the teachers than the director, their assistance was invaluable.

*Selection of the Staff.*—One of the most important responsibilities in planning a community workshop is the selection of staff. It is highly important to have persons who are skillful in workshop techniques, who comprehend the peculiar functions of a community workshop, and who can enlist the confidence of and work satisfyingly with the people of rural communities. After the basic functions and areas of emphasis had been determined for each workshop, the director of each workshop cooperated with the dean of the school of education of the university sponsoring the particular workshop in arriving at the roster of individuals to whom invitations might be extended. In each university the dean enlisted the cooperation of the chairmen of the various departments within which course registrations were to take place. It is significant that the sponsorship of these workshops involved the cooperative planning of two large universities and of several departments within each university.

*Library Facilities.*—Another phase of planning the workshops involved the provision of adequate professional library materials. Although it is common practice for local schools to maintain a small professional library for teachers, it could hardly be expected that a single school district or several school districts together would have an adequate supply of materials appropriate for a specific type of workshop involving from fifty to seventy-five teachers. Steps were therefore taken by the workshop directors to supplement local library resources.

Soon after the nature of the four workshops had been determined and a generous sampling of teachers had been interviewed to indicate the nature of the library problem, the directors collaborated in the preparation of a bibliography of professional books and pamphlets appropriate for each workshop. Each list included about 475 titles. These lists were then submitted to each staff member for review and additions. This process resulted in each workshop's having a professional library of about 500 titles. Several copies were provided of many of the titles. Practically all of these materials were on hand at the opening of the workshop. Some titles had been provided by local schools, some had been borrowed from state and university libraries, some were loaned from the personal libraries of staff members, and the remainder (about 400 titles) were provided by the library of the W. K. Kellogg Foundation. In each instance the county requested that this latter collection be left in the county during the ensuing year to serve as the nucleus for a professional study center for the teachers of the county.

*Selection of a Community.*—In each county there were several villages or cities which had extended an invitation to have the workshop held there. The directors soon realized that certain conditions would have to prevail if a workshop were to operate successfully in a given community. They developed the following list of criteria in terms of which the resources of each community could be reviewed:

1. Does the village under consideration have the unique facilities required for the workshop that is being planned? Are those facilities available for use by the workshop?

2. Will children of the age groups desired for the laboratory school be available?

3. Is the community conveniently located for the teachers who wish to commute?

4. Are there rooming accommodations for those who wish to get rooms in town?

5. Are the eating accommodations adequate and satisfactory?

6. Do the school administrators and board of education wish the course to be held there?

7. Will the board of education provide heat, light, janitor service, books, and library facilities for the workshop and for the children of the laboratory school?

8. What contribution, if any, will the board of education make toward the salaries of teachers for the laboratory school?

9. Do the parents of the community wish the workshop to be held there? Will they participate in the program?

These criteria were applied to several communities in each county. The village finally selected in each case was the one in which all of the factors gave greatest promise of a successful program.

*Preparation of the Local Community.*—After the locale for each workshop had been determined, a variety of steps were taken to get the local situation in readiness for the summer program. Each chapter describes these procedures in detail.

### THE FOUR COMMUNITY WORKSHOPS

The next four chapters in this monograph give detailed descriptions of the four community workshops conducted in the area of the Michigan Community Health Project during the summer of 1941. From each chapter are omitted those elements which were common to all four workshops and which have already been set forth in this chapter. In each of the succeeding chapters is illustrated, however, the application in specific situations of the general principles outlined in this chapter.

# CHAPTER II

# THE COMMUNITY WORKSHOP DEALING WITH PROBLEMS IN HEALTH EDUCATION[1]

A community workshop designed to help teachers with problems relating to child health was centered in Calhoun County at Marshall, Michigan, for two successive summers, 1940 and 1941. Teachers recognized the need for applying the achievements in the field of the health sciences to problems existing in their school and community. The unusual value which participants in the 1940 workshop[2] placed on this type of in-service experience led others to request a similar workshop during the summer of 1941.

Steps in arranging for a community workshop and in preparing teachers who anticipated attending the workshop were similar to those described in Chapter I. The director met with interested teachers the evening of April 1 to discuss informally the nature of a community workshop,[3] the registration areas,[4] and techniques which might be helpful in identifying a problem or special interest for intensive study.

## CONFERENCES WITH TEACHERS IN THE CLASSROOM

Individual conferences which were held with teachers in their schools or classrooms proved to be highly valuable in preparing director, staff, and participants for the summer's experience. It helped the director to see problems first hand, to know the teachers' interpretations of them, and to think through the kinds of materials and resources that should be available in solving them. It encouraged and stimulated the participants to do more thinking about their special interests or problems. It provided an opportunity to answer

[1] This chapter was prepared by Miss Vivan Drenckhahn, director of the workshop at Marshall during the Summer Session of 1941. Miss Drenckhahn had charge of a similar workshop in the Summer Session of 1940, and has been engaged as a consultant in the Michigan Community Health Project since March, 1939.

[2] Vivian V. Drenckhahn, "A Summer Course in Health Education," *University of Michigan School of Education Bulletin,* XII (January, 1941), 52–56.

[3] *Recommendations of M. E. A. Teacher Education Committees* (Allegan, Barry, Branch, Calhoun, Eaton, Hillsdale, Van Buren County Districts) *for Workshops for Teachers in Elementary and Secondary Education for Summer,* 1941. Lansing: Michigan Education Association.

[4] Participants could register in any three of the following four registration areas: Hygiene 115, Methods and Materials in Health Education, credit two semester hours; Hygiene 131 or 201, Physiologic Hygiene, credit two semester hours; Hygiene 132 or 202, Communicable Diseases and Epidemiology, credit two semester hours; and Education A130, Problems in Educational Sociology, credit two semester hours.

questions that teachers had in regard to the problems they had selected and ways in which they could prepare for the summer's work. These conferences were also a means of indicating to the teachers that the workshop staff was interested in them as individuals, as well as in their professional problems. Knowing something about the teacher's responsibility for special activities in the community and her special interests, as well as problems arising out of her teaching program, proved very helpful later. For instance, Mrs. A, a teacher of junior high school pupils, was in charge of their work in English and history. Among her special interests were dramatics, choric reading, and music, especially singing. She took an active part in community work, serving during the preceding year as president of a local branch of the American Association of University Women. She would be one of a group of seven teachers from the same school system attending the workshop. Although her primary interest was not in earning credits, she was working toward a master's degree. She was urged to write to the university to learn if the credits she could earn at the workshop would be acceptable. Her special interest as stated at the time of the conference was "doing more in the field of guidance, particularly with unadjusted children." Many pupils with whom she worked had poor reading ability. She wished to know more about child health and development.

In a conference with Mr. B, a high school principal in a village school, it was learned that he worked with high school boys and girls in civics, economics, shop, and social studies. He coached basket ball and was the newly elected president of his district in the Michigan Education Association. He directed recreational work in the community, was a member of the town service committee, and president of the Little C Conference in which eight schools participate. His academic rating at the university was that of a graduate student. His special problem was first to determine the health needs of his junior and senior high school people and then to plan a program to meet these needs. As a member of the service committee, he was also interested in health problems of the preschool group.

In calling on a rural teacher, Mrs. C, it was learned that she was very much interested in attending the workshop and that she wished to work on plans for a health education program in her school, in which the health needs of her pupils would be met. She was not certain of her academic standing, but she would write for this information. Her big problem, however, was knowing what to do with her two children, ages twelve and six, while she was attending the workshop. The suggestion that she bring the children with her and enroll them in the Children's Division of the workshop met with the approval of the entire family. Mrs. C realized how valuable this experience might be for her children, both of whom attended the school she taught. She greatly appreciated the fact that a housing committee in Marshall would help her locate an apartment.

Of the fifty-two teachers who later enrolled in the workshop, all were visited except eleven. Four of the eleven were from outside the area and special arrangements were made through correspondence for them to enter the workshop.[1] The seven other students decided to enter the workshop at such a late date that it was impossible to interview them personally.

## LOCATION OF THE WORKSHOP

The superintendent of the Marshall school system, who was also chairman of the Calhoun County teacher education committee, again invited the 1941 workshop to Marshall. The board of education, the teachers, and the community were genuinely enthusiastic over the type of educational opportunities made possible through a community workshop.

Marshall, a city with a population of 5,253, is centrally situated in Calhoun County. It is the county seat and in addition to the court house, the offices of the county agricultural extension service, the health department, the commissioner of schools and welfare services are located there. Its school facilities were adequate in every way to meet the needs of a large group of teachers during the workshop session.

Marshall itself is rich in history. The first permanent settlers came from New York State in 1831 and many others came soon afterward from Connecticut and Vermont as well as from New York.[2] They left many beautiful structures, colonial in design, in residential and business districts. Before the capitol was moved from Detroit to Lansing, in 1847, Marshall on successive ballots narrowly missed being selected as the capitol city.[3] A site had already

---

[1] In order to enroll in the workshop, these four teachers paid a tuition fee of $60.00, the amount of the scholarships which teachers in the area received.

[2] *History of Calhoun County, Michigan*, 1830–1877, pp. 56–57. Philadelphia: L. H. Everets Company, 1877.

[3] *Inventory of the County Archives of Michigan*. No. 13 Calhoun County (Marshall). Detroit: The Michigan Historical Records Survey, Project, 1941.

been chosen for the capitol building, and the school which was built nearby in 1860 is called Capitol Hill School. Marshall is proud, too, of being the home of Isaac E. Crary and of John D. Pierce, founders of the Michigan public school system, which was planned in 1834. In 1836, Mr. Pierce became the first superintendent of public instruction in Michigan. Mr. Crary was Michigan's first representative to Congress.

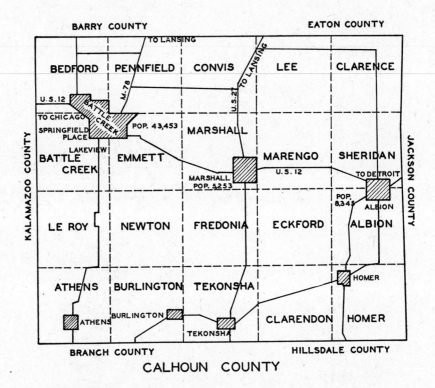

*Calhoun County has a population of 94,206. It ranks twelfth in the state in population density and tenth in taxable wealth. Agriculture is the leading occupation, with grain and fruit as important products. Battle Creek, its largest city, contains 65 percent of the county's wealth. It is an industrial center known for making cereal products and farm machinery. Calhoun County, exclusive of Battle Creek, has a population of 50,743 people, and has 385 teachers for its 9,000 pupils. The largest school systems are Albion with 71 teachers, Lakeview with 53 teachers, and Marshall with 41 teachers. There are 130 one- and two-teacher schools and 10 schools with from 4 to 17 teachers.*

## GETTING CHILDREN TO PARTICIPATE

Responsibility for enrolling children in the laboratory school, or as it was more generally called, the Children's and Young People's Division of the workshop, was assumed by Mr. Harley W. Holmes, superintendent of the Marshall school system, and Miss Kathryn Leeke, elementary supervisor. They met with each of the parent-teacher organizations in the four elementary schools to explain the summer program and to give parents an opportunity to enroll children for forenoon sessions in the school. Since these organizations met in the afternoon, fathers were not present for the discussions. At another time, slides showing workshop activities of the past summer were shown to interested parents and children. Other groups in Marshall with whom the summer's program was discussed included the Community Council, the University of Michigan Club, the Monday Club, the Junior Chamber of Commerce, the Rotary Club, several church groups, and the faculty itself. Enrollments of children were secured largely through the teachers who distributed registration blanks for the children to take home. Since nearly half of the elementary grade teachers attended the workshop the preceding year and were familiar with the nature of the program, they were able skillfully to interpret it to their children.

Many more children of elementary school age wished to enter the summer program than the laboratory school was able to accommodate. There was real difficulty, however, in securing pupils from the groups of high school age. Since there was no high school parent-teacher association, these parents were not reached except indirectly through students and newspapers. A committee of parents could probably have developed a more effective plan for establishing contact with parents of high school students and for securing enrollments. Since some of the junior and senior high school students wished to learn more about the nature of the summer's program and since the staff members who were planning to work with these groups wanted to know something of their interests, meetings for this purpose were arranged during the last week in May. The superintendent had previously met with these students to talk over such questions as credit, the length of the summer session, and the type of activities to be developed.

Although there were many advantages in having a workshop the second year in the same community, there were also disadvantages

# Quiet Town Of Marshall Is Home Of School Of Education Workshop

(Editor's Note: This is the first of three articles on the School of Education's Community Workshop at Marshall. The remaining articles of the series will appear tomorrow and Sunday.)

**By PAUL CHRISTMANN**

If you should drop in some day at the Marshall High School you would have one of the unique experiences of your life. Here in operation is the Community Workshop sponsored by the University of Michigan.

Marshall is a quiet town of some 5,000 population about 30 miles west of Jackson on US 12. This is the second year that the Community Workshop has been held here.

Well, you ask, just what would I see if I paid the Workshop a visit? As you enter the lobby of Marshall's modern high school you are greeted by a large lighted exhibit. Across the top it says, "A Summer 'Workshop' in Health Education for Teachers." Below are a number of large pictures telling in visual form the activity of Marshall's Workshop last year.

On either side comfortable looking chairs stand as if they were saying "Welcome." A small sign informs you to take one, and you reach to a stand to pick up a reprint from The University of Michigan School of Education Bulletin, an article till now in a word picture, the story of last year's workshop.

**Key Word Is 'Welcome'**

Already you have been given the key, silently, but surely, the key of a sincere welcome.

Having been directed to the second floor you walk into a long pleasant room. Here you receive the welcome again—now personally from Miss Vivian V. Drenckhahn, a charming and gracious person. Miss Drenckhahn, you learn later, is director of the Workshop, a difficult and responsible position, which she capably fills.

Enthusiastically Miss Drenckhahn tells you the purpose, philosophy, and the machinery of the Workshop. The aim is to give the teachers and administrators practice in methods and techniques of studying health problems in their broadest sense, That is, health in relation to community implication, the total personality of the child, the sociological aspects, integration with subject matter, or tapping human resources.

**Talk Over Plans**

Participants were prepared. Several months before the session actually started each teacher received a personal visit from Miss Drenckhahn.

## Workshop Group Studies Housing

**All-Day Trip Wednesday Is Made by Staff and Participants in Marshall Area.**

MARSHALL—A group of participants and staff of the University of Michigan Community Workshop here made an all-day trip Wednesday to study community projects in housing, sanitation and education. Ralph Witherspoon of the university staff and Herbert Dunsmore of the Calhoun county health department accompanied the group.

On Friday, a group of teachers accompanied by Meredith Darlington will visit schools to discuss educational resources available in each community and ways in which these resources can be incorporated in the teaching program.

This morning, parents and all interested individuals in the community were invited to a meeting in the high school library. Children's books and reading materials were discussed at the meeting. Mrs. Zoe Wright, Kellogg Foundation librarian, aided in the discussion.

Residents and professional workers in Marshall are participating in numerous workshop activities. Dr. Earl C. Peabody and Dr. Hugh Robbins are attending discussion meetings today. Dr. Peabody will help with problems in the field of dental health, while Dr. Robbins will discuss the ways of working together in solving community problems.

Ralph Helm, county agricultural agent, and B. E. Henry, 4-H club leader, have secured new films from the United States department of agriculture. Some of the films already have been shown at the workshop, and others will be shown before the project is completed. The state health department has provided films on health problems under study

## PARENTS MEET WITH HEADS OF WORKSHOP

**Become Acquainted With Summer School Program**

One of the essential features of the Community Workshop in Education which is being held in Marshall for teachers from the area of the Michigan Community Health Project during this summer under the sponsorship of the University of Michigan is the correlating and integrating of the activities of teachers, boys and girls, and staff, with the available resources of the community. In addition to the work with teachers enrolled in the course there is also being conducted a children's and young people's school which is in session only in the forenoon. Friday morning about 35 parents, teachers, and staff members met in the library at the high school building to meet the staff and become acquainted with the summer school program.

Arrangements for this meeting were worked out by a committee made up of Mrs. Lillian Mulvany, Mrs. Geraldine Cobb and Mrs. Edna Crawford, assisted by Mrs. Mary Mills, Mrs Effa Black, Lester Swartz and Mrs. Florence Sweet.

**Miss Drenckhahn In Charge**

The conference was in charge of Miss Vivian Drenckhahn of the University of Michigan who is director of the workshop. Some of the topics discussed were: (1) An explanation of the nature of the summer school, its aims, methods and (Concluded Page 3, Column 3)

*Michigan Daily*
*Friday*
*August 1, 1941*

*Battle Creek*
*Enquirer and News*
*Thursday*
*July 24, 1941*

*Marshall*
*Evening Chronicle*
*June 28, 1941*

in having a program in which the same registration areas were repeated. The local teachers who enrolled in the previous workshop, for example, were not able to take the second one for course credit.

### COMMUNITY PREPARATION FOR THE WORKSHOP

*The Newspapers.*—The newspapers in Calhoun County, particularly the Marshall *Evening Chronicle* and the Battle Creek *Enquirer and News*, did much to prepare the community for the workshop and to interpret it while it was in session. Beginning on the first of May, the Marshall *Evening Chronicle* ran a series of six front-page articles. Throughout the summer session the newspapers generously gave space to articles interpreting the program to the community. Eighteen articles, twelve of which appeared on the front page, were printed during this time by the Marshall paper. The Battle Creek *Enquirer and News*, which is widely read in Calhoun county, was likewise exceedingly generous in the space that it gave to workshop activities. On two successive Sundays this paper ran feature articles, one of which was illustrated with six photographs. Local newspaper reporters called daily upon the publicity committee for news. A series of three articles was featured in the *Michigan Daily*, the University campus newspaper. The articles reproduced on the opposite page are typical of the publicity the newspapers gave.

*Community Resources.*—The director of the workshop visited the Calhoun County Health Department, the Michigan Department of Health, the Calhoun County Agricultural Extension Service, the Marshall school library, and the County Laboratory before the opening of the workshop to explore ways in which the personnel of these agencies could work with the participants. No commitments were made at this time, however, for it was understood that requests for various kinds of services were usually to be made directly by participants so that they might learn about available resources and how to use them. It was discovered through these contacts that excellent films could be secured from the U. S. Department of Agriculture through the county agricultural agent and the 4-H Club leader, and that certain facilities such as portable blackboards and electric plates, as well as literature on many pertinent problems, were also available. The County Laboratory had technical equipment that could be used for certain experiments. The Michigan Department of Health had exhibits and films. The personnel in all of these organizations, particularly the County Health Department, was willing to work with individuals or groups on their problems as the occasion arose. The same procedure was followed in making plans for using recreational facilities and the services of the community recreational leader.

*The Board of Education.*—The board of education, working through the superintendent, contributed much to make the workshop possible.

*Marshall High School was one of the three school buildings in which workshop activities were centered.*

Its attitude was well expressed in a communication from the superintendent of schools: "The Marshall school faculty, board of education, and community appreciate very much the services rendered to the community and have endeavored to provide the necessary local assistance that would contribute to a successful workshop."

This assistance was most generously given. The actual cost for housing the workshop is difficult to estimate. The auditorium, for instance, rents for twenty-five dollars a night. One janitor, in addition to the two regular workers, was employed during the six-week period. Necessary equipment was trucked from one building to another. Electricity, soap, towels, water, gas for cooking and experimental work, typewriters, and telephones were used. Three buildings, the High School, the Central School adjoining it, and the Capitol Hill School were used. The rooms used by the workshop were thoroughly cleaned beforehand. Although the janitors were busy with refinishing and repainting, they were most cooperative in helping to make the group comfortable. School equipment of all kinds was required by both participants and children. The high school librarian took charge of accessioning about five hundred new

*Capitol Hill School, a two-room school, was used as the rural school demonstration center. This school was built in 1860.*

books for the workshop. She arranged the nine hundred books selected by the staff according to the classifications used for the group—philosophy of education, curriculum planning, adolescent psychology, student needs and counseling, regional and community life, techniques for the study of community life, improvement of reading ability, literature and language arts, foreign languages, consumer education, health and physical education, safety education, mathematics, science, social studies, visual education, evaluation and research, and administration of the school—and she also served as librarian during the first half of the workshop.

*Housing.*—The superintendent and his office assistant prepared a mimeographed list of available rooms and apartments to help participants who were planning to live in Marshall find comfortable living arrangements.

Typical of the problems which participants brought to the workshop are the following, expressed here as stated by the members at the outset:

How to integrate health sciences in a modern educational program that meets the needs of boys and girls

How to make the transition from traditional to modern teaching

Health education in a high school program, with emphasis on the application of the principles of science to living in the community

To develop a technique of appraisal of the school situation at the time of visitation. Items to be considered include the teacher and her part, pupil attitudes and responses to the situation, and the physical condition of the building and grounds

The problem of using the local community in the school program

How and what health problems can be carried on throughout a rural school so that every child will be interested and will contribute to that problem

A hot lunch program in a small school

Most of the numerous problems brought to the workshop by the fifty-two participants[1] were related closely to their school and community health programs. For instance, six teachers from the high school group were interested in working out a health education program as a part of the daily experiences of students and teachers, particularly in the areas of learning for which each teacher was responsible. They also were concerned about developing techniques for securing cooperation among administration, teaching staff, and community in making a reality out of any plans that were formulated. Eighteen teachers from rural and elementary schools wished to work on a health education program for their particular schools, grades, or groups of children. Fifteen were interested in learning about the community resources to use in school activities and in developing techniques of working with parents and community groups. Seven selected as their problem nutrition, food habits, and the school lunch program. Nine wanted help in such educational problems as making the transition from traditional to newer ways of

---

[1] This group included 25 rural teachers, 16 city or village elementary school teachers, a commissioner of schools, 4 junior high school teachers, and 6 high school teachers including a dean of women and a senior high school principal.

teaching, planning for an experience curriculum, developing units of work, discovering child needs and interests, preparing a core curriculum for junior high school groups, or teaching the fundamentals better through an indirect approach. Four wanted help in teaching activities for primary grade children in rural school situations. Three had difficulties with the teaching of reading and another three wanted to work on problems of evaluation. Other interests of participants were guidance, communicable disease control, first aid, arts and crafts, lighting, and student government.

### STAFF PREPARATION FOR THE WORKSHOP

Conferences which were arranged occasionally with the directors of four other workshops to be held in the area proved most profitable. Discussions related to such common interests as organizing a workshop according to democratic procedures, preparing the participant for the summer's work, kinds of resources and materials to make available to participants, types of records, and selection of professional books. These general procedures are described in Chapter I.

The directors attended a two-day staff conference conducted by the Workshop Advisory Service sponsored by the University of Chicago early in April. A one-day meeting was held in May for directors of fourteen workshops scheduled in Michigan for the summer of 1941. At this time, plans of organization for the different workshops were explained and various problems, such as the use of part-time personnel and evaluation of work, were discussed.

*Selection of the Staff.*—The assistance and cooperation of Dr. J. B. Edmonson, Dean of the School of Education, Dr. John Sundwall, head of the Department of Hygiene and Public Health, University of Michigan, and Dr. Henry J. Otto of the W. K. Kellogg Foundation made it possible to secure a staff excellently trained, versatile, imbued with a spirit of education for a social democracy, and particularly gifted by personality to work with people. Staff members looked upon their appointments as exceptional opportunities and wholeheartedly accepted the challenge to participate in a venture which they believed would prove full of social and educational significance.

Of the eight staff members, all were employed on a full-time basis except one. Four staff members worked with children and young people in the laboratory school; they were selected for their special

training in child growth and development, their work in the fields
of science, and their rich background of teaching experience. Staff
members who were responsible for a certain registration area were,
of course, thoroughly familiar with the University requirements.
These areas of learning were explored and made to function in relation to the problems being solved. A brief description of the background of each staff member follows.

Otto K. Engelke, M.D., M.S.P.H., studied medicine at the University of Cincinnati and public health at the University of Michigan. He served as health officer for Adams County, Ohio, and
practiced medicine in Dearborn and Detroit, Michigan. During a
year's fellowship in the Michigan Community Health Project area,
he served as acting director of the health departments of Branch
and Allegan counties. During the workshop, it was necessary for
Dr. Engelke to leave for Ann Arbor to assume his responsibility as
director of the newly organized Washtenaw County Health Department. The University then appointed Morley B. Beckett, M.D.,
M.P.H., director of the Allegan County Health Department, to fill
the vacancy. Dr. Beckett had previously worked with the Michigan
State Department of Health. He received his medical training at
the University of Toronto and his public health training at Johns
Hopkins University. Dr. Engelke and Dr. Beckett were the resource
staff members in two registration areas: Hygiene 131 or 201, Physiologic Hygiene; and Hygiene 132 or 202, Communicable Diseases and
Epidemiology.

Meredith W. Darlington, B.S., M.A., formerly of Teachers College, University of Nebraska, is at present serving as assistant professor of education in Oklahoma Agricultural and Mechanical College, Stillwater. Mr. Darlington has also done field work sponsored
jointly by the University of Nebraska and the Teacher Education
Commission. In the workshop, he served as generalist in education
and resource person in Education A130, Problems in Educational
Sociology.

Miss Miriam Kangas, B.S. in home economics, has studied as a
graduate student at the University of Michigan, at the University
of Chicago, and at Iowa State College. She came with a rich background of experience in high school teaching and in parent education. At present she is teaching in the Lakeview consolidated
school in Calhoun County. She was the teacher of the senior high
school laboratory group.

Ralph Witherspoon, B.S., M.A., was an assistant in elementary education, School of Education, University of Michigan, while completing work for his doctorate in the fields of human development and educational psychology. Mr. Witherspoon has taught in rural schools, in junior high school, and in senior high school. He worked with boys and girls in the junior high school laboratory group.

Miss Kathryn Leeke, B.A., M.A., supervisor of the elementary grades in the Marshall school system, has had experience as a rural teacher, a graded school teacher, a county normal teacher, and a critic teacher at Michigan State Normal College. Miss Leeke had charge of the young elementary school children in grades one to four.

Miss Amy Person, B.A., M.A., supervising principal in an elementary school in Wyandotte, Michigan, has been a county normal principal, a critic teacher in a rural training school, and a teacher of science. She worked with the children in the rural school group.

Dean Chamberlin, M. A. Assistant Dean of Men and Professor of English in Dartmouth College, worked in the area of arts and crafts and recreation for two days a week. His time was shared between the Hillsdale and Marshall workshops.

The director of the workshop, Miss Vivian V. Drenckhahn, M.S., C.P.H., had been working with elementary school teachers in Calhoun and Van Buren counties on a consultative basis, with an appointment on the University of Michigan staff, during the preceding two years. She served as resource staff member in Hygiene 115, Methods and Materials of Health Education.

Two secretaries, employed on a full-time basis, contributed greatly to the efficiency of the workshop. They made it possible to produce materials as developed or needed by staff and participants. They also made possible a more complete record of all phases of workshop activities including the diaries of the staff, the developments at group discussions, and lecture notes. At the end of the workshop, they assembled materials developed in the workshop; this ninety-page mimeographed book was distributed to all participants.

*Orientation of Staff to Local Problems.*—Conferences were arranged with all staff members long before the opening of the workshop. Most of the staff visited schools in Calhoun County with the director. They all had the opportunity to help compile the bibliography. Problems were also discussed through correspondence.

Finally a three-day working session for staff took place beginning on Thursday of the week before the workshop opened. A tour of

the school buildings was made to review the facilities. Staff members
became acquainted with the superintendent, school librarian, community recreation leader, janitors, newspaper reporters, and other
people in the community. There was discussion of the primary responsibilities of each staff member, different ways in which the
teachers in the laboratory school might work with participants, and
ways in which the staff not teaching in the laboratory school might
serve it.

The interests and problems of teachers as expressed during the
conferences held in their schools were reviewed. Consideration was
given to democratic procedures in organizing the six-week session
so that individuals in the group could take an active part in planning
and in assuming responsibility for carrying out various activities.
Events were planned for the first two days to nurture and encourage
such developments. A typical day was also anticipated, as well as
the types of problems which would arise in connection with the use
of library books, observation and participation in the laboratory
school, and the scheduling of general and special group meetings,
noon luncheons, field trips, visitors, records, and reports. The staff
frequently disagreed as to the best procedure, and all decisions relating to the participants were left to the members of the workshop,
either as a group, or through a committee to be elected by the group.
The staff discussed records and agreed to keep a diary. A pictorial
record of activities was also to be kept either by one of the staff or
a participant interested in visual education and photography. All
pictures were later taken by Mr. Ernest Cutting, a participant, and
Mr. Ralph Witherspoon, a member of the staff. Staff members had
time during the preworkshop conference to learn more about the community. They met with the staffs of the four other workshops to
hear the Foundation's Consultant in Education, Dr. Henry J. Otto,
describe the broad educational program sponsored by the Foundation in the area of the Michigan Community Health Project, and
at the close of this three-day orientation period held a picnic.


### ORGANIZATION OF THE WORKSHOP SCHEDULE

Daily activities were guided by the bulletin boards in the general
meeting room and by the frequent planning sessions. Early in the
workshop, the members decided not to have a planning or steering
committee; they thought the group was small enough (fifty-two

participants and eight staff members) that all could participate in planning meetings to be held once or twice a week. Since many of the staff felt that a planning committee had an important place in the workshop and that the group had not understood its function, this subject was brought up at subsequent meetings but each time voted down. The group sincerely felt that they all wanted a part in planning, for it was more "democratic." Surprisingly enough, this plan functioned exceedingly well. The group efficiently delegated certain responsibilities to committees which in turn reported to them or kept them informed through announcements or messages on the bulletin board. A six-week calendar was posted on one of the bulletin boards, which served as the place to schedule events and to inform participants about them. A "Suggestion Box" was placed in a prominent position in the general meeting room, but only three suggestions were made through it.

*Evaluation of Daily Activities.*—At an early meeting, when the question of reports and grades was discussed, members of the workshop agreed to keep a diary, in which progress in solving problems would be recorded, events in terms of individual growth would be evaluated, and reactions toward daily activities, such as conferences, discussions, trips, or observations, would be recorded.

*Selection of an Adviser.*—Not until the second week, after participants and staff had an opportunity to know each other better, did each participant select an adviser. The staff member selected was usually the one with whom previous conferences had been scheduled on the first day of the workshop. The adviser kept in touch with the individual's daily program and with the progress he was making in work on his problem or special interest. Although all staff people were eager to help any participant, it was to the adviser that the participant went most often to discuss progress in solving his problem, ways of improving the diary, or the selection of reference material. Usually the adviser visited the school with the participant to study a problem further and to discuss local resources in terms of the educational program.

*The Daily Program.*—The workshop day began early, at eight o'clock in the morning, although many of the teachers had household duties to perform at home. Sixteen of the fifty-two participants lived in Marshall during the summer. Many could reach Marshall High School by a few minutes walk or drive, but some had longer drives—as much as thirty-five miles. Even so, eight o'clock found many already at work, attending a committee meeting, having a conference with a member of the staff, participating in a group meeting, or delving deeper into special interests or problems. By nine o'clock, the workshop was in full swing for everyone, with about half of the group observing and participating in the Children's and Young People's School. These classrooms were in session from nine

*On the first days in school the children and teachers arranged furniture, measured the light, tested vision, weighed and measured, and became acquainted with each other and their school. Out of these activities, working groups were organized to meet the interests and needs which were discovered.*

until eleven-thirty o'clock, except during the days when hot lunches were served at school. After the children left, observers and staff discussed the experiences of the forenoon and the development of the children through these experiences. They discussed growth and behavior. They asked questions about the teacher's reasons for handling situations as she did. As progress was made, it was noted. Together they made suggestions and planned for future work. It was a free, informal period and, for many observers, "the highlight of the morning," for they were able to talk over their own problems as teachers.

Participants who were not observing were equally busy at one of several activities. They might be meeting with a small group working on problems such as the school lunch, first aid, communicable disease, community resources, or parent relationships. They might be out in their own school district visiting people to get help or information necessary in developing plans for the coming year. They

*Participants could observe and help in the four classrooms of the laboratory school which were in session from nine to eleven-thirty.*

might go on a half-day or all-day trip to study sanitation of milk and water, methods of sewage disposal, housing, school modernization, or school equipment. They might be reading in the library, having a conference, preparing an exhibit or demonstration, writing a report, or previewing a movie before arranging to show it to the group. They might be working in the shop, learning a new craft, or making an art object. They might be in their community, studying their own particular school with the assistance of a member of the staff.

Two luncheons a week were arranged in a special room of the Marshall Tavern. This was the time for group singing and other music, readings, and laughter. Occasionally visitors gave short talks.

Afternoon sessions included general meetings for discussions of problems in which the entire group was interested, such as child development, the organization and services of the health department, school environmental problems such as lighting, heating and ventilation, bacteriology as applied to sanitation and communicable diseases, communicable disease control, the medical examination, the

*A committee made arrangements for group luncheons twice a week. Much talent was discovered through the informal and often impromptu entertainment.*

medical program in the area, dental health, cumulative records, and committee reports on various subjects studied, such as nutrition, visual aids, and parent-teacher work. In the afternoon, participants also worked individually and in small interest groups. Usually group activities came to an end around four o'clock, although sometimes meetings ended earlier or continued longer. The activities which were scheduled during two days of the workshop follow.

### ACTIVITIES ON THURSDAY, JULY 3, 1941

8:30–11:00    A tour to observe food sanitation in restaurants. It was one of four similar tours with not more than ten in a group conducted by a public health engineer from the County Health Department and a member of the staff. These tours were scheduled before the workshop began serving hot lunches in the laboratory school.

9:00–12:00 Observation in the laboratory school and group conferences with classroom teachers following the school session

9:00– 1:30 Trip to the Athens High School. Four members of the high school group, a staff member, and a public health engineer from the County Health Department visited the Athens High School to study environmental problems and their educational implications.

8:30–10:30 Group meetings to evaluate magazine articles on communicable diseases

1:30 Meeting of the recreation committee to plan for workshop recreation

2:30– 3:30 General meeting of staff and participants. Discussion of slides on school environmental problems

3:30 Movie on child guidance, *You and Your Child*

### ACTIVITIES ON TUESDAY, JULY 15, 1941

8:30–10:00 Meeting of six members of high school group with three members of staff

9:30–12:00 Seven teachers make trip to two rural schools to discuss school problems, community resources, and educational implications.

9:00–12:00 Conferences. Committee meetings. Reading in library. Work on problems. Observation in laboratory school and group conferences following observation

12:00 Luncheon in charge of committee working on school lunch problems. Following lunch, the committee led a discussion on problems relating to the preparing and serving of school lunches.

1:30 Meeting of public relations group

1:30 Meeting of parents of school children and staff working with children

3:00 Meeting on evaluation of films on tuberculosis

### TYPES OF WORKING GROUPS AND COMMITTEES

Conferences with participants before the opening of the summer session gave the staff leads as to possible working groups and committees. Even before the workshop opened, the publicity and recreation committees were under way. Beginning with the first day, new needs and interests arose. Participants volunteered to serve as hostesses on a weekly basis. A luncheon committee investigated possibilities for eating together and made arrangements to do so.

A group interested in movies and slides assumed the responsibility for ordering and previewing all movies throughout the summer. The high school people formed a group which continued to work together

*A local physician meets with the entire group to discuss the medical examinations for children and adults.*

*A group working on bacteriology, as applied to problems in school sanitation.*

closely. So many were interested in nutrition and the school lunch that it was necessary to organize four groups concerned with different problems. Another large group was interested in developing better school and community relationships. This group continued throughout the summer session and sponsored discussions of the work of the parent-teacher organizations, service committees, and health de-

*A committee making plans for group recreation. A portion of the workshop library can be seen in the background.*

partments. They were interested in school finances, in meetings with parents, and in making better use of the community resources.

Other groups which met frequently were rural teachers, grade teachers, and teachers from the same school system, so they could discuss educational problems peculiar to their situations. A commissioner of schools and a group of rural teachers worked on an appraisal form which could be used by the commissioner during visits to schools. Teachers interested in evaluation worked out procedures and forms to use in appraising the workshop.

The recreation committee planned picnics, games, a smorgasbord luncheon, a "fun" program, and the trip to Clear Lake Camp. The committee found it difficult to plan recreation activities because the weather was very hot during most of the session. Teachers planned busy workshop schedules and many (thirty-six in all) drove to and from their homes daily. The participants working in the shop on arts and crafts prepared an exhibit of articles which children could make. Another committee or group interpreted workshop experiences to visitors through a panel discussion. Some committees or groups worked for a short time—three days or a week—while others continued throughout the six-week period. The work of these groups is illustrated by the following three progress reports.

*A member of the staff was in the shop two days a week to work with participants on arts and crafts. Many of the articles in this exhibit were made during the summer session.*

*The Nutrition and School Lunch Group.*—One of these three groups was concerned with the study of nutrition and school lunches. It met during the first week of the workshop, and the problems raised at that meeting (and recorded by a group secretary) were:

1. Does a good school lunch have to be a hot lunch?
2. How are hot lunches prepared in a one-room school? in larger schools?
3. What can be done about selecting adequate lunches when students buy at stores or restaurants?
4. How are good eating habits encouraged? How do children learn to like different foods?
5. What can be done about children who eat most or all of lunch at recess time? no lunch? stealing lunch? trading for lunch?

6. Should food be served at school in the morning for breakfast or at noon?

7. What can be done about dieting among junior and senior high school students and teachers?

8. What are the recreational problems in relation to noon lunch and pupil health? (10–15 minute eating periods; eating outdoors)

9. What are the standards for a good lunch room?

10. What are the food needs of boys and girls?

11. Do we need a lunch program?

12. Why should we have one?

*Nutrition was one of the problems studied in the workshop. Graphs were used to compare different food values.*

13. How do we go about getting the food, money, equipment, and interest for a lunch program?

14. What kind of educational program can be developed with parents, children, school board, teachers, community groups, and press?

15. How much pupil participation should there be?

16. During what part of the year should hot lunch be served? all year?

17. What is the advisability of serving milk and graham crackers or tomato juice at 9:30 or 2:30? Does it interfere with noon lunches?

18. What are standards for the care and handling of food?

19. How should food be cared for with respect to storage and refrigeration?

20. What are standards for dishwashing?

21. How should we avoid embarrassment for children who need milk and breakfasts?

22. On what basis should children be selected for special feeding?

Only two of these problems were settled to satisfaction at this first meeting; namely, that a mid-morning lunch of milk or fruit juice served early enough so as not to interfere with noon lunch was thought desirable for some of the children, and that the reason for using only pasteurized milk in a school lunch program is to prevent the spread of certain communicable diseases. Since the participants who were observing in the laboratory school were unable to attend

*The group had the experience of learning more about a hot lunch program through participating in one. A committee prepared a hot dish to supplement the packed lunches brought by participants.*

this discussion, a similar meeting was scheduled for them. During the second week the group met to work out procedures for solving the problems that had been raised, and the problems were classified into the following groups:

1. Study of food needs in relation to an adequate diet
2. Survey of resources available in a community to meet nutritional needs, particularly in the school lunch program
3. The organization of a school lunch program
4. The educational activities which may go hand in hand with the school lunch program with particular reference to school personnel, children, parents, and community groups

The techniques listed for helping to solve these problems included consultation with experts, discussion with participants who had already made some progress in this problem, slides and movies showing desirable practices, reading books and pamphlets, visits to a school to observe a program, observations in the classrooms of the workshop during lunch period, and surveys of local eating habits and food needs. Participants organized themselves into working committees according to their special interests. Committees began their work on July 3, and arranged for the following experiences which were made available to the workshop as a whole:

July 11, 9:00 A.M. The discussion of adequate diet was centered around making graphs indicating relative food values. This session was conducted by one of the nurses from the County Health Department.
   1:00 P.M. The above working session was repeated for a different group.
July 15, 12:00 M. A committee of five demonstrated the planning, preparation, and serving of a school lunch with participants as "pupils." In the discussion which followed, many educational activities were illustrated.
July 18, 2:30 P.M. Material summarizing nutritional needs and adequate diets was presented by another group. Exhibits pertaining to an adequate diet were also arranged.
July 21, 2:00 P.M. A committee presented reports on the cost of suitable equipment for rural school lunch programs. Charts illustrating the community resources which are available were placed on exhibit. A further discussion of school lunch equipment and sanitation was led by the public health engineer of the County Health Department. Slides were used in the discussion.
July 25, 8:30 A.M. A panel discussed school and community education activities in connection with the teaching of nutrition and school lunches. An exhibit of educational materials for reference use in the teaching program was also arranged by this committee.
July 31, 9:30 A.M. A demonstration of canning by 4-H Club girls was arranged with the cooperation of the 4-H Club leader.
   3:15 P.M. Panel discussion. The discussion on July 25 aroused a great deal of interest and this second meeting was arranged to provide for further consideration of certain problems. This activity completed the work of the committees working in nutrition.

The members of the workshop had the opportunity to take part in all phases of the lunch program carried on in the laboratory school, and during visits to other schools they appraised the lunch equipment. Conferences were scheduled frequently to help teachers with specific lunch situations or problems.

*The Committee on Visual Aids.*—A small group who were interested in assembling a bibliography of films and slides which could be used with boys and girls and community groups had their first meeting at 8:30 A.M. on July 2. This group decided to investigate local sources of films and slides and visited the offices of the County Health Department, the Commissioner of Schools, and the Agricultural Extension Service. They began to investigate state and national sources.

Films were usually ordered through this committee. During the six weeks they previewed and arranged for the showing of fourteen

*Participants take part in a panel discussion on the educational implications of the movie, "And So They Live." All movies and slides were evaluated after showing.*

different films,[1] which the committee explained to the group before showing, and evaluated afterward. The committee also compiled and mimeographed information on sources of films and slides and secured for each participant a folder of material and catalogs listing the films available from these sources.

Through efforts of the committee and with the cooperation of the manager of the Garden Theater, the state Department of Health,

---

[1] The films shown were: *With These Weapons, In Defense of the Nation, You and Your Child, Let My People Live, Good-bye Mr. Germ, On the Firing Line, And So They Live, Choose to Live, Safe Drinking Water from Small Water Supplies, The Plow, Vitamins on Parade, The Heritage We Guard, The River,* and *The Proof of the Pudding.*

and the Metropolitan Life Insurance Company, one of the highlights of the summer was securing the movie, *The Proof of the Pudding*, for community showing at the Garden Theater in Marshall. This technicolor film on nutrition was shown only in theaters. For the occasion, a "theater party" was planned, to which the County Health Department staff, families, and friends were invited.

Finally, the committee presented a report, later mimeographed, which included general background material about films and their use in the educational program as well as findings of research in this field, the sources of films and slides with many catalog listings, and description and evaluation of the films which the committee previewed and arranged for showing, along with suggestions for presentation. In addition to these films, ten different series of slides[1] were shown.

*The High School Group.*—Six participants from the high school field formed another group. Its members were a principal, two teachers, and a dean of women from senior high schools, and two teaching principals from junior high schools. Their activities included the following items:

June 23, 2:30 P.M. Met with staff member in charge of work with high school students to plan for their summer school experience.

June 24, 9:00 A.M. Continued to work with staff member in preparing for high school students who were to start summer school the next day.

June 25 to 27, 9:00 A.M. to 12:00 M. Observed a teacher working with boys and girls in a classroom situation, for busy teaching schedules did not provide the opportunity to observe during the school year.

July 3, 8:30 A.M. to 1:00 P.M. Visited Athens High School. The conference which followed indicated that problems already of interest now assumed larger proportions. The group began work on definite plans to meet specific problems in their own schools.

July 7 to 11, 9:00 A.M. to 12:00 M. Observed during the forenoons in junior high school room. They asked questions about the experience curriculum and the informal teaching program being developed with the boys and girls.

July 15. Met with four members of staff. The problem of developing a health education program now seemed so large that they reached the decision that each one would work on some phase of the high school program. Later they would share their reports.

July 21 to 28. Observed during the forenoons in the senior high school room.

[1] The slides shown included series on *Communicable Disease Control, Overview of Activities of the W. K. Kellogg Foundation, Rural School Modernization, Camp Activities, Water Supply, School Equipment, Dental Health Activities, Hot Lunch Programs,* and *Marshall Workshop Activities in* 1940 *and* 1941.

*Problems of sanitation affecting the health of children are studied. Here the group examines the school pump and well covering.*

*The condition and care of toilets are discussed, as well as their proper construction.*

July 22. Met with high school group to give a progress report. Questions relating to planning for a high-school program were brought up.

July 29. Discussed material that this group developed, assembled in a fifty-five-page typewritten report. The decision was reached that the material was only experimental, that there was a need to work further in their own communities and with their respective staffs; therefore, steps for working with local staffs were considered and outlined.

### VISITS TO TEACHERS' OWN SCHOOLS AND COMMUNITIES

Practically all of the participants visited their own schools with a member of the staff, usually with other participants and the public health engineer from the County Health Department. Before each

*School health problems are discussed in the school. Many of the participants*
*visited their own schools during the workshop with a member of the staff and*
*the public health engineer from the County Health Department.*

visit, the teacher acquainted the superintendent or school board, and sometimes both, with the purpose of the visit. There were many half-day trips with small groups visiting one or two schools, and one all-day trip on which twenty-six teachers took picnic lunches and visited five schools. In visits to their own school situations, teachers now observed things which hitherto had gone unnoticed.

They were looking at familiar conditions, but with a different point of view.

An incident illustrates the kind of change that took place. After seeing slides on rural school equipment problems, one group of rural teachers early in the summer session became most enthusiastic over the idea of arranging a "model" rural school in one of the Marshall High School classrooms. They wished to assemble file case, school lunch equipment, hand-washing and drinking equipment, library materials, scales, first-aid kit, and so on. Before long, however, they began to look at their own schools with new eyes and were challenged by work on real problems, with no further thought of the "model" rural schoolroom they had planned to set up in the high school.

References to visits to the teacher's school or community were frequently made in the diaries. Typical comments follow.

One teacher writes:

> Since this section is "home base" to me, the middle part of our trip was through very familiar territory. I was particularly interested in the comments and reactions of other people on our well-known section . . . Mr. A said that there were 150 families in three acres down there with individual sewage disposals and water supplies. These facts I did not know and as I rode with the "procession" through this section, I tried to look at it through a stranger's eyes. I saw many things that had gone unobserved during my previous home calls. Then I thought of the slogan "Know your community" and I wondered—what can I do? Probably one-fifth of our room each year has this section for a home. Do we make our school activities fit their needs, or do we meet the requirements of people from our better section? Which is more important in the making of good citizens? Does our school help them any more than the school helped the people in *And So They Live?*

Another teacher writes:

> Following my conference, I returned to our school late in the afternoon and tried to locate all types of records and materials which we have that would contribute to our picture of the whole child, thus aiding in his guidance.

A staff member writes about one of his trips with a group of teachers:

> Aside from Mrs. A's flat tire, our field trip went off as planned. B School certainly has its problems which appear somewhat hard to solve. Miss C proved to us that about the only place she could talk confidentially to patrons was "in the coal bin." We had an interesting discussion on the problems in safety. It would seem to me that a traffic light should be obtained at such a hazardous corner. The nature of the building also presented many problems in safety. Many lunch problems were discussed.
>
> The situation at Miss D's school doesn't appear so hopeless after all. The

teacher who will work with Miss D (not enrolled in the workshop) accompanied us. There seems to be every evidence of cooperation for next year. A large part of our time was spent in thinking of ways to get the lunch program out of the furnace room.

## Another staff member describes a trip as follows:

Mr. A and I went to - - - - - - for a building survey. Mr. B, principal of the high school, and three other high school teachers were there. Mr. A spent about three hours in going over the entire school plant. , Criticisms and suggestions were made concerning the heating system, the ventilation system, the plumbing system, lighting, window curtains, and other such things. The group then went to each classroom where time was given to considering the building and health needs necessary for this particular room. Mr. B has a rather complete set of notes as to the needs of the public school building.

Mr. B is to confer with his superintendent of schools as to the method of presenting these building needs to the board of education, and to the people at large. It may be that Mr. B will prepare some type of booklet which will portray the building situation in its present condition, its future needs, the reasons for certain changes, and the estimate of costs for the changes or improvements recommended.

## This same staff member writes at another time:

At 9:30, seven of the teachers, Mr. A and myself went to the B School which Mrs. C is to teach next year. Mr. A went over the buildings and grounds very carefully with the teachers, calling their attention to, and giving them an opportunity to talk about, and ask questions on, the walls, the ceiling, the windows, the electric light fixtures and arrangement, the floors, the seating arrangement, the drinking and washing facilities, the hot lunch equipment, the heating system, ventilation and safety features of the school building, the steps and front porch, the well, the toilets, playground equipment, and the general layout of the school grounds. . . . Some of the suggestions made were: get the pupils to study certain features of the school building and grounds from a safety or health point of view; take some of the pupils to visit other school buildings and grounds that are more attractive and desirable; take some of the parents or mothers' club to visit other school buildings and grounds; have the mothers' club make a study of certain features of the school buildings and grounds, call the attention of people to certain conditions, such as the steps, when they come to visit school. Have the county school commissioner come out and talk to the school pupils, the patrons of the community, or other community people, about the school buildings and grounds. . . . This group plans to meet tomorrow in the library to talk about educational implications. . . .

A study of school problems was particularly significant at this time, for Calhoun County was preparing for a school modernization project during the coming year. Every opportunity, therefore, was used to emphasize the need for working with school boards, parents, and children in the community in developing an understanding of education to meet existing needs and the way in which the school facilities might contribute to such an educational program. It was brought out that schools whose programs and facilities are good in terms of the traditional pattern, often are not well suited to today's needs. Studying the school program in the school situation had the added value of bringing the staff to see the problems of the teacher vividly and forcibly. This experience alone was of inestimable value to both staff and participants. It presented a challenge which the workshop group were trying to meet throughout the session.

*A group visits the County Health Department to secure*
*help on problems of school sanitation.*

### THE USE OF LOCAL RESOURCES

Every community has resources that are of marked educational value, but the extent to which these values are understood and realized depends largely on the teacher. For this reason, the participants themselves arranged for the utilization of resources as the opportunity arose. Many professionally trained leaders from the community helped with certain problems. This group[1] included the

[1] They were respectively Dr. Hugh Robins, Mr. Herbert Dunsmore, Mr. Robert Cameron, and Misses Mildred Tuttle, Roberta Foote, Thelma Meckfessel, and Janet Davidson, all from the Calhoun County Health Department; Dr. D. B. Morrison, Dr. Earl Peabody, Mr. B. E. Henry, Dr. Henry J. Otto, and Mrs. Zoe Wright.

county health officer, two public health engineers, and four public health nurses, all from the County Health Department; a physician, a dentist, the county 4-H Club leader, and the Consultant in Education and the librarian from the W. K. Kellogg Foundation, and a number of lay leaders in parent-teacher and other community organizations.

Restaurants in Marshall agreed to have groups of teachers visit them on tours of inspection. Dairy barn and pasteurizing plant

*A public health nurse discusses with parents and teachers*
*health problems of the school child.*

operators received groups on two occasions. The County Health Department staff, in addition to helping individuals and groups, entertained the participants at a tea in the library of the W. K. Kellogg Foundation. Some of the business and professional men in Marshall made no charge for some services or for some materials used by the children in the workshop.

Clear Lake Camp, Federal Housing Authority projects, Wilder Creek Park, the Battle Creek sewage disposal plant, and the Marshall sewage disposal and water systems were among the places visited. The Calhoun County Tuberculosis Association, the Michigan Department of Health, the County Laboratory, and the County Agri-

*Girls in 4-H Club work demonstrate the canning of vegetables
to be used in the school lunch program.*

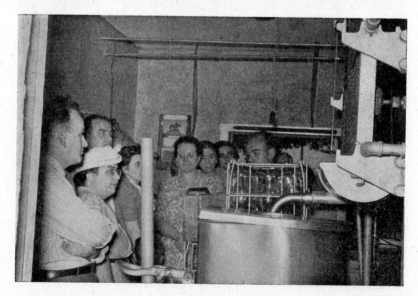

*During a study of milk and milk-borne diseases, a local dairy barn and
pasteurizing plant are visited to observe the handling and care of milk.*

cultural Extension Service helped with certain problems. The manager of the Garden Theater, the local school superintendents, principals, school boards, and other leaders assisted from time to time.

*Utilizing Resources in Solving School Problems.*—As different school problems were discussed, the resources available for helping with the solution of them were explored. For instance, in the following school situations[1] it was necessary to draw upon information relating to

*Participants studied the relationship of housing to health. While visiting a low cost housing project, they see a septic tank being constructed.*

the public health sciences as well as the community resources in order to solve the problem satisfactorily.

1. Plans for a school lunch have been made, but it was found that a pasteurized milk supply is not available.

2. Child in a schoolroom develops a chronic cough, is pale, and his work begins to slow up. Medical examination is obtained, but no definite diagnosis made. Neighbor tells the teacher that the child's mother has tuberculosis.

3. Continuing the above situation, a positive diagnosis of tuberculosis is made on the child. What of the school, community, children, and teacher?

4. Child listless on Friday afternoon. Monday morning child absent, but

[1] Compiled by Dr. M. B. Beckett.

sister comes to school and complains of headache.  Sister says brother at home has a rash.

5. Continuing above situation, medical diagnosis of scarlet fever is made. What of pupils, school, school board, and the community?

6. Teacher wishes to promote a dental program.  What are her resources and should she use a screening program with the help of the school nurse?

7. A case of measles breaks out in school.  What responsibility has the teacher to parents of other children?  Is this responsibility greater for measles than possibly for some other diseases?  What diseases may be prevented after actual exposure?

8. Dog runs through school yard and snaps at a child, leaving teeth marks. Mixed story from children as to reason for dog biting.  Child sent home and father comes in ready to hunt down dog and shoot him.  What education can the teacher practice?  What resources should she call upon and what action should be taken?

9. There is impetigo in the school.  Parents complain because a family does not treat the child.  What can the teacher do and how far may she go in helping to clear up the condition?

10. Teacher and school board receive notice that the school well is contaminated.  School board refuses to act and tells the teacher to carry water from the next farm.

11. School board has $100.00 to spend for improvements.  They agree on a merry-go-round.  The teacher knows the school needs new toilets, new well, new lighting.  What can be her actions?

### THE LABORATORY SCHOOL IN OPERATION

The children met in four groups including a rural school, a high school, a younger elementary, and an upper elementary group.  In all, eighty children were enrolled, four of whom were brought by teachers from outside of Marshall.  Almost twice as many children from the lower elementary age group wished to enroll, but the workshop staff was not large enough to accommodate them.  Twenty-five was the limit set for each room, but the high school enrollment was far below this number with only nine regular students in attendance.

The work for children started on Thursday of the first week and continued through Wednesday of the sixth week, making a five-week period.  School was in session from nine o'clock until eleven-thirty, except for the five days when everyone stayed for luncheon. An experience curriculum, starting with the interests and problems of the children, was developed.  Health sciences and citizenship received considerable emphasis and were integrated throughout the program.  The observers were much interested in observing the growth processes of children and in discussing their observations afterward with staff members. Even if teachers were unable to observe in the morning, they made a real effort to attend one of these discussion periods.

Parents preferred being able to observe at their convenience and this they were cordially invited and urged to do. They were also invited from time to time to attend special meetings, luncheons, or other visits to school.

*Parents visit the young people at work in their classroom. Parents and others from the community were urged to participate in workshop activities.*

The workshop group on several occasions discussed the best use of the laboratory school, but wisely formulated no rules to govern its use. They agreed that it was desirable to observe in smaller groups of six or seven, largely so they would be less conspicuous and so they could participate more fully in both planning and helping with activities. As a result, the participants, for the most part, decided to observe a week at a time, and during alternate weeks. Some, however, spent considerably more time in the laboratory school than others.

A summary[1] of kinds of experiences which children had in the laboratory school follows.

[1] This summary was prepared by the staff members working with the young people, Misses Kathryn Leeke, Miriam Kangas, and Amy Person, and Mr. Ralph Witherspoon.

*High School Students.*—At the outset of the program, the interests of the high school students were inventoried and the students then made selections of the work in which they wanted to have experience. Group work was organized into projects and as progress was made each student reported to the whole group. Some of the projects of students were:

A study of the Marshall sewage disposal system and water supply. As a result of this study, the whole class studied techniques to use in informing the people of Marshall about this problem.

*Many visitors from the local community as well as from a distance came to observe the work. Here a high school boy tells about his interest in conservation which he hopes to make his life work. He discusses the habits of a pet raccoon.*

A study of conservation. Informative talks on wild animals were given and the problems of conserving them were discussed.

A study of personality development. The importance of good general appearance, good posture and carriage, and proper manners was emphasized. During this project, community people were called in to help. A shoe dealer gave many points to look for in buying shoes. A local saleswoman talked to the group on the appropriateness of clothes, color, and design, to the individual.

A study of lunchroom management. The high school group managed a lunchroom in relation to a project in school lunches. Balanced, attractive, and inexpensive noon lunches were served to the teachers in the workshop for a three-day period. The requirements of planning, preparing, and serving, of being host and hostess, of being waiter and waitress, or cashier, were studied and the activities practiced. The group entertained parents and guests at one luncheon on the profits made in their lunchroom. At this time students explained the work done in their group.

Other projects were a newspaper on workshop activities, and undertakings in shop work for boys and girls.

In evaluating their work and discussing young people's responsibility in the community, it was concluded that they should find

*Through experimenting, children discover the properties of light. They became interested in this problem through using a light meter to determine the amount of light on their desks and in various parts of the classroom.*

something worthwhile to do, keep themselves healthy, and be good citizens.

*Boys and Girls in Grades Five to Eight.*—Living together happily became the theme of the summer's activities for children in intermediate grades. Regular school subjects, such as arithmetic, reading, and writing, became an integral part of the activities in which health sciences were considered the foundation on which happy, cooperative living was built.

Since many teachers, thirty-five in all, observed and participated in the activities of the room, the children took advantage of the opportunity to become acquainted with them and to help make the teachers feel interested in them and their work.

One of the most interesting activities began when the children obtained the use of a light meter from the local health department and measured the light on their individual desks and committee tables, under various lighting conditions, to determine whether there was enough light to meet hygienic standards for the kind of work

*As a part of the study of light, boys and girls make a drop-of-water-lens which was later compared with a real microscope.*

to be done. This led to a complete rearrangement of the room and then to a study of light as it affects man, plants, and animals. Experiments were conducted to show the properties of light, the formation of colors, the causes of day and night and the seasons, and finally into practical applications, such as the construction of a drop-of-water-lens microscope and blueprinting. The microscope experiment was extended to include the use of a real microscope and studying its use in protecting the health of man. Blueprints were made of leaves of food plants, many of which were leaves of plants which furnished food for the school lunches.

A study of the value to the body of various foods was undertaken in anticipation of the school lunches to be prepared at school. The children constructed a set of graphs showing the composition of various foods, and another set illustrating the vitamin content of the same foods. Committees of children participated in preparing, cooking, and serving the school lunches, and determining their cost. Children acted as hosts and hostesses and table etiquette was studied and practiced. Each day, teachers and visitors were guests of the children.

*In preparing for work with food, the boys and girls study food values through constructing graphs in an arithmetic period.*

A study of the digestive system was highlighted by several experiments showing the digestive process and by x-ray pictures of the parts of the digestive system.

Throughout the summer, activities stressing and practicing safety and first aid were integrated with the regular work, as the opportunity or need arose. As a part of this study, a first-aid box was built and outfitted. Directions for using first-aid materials were studied and mimeographed, and later explained to the other groups of children.

During all the activities, the children took every opportunity to explore the aspects of the projects which related to bettering health and citizenship. They watched for problems of cleanliness, nutrition, rest, and sanitation, discovering for themselves the facts through participation in scientific experiments. Cooperative planning of the many activities, followed by sharing of experiences, was the procedure most commonly used to solve the problems which were encountered; likewise, the room organization and the recreational activities were planned cooperatively by the group as a whole. In this way each child had the chance to follow his own interests and at the same time to participate in group living.

*On some days the children in all the classrooms prepared a hot dish to supplement a packed lunch brought from home. On other days they ate at home. The children thoroughly enjoyed their school lunch experiences.*

*The Kindergarten-Primary Group.*—On the first day of school, each child in the kindergarten-primary group told the other children what he wanted to do during the summer. Since their interests related to community workers, and one of the boys wanted to be a dentist, the first group activity was concerned with dental hygiene, in a study of the teeth and their care.

The older children did much reading and made reports to the group on the structure, number, and kinds of teeth, on how children should care for their own teeth, and on how the dentist could help them to have strong teeth.

In one corner of the room the younger children built a dentist's office of building blocks and made furniture for it. The girls made uniforms and learned of ways of being a dentist's assistant. All the children had been to the dentist, some very recently. One youngster was having her teeth cleaned and filled at the dentist's during this study, so she contributed a fine story of her visit to the dentist.

In preparation for the lunches there was an exhibit, provided and arranged by children, of foods that are good to eat every day. Since

*Among the stories which the young children enjoyed were those about helpers in the community. This was one of their interests during the summer.*

milk is one of the essential foods for children, it was studied in detail and related to the milkman as a community worker. The children learned about cows, their care, the dairy barn, care of milk, pasteurization, and foods made mostly from milk. They prepared an exhibit of milk and foods made from milk.

The study of milk had helped to prepare the children for the school lunch activity, when children ate their lunches at school. They made menus, studied the handling, care, and preparation of foods, made place doilies and place cards for their tables, made aprons for the waiters, and learned how to set the table properly, to serve the food, and to use proper manners at the table. A hostess at each table was responsible for the five guests at her table.

The children brought their own sandwiches and a simple dessert, such as fruit. A hot dish, some raw vegetables, and a drink were furnished. A committee of children prepared and cooked the hot dish and prepared the raw vegetable. Another committee set the tables, served the food and drink, and cleared the tables after lunch. Another committee washed the dishes and put the room in order.

*Children in the rural group brought their pets to school. From an interest in feeding their pets, the children turned to a study of their own health habits.*

During the last week two children developed severe colds, and this seemed the logical time to consider another community helper—the doctor. They discussed how the doctor helps us to keep well. The group visited the office of a local physician to learn about his work as a community helper. Finally, they planned and built a doctor's office.

*Rural School Group.*—Many of the rural children at Capitol Hill School began discussing their pets the first day of school. The interest continued during the summer and most of the children's activities were related to them. Pets were brought to school—puppies, kittens, ducklings, white rats, rabbits, and turtles. The children observed them during the day and discussed their habits—sleep, play, how they ate, how they kept clean. The younger children made pet books with pictures and stories of their observations. Together they read stories and poems.

All the children were keenly interested in their pets' food habits and in proper foods for them. A group of boys built a "Pet Food Store" and stocked it with the foods that pet books had recommended. They performed radio programs advertising "specials" for

*During a study of pets, children built an observation coop so their animals would be given proper care.*

particular pets. When a rabbit showed that he liked their "special" of vegetables and grain, they considered him wise. And a kitten showed good judgment in liking their advertised milk and cereal. These boys also built a large observation cage with compartments for three animals.

The younger children made an exhibit of pets and their foods, using clay models for the animals. They made ink footprints of each pet brought to school and discussed how the animals used their feet. In observing the teeth of their pets, the children noted great differences in kind and use. They made soap and plaster of Paris models to show the gnawing teeth of the rabbit and rat, and the tearing teeth of the puppy and kitten. The care of pets at school brought up the questions of proper handling, providing fresh drinking water, and washing hands after handling the pets.

These activities culminated in a pet show and parade on the grounds of the Capitol Hill School. The other children in the Young People's School were invited to participate. Ribbons were offered for the best pet of its kind, the prettiest pet, the strangest pet, the funniest

*The children enrolled in the rural school group arrange a pet show for other children and for participants in the workshop, parents, and interested friends in the community. In the background are several of the many exhibits summarizing their study of food for pets.*

pet, the best-trained pet, the best in the parade, and for all who brought pets. A band composed of the younger children led the parade. The show included an exhibit of good foods for pets, and models of pets' teeth.

The children enjoyed many new experiences in connection with the study of foods. They planned menus for hot lunches which were submitted to the workshop nutrition committee. From these menus were selected some to be used during the week of hot lunches in the Children's Division of the workshop. The children participated in buying food, keeping record books of all costs and recipes, and preparing and serving food. Mothers and teachers visited during these activities.

In the many experiences in which science, health, and citizenship were emphasized, the children did much reading and writing, solved arithmetic problems, engaged in art activities, and even learned much history through interest in the Capitol Hill School, which was built in 1860.

*First aid is studied by participants. The physician on the staff discussed the use of first-aid supplies.*

### INTRAWORKSHOP RELATIONSHIPS

Although each member of the staff had definite responsibilities in conducting the workshop, all worked especially well together as a group in all kinds of working sessions, either with members of the workshop or with individuals from the community. The four members of the staff in the laboratory school utilized the help of the other four members frequently as the occasions arose. All staff members, except one spending only half-time in the workshop, served as advisers of participants.

Such cooperative efforts required long hours and many working sessions for the staff, but it made possible the steady development of the workshop as a unit, and remarkable progress of individuals, both in gaining a background in the health sciences and in working out special problems. The staff met daily the first week and about two or three times a week after that to discuss the workshop program and to pool suggestions for it.

The work in first aid illustrates the way in which the staff worked together. During the first week, a group of participants were interested in the selection of first-aid equipment and its use. At the same

*Children, too, studied first aid and worked with staff members in this project.*

time, a group of children were interested in safety. Excerpts from diaries indicate the developments which took place in meeting these interests.

June 25. A small group of participants met to set up a first-aid kit. The prevention of accidents was taken up as an introduction to the subject. The most important topic seemed to be the medico-legal aspects of first aid. A committee decided to question the prosecuting attorney about the matter. Another committee elected to purchase the needed equipment.

June 26. The second first-aid discussion was really tossed about by a peppy group. A committee of participants agreed to shop for the essential equipment.

June 30. This week the children in my room arrived at an agreement to have the following committees: safety, animals, light, reception, and recreation.

July 3. The many possible Fourth of July accidents brought forth everything from first aid to superstition as to the way to handle the situation. Dr. E was brought in. A thrilling demonstration of traffic, using chairs for automobiles, followed. Dr. E offered to give any first aid to anyone in the room, but all injuries offered were passed up because they would be second or third aid. A committee was formed to work with Dr. E next week and to build some first-aid cabinets.

*While the children studied first aid, they decided they needed
a cabinet for their supplies.*

July 3. The children in Mr. W's group were certainly something to talk about. I took the first-aid material to them to see what they would do with it. They didn't miss a trick. Questions were popped at me from all angles. They were good ones, too. If you do not believe me, try walking into that bunch of live wires with a kit under your arm! In about fifteen minutes, a committee was set up to build a proper cabinet. Another was set up to present questions on first aid to me for reporting back to the group. And Dr. E was walking on eggs, trying to help them find a way to a safer Fourth of July!

July 8. After a brief and happy recess, our first-aid committee called on Dr. E and made plans for a good first-aid box and made an appointment to return to find out more about first aid. The group had appointed a secretary and brought back detailed minutes of the meeting.

July 9. The first-aid committee visited Mr. C this morning to get materials for the first-aid box which they had planned with Dr. E. They returned quite dissatisfied because Mr. C would not use the power saw and make all the pieces fit. However, they went to work and found it necessary to return for more tools only three times.

July 10.   Fred, Jean, and Bob called on Dr. E with a list of all the materials in the first-aid kit. The committee that had met with Dr. E returned and reported on the use of the various items in the first-aid cabinet. The boys demonstrated each article while Jean told how the article would be used by the teacher or by the doctor in giving first aid.

*The study of first-aid practices motivated some of the children to build their own cabinet for supplies.*

July 29.   The youngsters returned to their room thoroughly anxious to complete their pictures and their revamped first-aid box and a few experiments which they had not written up in their plan books.

July 30.   Bob and Fred went right ahead finishing the first-aid cabinet.

July 30.   Jean Ann was able to get the suggestions which the committee developed on the use of the first-aid material mimeographed and these she distributed to all the children enrolled in the summer school as well as to the participants in the workshop. Bob and Fred proudly presented the cabinet which they built, filled with first-aid supplies, to me this morning.

Integrated efforts toward working together were illustrated in many areas. For instance, while studying light, teacher, children, the physician on the staff, the County Health Department, the high school, and a hospital laboratory cooperated in making available various supplies, such as the light meter, the microscopes, and x-ray plates.

In the rural school, when flies became a nuisance during the serving of school lunches, the children, the workshop staff, and the superintendent of schools and Marshall Board of Education cooperated in providing screens for the windows.

A pet coop was planned by some of the boys in connection with a study of pets. By working with Mr. Chamberlin in the shop and by securing contributions of scrap lumber from business men in Marshall, these boys were able to make a fine pet coop which was used in the study of pets and in the pet show later in the summer.

### PROGRESS MADE BY PARTICIPANTS

The location of a workshop in the community made it possible for some teachers to enroll who would not otherwise have been able to attend a summer course because of economic factors and family responsibilities. Many teachers, particularly in rural areas, receive a low income. The convenience of attending the Marshall workshop resulted in some teachers' expressing an overt interest in a problem relating to health education. It was decided, therefore, to help these people translate this apparent interest into a genuine problem. Others, of course, came to the workshop with real problems already formulated.

It was a matter of days, in some cases extending into the second week, before certain of the participants became adjusted to the informal situation in which they could utilize to the fullest advantage all of the opportunities and resources which were available in solving their particular problems. In order to help individuals plan a daily program in terms of their special interests or problems, participants were asked during the second week of the workshop to indicate the progress they had made to date, the difficulties they had encountered, and the steps which they were planning to take in solving their problems.

Two case reports are given below to illustrate teacher growth and progress in solving a problem during the workshop. In Case A, the participant came with a well-defined problem, in the area of the health services, on which steady progress was made. On the other hand, it was not until the second week that Case C had realized that her fundamental problem was neither "being bothered by noise" nor "changing from traditional teaching." Instead, she found that she needed to understand child growth and development, and it was only after she recognized this need that progress was made in solving her problem.

In both instances the participants had developed a plan of action by the end of the workshop. In the staff's evaluation of the work of all participants, it was felt that with one or two exceptions all made real progress with the problems brought to the workshop and that everyone had a sense of accomplishment at the end of the six-week period.

*Case Report of Mrs. A.*[1]—Mrs. A, a second-grade teacher in a seven-teacher school in a suburban area, had, in addition to her regular group, a class in remedial reading consisting of retarded pupils from the other elementary grade rooms. In working with her own pupils and with the special reading class, Mrs. A observed that many of the children, especially those in the special group, seemed to have some poor health condition or physical defect, sometimes of a minor nature, and in other cases of a more serious nature.

She raised these questions:

1. If the child's health were improved or if the defect were removed, would it help the pupil in his school work?

2. Are the regular classroom teachers aware of their pupils' health and is any effort made to correct it or report it to the family health counselor?

3. What pupils, if any, were suffering from malnutrition and lack of proper rest and sleep?

4. What could a teacher do in working with a pupil and his home to make his school work and experiences happier and more successful?

During the course of the year Mrs. A discussed with the superintendent her observations and made a number of home calls which proved of some value, since there was definite follow-up and corrective work by the family physician. She also made adjustments, many seemingly minor, within her own schoolroom, which often benefited the individual pupil. The year's work was successful. Mrs. A had the vision of what could be done for all children, if the teachers understood them. She also sensed the values and benefits that other teachers could bring to their pupils if they, too, were able to observe and to understand children.

In her first conference with the faculty adviser Mrs. A told of her

---

[1] As reported by Mr. Meredith W. Darlington, adviser.

previous year's work.  She indicated that she wished to make a special study of the common physical handicaps and health problems that a teacher should notice in her pupils and to develop a corresponding list of educational implications to guide her in making the necessary adjustments.  For the initial step in this study she and her adviser made a tentative list of the work that could be done immediately: (1) confer with other staff members, especially the physician of the workshop staff; (2) check the library for any materials that might be helpful or suggestive; and (3) talk with other members of the workshop about the problem in an attempt to determine an organization of her material that would be helpful to all teachers.  Mrs. A had previously expressed the opinion that the other teachers in her own school should have the benefit of the type of information she was seeking in order that they might deal with their  pupils more effectively and successfully.

At the close of this first conference Mrs. A rather hesitatingly said that she was somewhat timid and had difficulty, not only in talking and conferring with new people, but in appearing before groups in any type of presentation.  The adviser voiced his doubts concerning her difficulty, since she had just demonstrated in the brief, clear, pleasant presentation and discussion of her own problem that she had excellent social abilities.  In order that Mrs. A might gain further confidence in herself and her ability to talk with new people, the adviser assured her that she not only could talk easily with people, but that she should talk with other staff members and workshop participants without any fear or hesitancy.  She then confided that the fact that she could tell her adviser of her difficulty would make it easier for her to talk with him, since he would now have a better understanding of situations that might arise from her self-consciousness.

This first conference and a carefully planned line of procedure on her stated problem seemed to provide the necessary impetus for Mrs. A's special study.  Not only did she begin to work enthusiastically, but her conferences with other staff members challenged her procedures and opened up broader horizons for her.  The library books she read proved stimulating and helpful.  The conferences she had with other workshop members encouraged her to drive forward.  Perhaps it was their own needs in the same field and their wholehearted cooperation that spurred her to make a serious study of this important problem of children's health.

In her second conference with the adviser, which occurred at the close of the first week, Mrs. A's report showed that she had been very successful in getting started in her study. The work that she had accomplished so far showed rather definitely that she had not wasted any time. She also had succeeded in some diplomatic manner in securing individual staff conferences despite the many demands on the staff this first week. She also displayed a certain scholarly ability in searching out helpful reference books and in getting materials applicable to her problem. The notes, the desirable books, and the many suggestions that she presented showed that she was availing herself of the resources at hand.

In the interim since the first conference, she had decided to broaden her problem to include, in addition to the health problems, a corresponding list of educational and home implications. This latter addition, she felt, would help a teacher know what approach to use at the home, the type of help or cooperation to seek, and the part that the parents and family might play in helping the pupil. Her work showed that the preparatory stage of her problem had been well done, and that she was now ready to proceed.

In the actual study of her problem, Mrs. A utilized every available resource. She talked again with her superintendent of schools, with a member of her board of education, the parents of several of her pupils, the local physician and the dentist, and with members from several community clubs, such as the Mothers' Club. By utilizing these many resources Mrs. A was not only learning richly herself, but was sensitizing many individuals in her community to the health problems of school children. Wisely, she selected individuals who were in a position to help actively. Through such activities Mrs. A had not only drawn the school and community into closer relationship, but was in a position to draw them into still closer cooperation during the next school year.

Her final report, consisting of approximately twenty-five pages, listed various health problems, the educational implications for the school, and home and family implications. Her material was accurate and helpful. It showed a satisfactory use of the workshop resources—staff, library, fellow participants—and of her community members—parents, physicians, dentists, superintendent, board of education, and others.

In working on her problem, Mrs. A had to make many individual contacts with new people. Before the close of the summer session

Mrs. A could meet and confer with individuals without fear or embarrassment. She also participated in a number of workshop committees. She was one of the five members who volunteered to assume responsibility for developing a program on "Interpretation of Marshall Workshop Experiences" to be presented to a community group, the special guests of the workshop. Later, in formulating the program, the committee asked Mrs. A to give a talk on the problem she brought to the workshop, how she happened to select the problem, and how she had proceeded to solve the problem. She accepted the assignment and made a most creditable presentation before a large group of people. This workshop experience was highly valuable from several points of view:

1. She made an excellent study of a vital problem, and as a result had a better understanding of the health conditions of pupils with which all teachers should be concerned.

2. She made many community contacts and realized through first-hand experiences the opportunities and many resources available to the alert teacher.

3. She prepared herself more adequately for meeting future problems of this nature, and made herself ready to utilize the resources in her own school and community during the next year.

4. She overcame, to a great extent, her feelings of timidity in meeting people or in appearing before groups.

5. Finally, in working on this problem, she developed materials on "What a Teacher Should Observe about Her Pupils and the Educational Implications for Child Health and Growth." She had this material to draw upon in her future teaching program and in her work with teachers and parents. Although the material was not complete, it could be expected to serve as a guide in discovering many child needs and in guiding experiences to meet these needs.

*Case Report of Mrs. C.*[1]—One of the first people to make herself known in the workshop was Mrs. C, fifth and sixth grade teacher in a suburban school. Mrs. C told about her difficulty in making the transition from old to new teaching—noise particularly bothered her—and said she came to the workshop to see what help she could get in helping her solve her discipline problem. Although she had not found observation helpful previously, she wanted to observe the children in the laboratory school. This she was encouraged to do. Mrs. C had been doing some house-cleaning and appeared tired and nervous.

In the first meetings before the children came, she appeared to be less interested in planning for their experiences than she was in seeing

[1] As reported by Mr. Ralph Witherspoon, adviser.

that they learned the three R's and behaved themselves. She insisted that there were always a number of youngsters that had to be disciplined and that one could not permit them to "carry on" in the room among the other children.

At this time a good deal was said about child growth and the behavior of early adolescent children. The first three days with the children went so smoothly that Mrs. C was convinced that there were no problem children in the group. However, when their behavior records were looked up, it was found that there was one girl whose school experience had never been happy, there was a boy who came because his parents made him come, and there were two or three who were quite retarded in their work.

It is interesting to note that at the end of the first week Mrs. C told the director that her problem was solved, for she now realized that she created a tense situation because she was too anxious to have all children accomplish the same things in school. This opportunity was used to talk with her about the development of children, their needs and interests, how they learn, and the relation of their health to their growth. The possibility was faced that the problem instead of being solved had in reality led into a bigger one.

Mrs. C observed in one classroom quite steadily throughout the five-week period that the children were in attendance. Out of this work grew discussions on fundamental problems of child development. For instance, Monday of the second week was a very unsuccessful day with the children. Many new ones had entered, among them two boys who acted just like Mrs. C said some of the youngsters in her room acted all the time. She said she felt sorry for the teacher and two or three times during the morning wanted to take the youngsters by the collar into the hall. It was pointed out that, instead, efforts would be directed to trying to find their interests and seeing if their behavior problems could be eliminated. The observation group, therefore, were interested in child study during the second week and wanted to see what would happen to the boys and the other children in the group.

Tuesday was a better day and each succeeding day grew better, for the boys were becoming interested in the work and accomplished many things which the observers thought were almost unbelievable. Among these strange phenomena was the boys' desire to read without being told when problems arose that might be solved through reading.

Mrs. C's evaluation of the second week's work was, "He [the teacher] is winning, but . . . "

At the beginning of the third week, a new observation group came to the room—mostly men. This Monday was more difficult than the preceding Monday and it looked as though there might be behavior problems that would be hard to handle. Mrs. C was very watchful. Again she was not convinced that difficulties were being handled as well as they might be. From then on, however, there were no behavior problems in the room, and Mrs. C was enthusiastic over the accomplishments of the former "problem children" when they did fine work in planning meals, studying table manners, taking part in the Pet Show, completing their plan books up to the end, recording experiments, taking part in the discussions and planning meetings, and otherwise making significant contributions to the group without having been subjected to the kind of discipline that some teachers had thought necessary.

During the second week in summer school, after she herself questioned whether her problem had been solved, Mrs. C came to talk over her previous work. She decided to develop plans for a unit which would be helpful to her in making "the transition from the old to new," part of her original problem. She was interested in a community study, "Roads and Where They Lead." She and her adviser discussed possible approaches beginning at the school. She thought of several places where the roads led in the immediate community and then extended them to the nearby city, southern Michigan, the state, and the possibility of going practically all over the world. She decided to put the emphasis on health education in the unit, with work in the health sciences as the core. In this way, even thought her original interest was not in health education, she was able to utilize the special resources offered in this field at the workshop. It is very interesting to note that she went to work with a real desire to accomplish something and that the product showed a great deal of careful planning and thinking. Her plans were fundamental and had enough scope to carry through at least one year's work, possibly two. They were, of course, subject to change. Much of what she had observed in the way of an experience curriculum was incorporated in her plans.

Since teachers' salaries have been low, Mrs. C's twenty-three years of teaching experience have been hard and accompanied by much work other than teaching. If the workshop had not been in the community, it is doubtful that she could have gone to school. Satisfactory progress on her problem was her summer's ambition, and she really put much effort into it and was able to collect a file of materials in addition to her written report. She was very grateful for the comments on her problem and remarked on how much good a little praise can do even an old teacher.

The work with Mrs. C was climaxed during a visit to her schoolroom. The group of six, including the principal and two co-workers, were very much interested in helping her solve some of the problems—and there were many—relating to school equipment, safety, nutrition, and organizing the teaching program.

Before the workshop closed she told her adviser that the work, especially her work in the observation school, had done more for her than the group could realize. She mentioned particularly the progress made in solving her own personal problems. Judging from the interest and enthusiasm she showed, her progress may be expected to continue and her teaching may be expected to show great improvement, for she had gained a better understanding of children and had made plans for developing a program that would reflect this understanding.

### VISITORS DAY

Even though many participants were continually seeking the help of leaders from their respective communities, the thought was often expressed that if community leaders knew more about the workshop program, there would be greater readiness in the fall to continue the efforts toward community betterment. To stimulate further interest in this continuation, participants invited to the workshop about fifty leaders from local communities, including superintendents, principals, school board members, medical directors from health departments, and leaders in community organizations. Discussion meetings of particular interest to these people were planned for the day, a smorgasbord luncheon was prepared by participants and staff, and a panel discussion was arranged as a vehicle for explaining workshop experiences. The schedule for the day, July 31, was:

8:30 to 10:30.   Discussion of cumulative records, stressing information need by the teacher in guiding the children's school experiences

9:30 to 10:30.   4-H Club canning demonstration arranged by committee working on community resources and school lunch program

10:30 to 12:00.   Discussion of school finances

10:30 to 12:00.   Check list on "Winning the Good Will of School Patrons"

12:00 to  1:30.   Smorgasbord luncheon, prepared and served by workshop group. Music arranged by participants
  1:30 to  3:15.   Panel discussion interpreting workshop experiences
  3:30 to  4:15.   Symposium on educational activities related to the noon lunch period in school

The high point of the program was reached when participants had the opportunity to discuss their summer's work and plans for next year with guests from local communities. Although the staff real-

*Leaders in the community were invited to a smorgasbord luncheon pre-*
*pared by a group of participants and staff members. Guests included*
*superintendents, health officers, commissioners of schools,*
*and other leaders in local communities.*

ized that many participants made extraordinary progress in working on their problems, they were quite unprepared for the sincere and skillful interpretation of workshop experiences given by the panel. The summer program was described in terms of individual development and professional growth. It was indeed a dramatic presentation, with every participant feeling the significance of the experiences interpreted and the challenge in meeting educational problems in local schools.

EVALUATING THE WORKSHOP

*The Diary.*—Early· in the session, staff and participants decided
to keep a diary in which they would record their reactions toward
daily events, such as discussion meetings, observation periods, conferences, trips, or books read, and appraise these activities in terms
of their own progress in solving problems. This day-by-day evaluation seemed to help participants in planning their programs more

*The chairman of the county teachers education committee, the commissioner
of schools, the director of the county health department, and the director
of the workshop discuss cooperative developments in health education.*

carefully and to stimulate greater responsibility in making use of the
resources available in the workshop. At the end of the summer
session, the diaries were given to the director.

The following accounts, written during the first, third, and last
weeks of the workshop, are taken from three diaries:

THURSDAY, JUNE 26

Armed with an outline covering the history of the attempt to establish health
education at S - - - -, I met with Miss D, Dr. E, and Mr. D. They lent most
friendly and sympathetic attention to my recital and then gave me some valuable
suggestions for a starter.

These suggestions were, first, to discuss the idea with the faculty. As I see it, that will probably be my most difficult task. Mr. D suggested that I plan a series of teachers meetings with this end in view. I think I could start, perhaps, with that.

Another approach seems to be to correlate the teaching of health in the various departments. It was suggested that a beginning might be made by interesting students in surveys—a dental survey, vaccination survey, etc.—to determine the health problems in our community. All were agreed that a health course as such, set aside, and perhaps receiving credit, is not the answer to my cry.

*Participants from the same school talk over the summer's work with their superintendent and make plans for the school year.*

The industrial arts group might be interested in the lighting problem of the school; the social science classes could study community agencies; the chemistry class, pasteurization and other experiments; the home economics classes, nutrition and child care; the mathematics classes could be the statistical department; the art classes could make the necessary charts; and the library could feature literature on the subject of health. All departments could write to the state department for visual aids.

All the above items can be made projects—the problem is to make them a natural and normal part of a course, to make everyone health conscious, but not bored with the idea.

### MONDAY, JULY 7

I enjoyed working on my problem this morning. The time passed very quickly and a great deal was accomplished. I feel that I am succeeding in that which I set out to do. Of course, there is a great deal more to be done, but at least I am on my way—and if that "runs out" I surely have many more to work on. Believe I get a great deal of stimulation from just talking with other teachers, too. An exchange of ideas is extremely valuable to me.

So much fun singing during lunch at the Tavern. Everyone liked it, I believe—hope we have more of these get-togethers. Wish I could play the piano like Betty and Milly!

Since "colds" are common problems with most of us and are often the basis of other contagious diseases, our discussion with Dr. E was certainly a profitable

*Participants made plans for a panel discussion to interpret workshop experiences to guests from local communities.*

experience. The problem of colds in the schoolroom is indeed a difficult one, and I learned how to handle the situation involving a sick child and working parents. Approve of the idea of getting the school board to help settle the legal points prior to the beginning of school year.

My main reaction to the business of controlling disease in the schoolroom is this: How about the teacher? Why not enforce thorough physical examinations for all teachers at least annually, and encourage them to stay out when they don't feel okay. Too many of us "don't dare" to be absent at times when we should be!

### FRIDAY, JULY 25

I accomplished a great deal on my problem this morning by working with different members of our school in planning for next year. Mrs. A and I organized movie material and wrote press notices. I surely hope we get a good turnout for *The Proof of the Pudding.* I am a little worried for fear people will not come.

I always enjoy a conference with Miss D and I always come from the conference with new ideas to try out. I do hope our parent meetings for next year will work out. As far as I can see, our large enrollment is the only thing that can hinder them.

Dr. B made some excellent suggestions for determining when a child is fatigued. I like his ideas for follow-up, too.

This schedule of study is really something. Mr. W is a fine help, but it is

*The committee which developed plans for evaluating their summer's experiences is shown at work.*

rather difficult to work out. I wish the universities would work out one system of evaluating credits and abide by these rules and regulations.

*Another Appraisal by Participants.*—Even with such a constant reminder for evaluating both individual and group work, participants began to think in terms of appraising the summer's experience as a unit. A group volunteered to work on a committee for such appraisal, but at the time scheduled for the meeting three more participants and a staff member joined them. The work of these eight people illustrated excellent group thinking.

Since the real value of the workshop can only be realized in terms of the individual's work in a particular community during the year or years to follow, the first recommendation was that some type of follow-up work through contact with the participant, or a report from him, be made during the next school year.  It was suggested that a letter, with self-addressed stamped envelope enclosed, be sent to each participant during December or January and again in April asking the teacher in a brief letter or report to indicate how well she was getting along with her problem, what progress was made, what difficulties were encountered, and what suggestions she now had of ways in which the past summer's experience could have been more functional in terms of her problem.  The *esprit de corps* which existed among the group was illustrated when it was suggested that these reports or letters be mimeographed for mailing to the participants, since everyone was interested in the work others were doing and since members might have helpful suggestions regarding difficulties that were encountered.  Follow-up work by someone on the workshop staff was considered highly desirable and was recommended.

Out of the wholehearted discussions and the group thinking on the subject of evaluation, the following points for evaluation were listed:

1. Discussion with fellow participants in the workshop
2. Group opportunities
3. Observation
4. Conferences
5. Visual aids
6. Field trips
7. Utilization of local resources
8. Opportunities for self-expression and leadership
9. Luncheon meetings
10. Recreation
11. Library facilities
12. Written reports on problem
13. Broadening horizons in the health sciences
14. Diary
15. Comparison of the workshop with regular college courses
16. Suggestions for future community workshops

In two subsequent meetings of this same committee, the arrangement and wording of the evaluation form were considered and set up for the typist.  The final form was seven pages long, and was arranged so that specific items could be checked under the headings of *very valuable, valuable, some value,* and *little value.*  In addition, space was allowed under each of the sixteen headings for comments and suggestions.

There was some discussion as to whether evaluation forms should or should not be signed.  It was thought by some members of the committee that the forms would be filled out more completely if they were signed. On the other hand, it was believed that a more candid evaluation might be forthcoming if the forms were not signed. The latter suggestion was accepted by the committee and recommendations to this effect were made to the group when the chairman presented evaluation forms to the group.

It appeared that the group received satisfaction in evaluating their summer's experience. The suggestions and comments which were made seemed to indicate that real teacher growth had taken place. Some excellent suggestions were made regarding their experiences and the organization of the workshop, and these suggestions should be valuable in planning a similar venture in the future. A summary of the participants' opinions follows.

1. *Discussion with Fellow Participants in the Workshop.*—It was the opinion of the group that the environment of the workshop was conducive to a free interchange of ideas, both as to practical problems and in the development of a philosophy of education. As one teacher commented, "We use luncheon hours, driving to and from B - - - -, for discussion. Often we carried on from some topic started earlier. Besides this, we frequently chatted with people during the day." The value they derived from discussion with fellow participants was indicated by the forty-eight unanimously favorable replies made about it. Typical comments were:

This discussion was very valuable. I received many excellent ideas from the experiences of other teachers.

I gained a wealth of ideas; I lost lots of self-consciousness and I planned further action.

2. *Group Opportunities.*—Everyone evaluated group opportunities as either "very valuable" or "helpful." Two-thirds of the group thought that one or two general meetings a week were desirable and that an hour was the best length of time for such a meeting. These suggestions were in keeping with the workshop plan. But while our general meetings were usually held in the early part of the afternoon, responses on the blanks indicated that almost half of the group would have preferred an early morning hour.

Forty-five of the group considered two or three movies advisable each week. Fourteen movies and ten sets of slides were shown during the summer session. It may be that too much material of this type was used in connection with discussion groups and general meetings.

Comments about outside speakers indicated a preference for using speakers only as they were needed in work on special interests or problems. This was the procedure generally followed in the workshop. In all, twenty persons, not including lay leaders or visitors, assisted in various ways in working sessions.

Over two-thirds of the group considered small group meetings "very valuable," while all others found them "helpful." As indicated through forty-one replies, the opinion was that small group meet-

*Dr. Henry J. Otto, of the W. K. Kellogg Foundation, discussed with the group various developments of the educational program in the area of the Michigan Community Health Project.*

ings should be the outgrowth of special interests or problems. Examples of the seventeen comments and suggestions regarding these meetings are:

I got so much from the small groups, for I was able to get to the "root" of my problem and thus was able to get more detailed help.

"Air" the different problems so that those with the same interests, but from different communities, may work together. I found out this week that there were others who would have worked with me on my problem.

Many meetings have been too long and fatiguing. Would suggest better follow-up on small group meetings rather than large group meetings.

3. *Observation.*—There was probably more difference of opinion expressed as to the use of the observation period and its value than almost any other experience which was evaluated. This variation was in keeping with the differences brought out in general meetings when discussing the use of the laboratory school. The problem created when a large group observed in a classroom was no doubt the reason for the suggestion that members take turns on a weekly basis in participating in the classrooms. No rules were made, however, and the use of this resource was based largely on individual needs. It was generally thought that observation should be planned either according to a problem unit the children were working on, or in terms of individual child study. Almost two-thirds of the group thought observation should be limited to one room while one-third thought it should be extended to different rooms. Again a small observing group of five to seven was thought to be most desirable. The majority preferred a two-hour observation period. Some thought a longer time was desirable. Practically all thought the conference period directly following observation should be about half an hour long. Most participants preferred the early forenoon for observation. Well over half of the group felt the observation periods were "very valuable," but two out of the group felt they were of "little value." Suggestions and comments regarding this experience were varied. Examples are:

The conference with the demonstration teacher was the highlight of the demonstration itself.

I do not think the observation period was the normal school situation and I felt it was of little value. Yet certain principles were seen in them, so they do have some value for some teachers.

The observing periods should depend upon the individual for the amount of time spent in that way.

Every moment spent was valuable, discussions likewise. The exposure to useful materials was of inestimable value.

Gained much help from observing in Miss P's room. I hope to improve my own teaching from this observation.

4. *Conferences.*—Everyone felt that the conferences with advisers were valuable. Two-thirds of the group considered them "very valuable." More than a third found difficulty in arranging for conferences with their advisers. About a third did not feel they had all the conferences they needed and some wished for longer conferences. All thought that they should have one, two, or three conferences each week with their adviser. Many of the thirty-five comments

and suggestions indicated that participants would like more conferences, longer conferences, and conferences that could be more easily arranged with the adviser. Typical suggestions and comments follow:

Some days were so crowded that it was not possible to have a conference. Could one day or one-half day per week be left open to make possible a greater availability of advisers?

I believe workshoppers need more conferences with advisers than we have been able to have this summer.

*Although staff members worked with everyone in the group, each participant selected an adviser from among the staff. Conferences were held frequently to discuss next steps in solving a problem.*

Conferences with the staff were a great help in solving our problem.

The difficulty was not in obtaining the cooperation of the adviser, but in finding time outside of group meetings for conferences.

Individual conferences are better than groups of three or four.

These conferences were stabilizing when participants, particularly those who are accustomed to having their work organized and charted for them, were thrown upon their own responsibility.

If my conferences were not satisfactory, the fault was my own. I was so busy that I had difficulty finding time for a conference.

My adviser gave very helpful and practical suggestions and showed a genuine interest in helping. My adviser also visited my school with me, which was most helpful.

5. *Visual Aids.*—Everyone in the group thought that the motion pictures were very valuable or at least helpful. Slides and exhibits were all considered very valuable, helpful, or of some value. All but one participant thought the exhibits prepared by members of the

*Participants show Dean J. B. Edmonson, of the School of Education, University of Michigan, an exhibit of health education materials that they arranged.*

workshop were valuable, helpful, or of some value. Thirty-six comments were made about the use of visual aids. These included:

Think the movies should be staggered more if possible. Also the slides. Too many were shown in a short time.

Have more discussion of the movie right after it is shown.

I felt we had used them satisfactorily. We had an introduction and interest in the subject. The film with comments and evaluation seems like a good procedure.

Slides were extremely helpful because they were nearer our situations.

6. *Field Trips.*—Visits to the Marshall and Battle Creek water supply and sewage disposal systems, trips to Ann Arbor during the New Education Fellowship Conference, and the visits to the teach-

ers' own particular schools were all considered very valuable or helpful. Other trips, such as the visits to the dairy and pasteurizing plant, the restaurant tours, the Clear Lake Camp, and the Kellogg Foundation Library, were generally considered very valuable or helpful. Among the twenty-eight comments and suggestions about the trips were:

I really gained much practical help from these trips. The evidence was right before me as the discussions were given. It was all so real and natural.

Trips were very helpful from the teachers' standpoint, for it gives a teacher ideas for excursions she might use in her own classrooms.

These trips were especially valuable for they gave us new experiences. More of these would be beneficial.

Field trips are very interesting and impressive, for we see actual situations accompanied by explanations.

7. *Utilization of Local Resources.*—The Marshall school system, the Kellogg Foundation, the County Health Department, and professional people in the community were considered very valuable or helpful in the summer program. County and city officers, extension workers, parents and lay leaders, Marshall itself, the teachers' own school boards and communities, and the University of Michigan services were among other resources used. Fifteen listed additional resources they should like to have used. Only twelve written comments or suggestions were made regarding this item.

8. *Opportunities for Self-expression.*—In reviewing the opportunities for self-expression and leadership, almost all the group felt they were given opportunities for self-expression and leadership through conferences with workshop members, committee meetings, conferences with staff, through the children's activities, through small and large group meetings, and through the special activities in the workshop. Although only twenty-five comments and suggestions were made in this section, they were particularly interesting. Examples are:

I have participated much more in this course than in any previous summer school experience.

It was especially valuable for me to have a part in all the ramifications of the workshop set-up. In this informal atmosphere *as in no other*, are opportunities for developing initiative and leadership in a sympathetic situation.

I many times did not say as much as I should, but that was my fault—not the workshop's. It is hard for me to express myself in a group and I think this type [of experience] is an ideal one for a person like that to grow in.

Never was anyone denied a chance to speak freely and contributions seemed welcome, which encouraged the more shy individual to expression.

9. *Luncheon Meetings.*—The luncheon meetings were thought valuable from a social point of view and, for the most part, the group thought that two luncheons a week such as we had were satisfactory. Some people did not like the food, but realized that it may have been necessary to pay more in order to have better food—and the group had decided on a price for luncheons.  Comments and suggestions made by twenty-five people included:

The luncheons were enjoyable.  They provided an opportunity for the group to get together and forget about their problems.

There was a development of good fellowship of a type afforded by no other situation.

*Opportunities for working with others in committees or small groups were numerous.  Here a committee meets with Dean Clarence S. Yoakum and Dr. John Sundwall, from the University of Michigan, to discuss the significance of their summer's experiences.*

10. *Recreation.*—In general the group were not as enthusiastic about their recreational activities as about other aspects of the program.  Suggestions as a whole were for more recreation.  Illustrative comments were:

I think there should have been more time for relaxation.  It was too strenuous at times.

I feel there is a need for more music in the workshop and more drama as well.
More picnics, excursions and things that get us better acquainted.
Program was too full to allow enough recreation.

11. *Library Facilities.*—Three members of the group did not feel
that library materials were adequate for the problems they were
working on, while eleven indicated they could not get materials
when they needed them. Although only two participants thought
the library, and aid which was given in using the library facilities,
inadequate, some members of the staff felt that a trained librarian
would have contributed much to the workshop. Comments and
suggestions were few, only eight in regard to the library, possibly
because the group felt the collection of books was quite adequate.
Two of the comments were:

A grand selection—an excellent opportunity—not enough time to use them.
I only wished I had had more time to make use of the professional books.

12. *Written Report on Problem.*—All of the forty-nine participants
who filled out evaluation forms indicated that they had a clearer
concept of their problems at the end of the workshop than at the
beginning. Twenty-six indicated that their problems changed while
they were working on them. All but one felt that writing out the
plan for work helped in the organization of material and in thinking through the problem. Ten felt that they did not have sufficient
help from adviser and staff in working on their particular problems.
All reported that they derived a sense of satisfaction from work on
their problems. The nineteen comments and suggestions included
the following:

Finding a solution to my problem was a grand experience. It gives me something to work with next fall.
I would have been more successful in working out my problem if members
of our faculty had been here. My problems were interests of a group rather
than an individual. I need help and cooperation from them.
My work has been very interesting because of the fact that I was working
on my own problem.
I have learned the right way to work out a problem and use the community
resources.
I feel confidence in myself and in my ability to work more efficiently.

13. *Broadening Horizons in the Health Sciences.*—The entire group
indicated that their knowledge of health science was increased, that
they felt they would be able to use this knowledge effectively, that
they had a better idea how to secure and how to use health resources
in their health education program, that they planned to use these

resources next year, that they had a better attitude toward and an appreciation of the health agencies in their community, and that they had a better idea of how to get teachers and community to cooperate in a health program. Most of the group indicated that they would like follow-up services next year in their educational program. Comments and suggestions in connection with this question were varied:

I have learned more about health sciences, but still have much to learn.

My whole being has been affected for the better.

I feel that my problem will work out without further assistance.

Much practical help was secured for my work in getting children into better physical condition.

14. *Diary.*—One-third of the group thought the diary took too much time, but the majority felt that it helped them to clarify thinking, to summarize experiences, to record changing points of view, and that it gave them an opportunity to review experiences and helped them to discover their attitudes toward experiences. The forty-three answers to the question, "What fears did you have concerning your diary?" were quite varied. Typical answers were:

I was not sure that it was written as a diary should be.

I was afraid that it might not tell what I really got out of the course.

At first I thought it might not be done as the staff expected it to be.

Sometimes I wondered if I dared be as honest as I was urged, for I wondered if others besides my adviser would be reading it.

I didn't wish to offend anyone. I was so anxious and so happy that I was afraid I might do [write] so much that I would seem insincere.

I am afraid I had no fears.

That it might be too critical and I would fail to record the most important points.

I liked the idea of writing a dairy and to use it for my classes next year.

The diary was well worth all time spent on it. In reading my entire diary last evening, the summer's work was reviewed.

15. *Comparison of Workshop with Regular College Courses.*—The students were almost universal in thinking that the workshop environment, more than regular college courses, helped them in developing initiative, in making their own work schedules, in learning to work better with staff and fellow members, in utilizing local resources to greater advantage, in working on their own problems, and in gaining new ideas and inspiration. Some of the forty-five comments regarding the major values received from the workshop were:

I feel refreshed this morning, instead of being sick of the whole thing. I feel

I want to get right at my planning for this coming year instead of wanting to get away from it. I have received a new inspiration to do the best work my ability will allow. I always had more fear of a mark than of the desire to really learn all I should.

I feel that I made progress on a piece of work for which I have never before had the time or the resources.

I learned the importance of health in the educational program; I received inspiration for next year; I now have more faith in my own capabilities.

I gained an understanding of workshop philosophy and procedure; I liked knowing the staff so informally; I gained greater understanding of public health; I gained greater understanding of rural and community problems.

I was able to work on my own particular interests and problems. I have collected more practical things from my summer experience which I can make use of in my classroom, rather than stacking a notebook of notes in a dark corner.

I have new courage to go on tackling the problems of a teacher. I have regained some of my conviction that we are teaching the whole child.

It was an opportunity to work out problems alone and with a group—to share with others—to think and act—and let others do likewise.

Many of the things which have happened have given me a chance to develop socially, a situation in which my home surroundings have always been limited.

This has been the most beneficial to me of any summer course I have ever taken. Very happy that I came.

I would have liked more talks by staff members. I felt that they had much to offer, but kept in the background.

No other educational experience has given me so many heartfelt satisfactions.

16. *Suggestions for Future Community Workshops.*—Thirty-seven participants made suggestions regarding future community workshops. Examples are:

I suggest making observation completely optional, as to time; that general meetings be called first thing in the morning; that there be more time for "seventh inning stretches"; that group discussions stop by three-thirty or four o'clock; that a panel such as we had Thursday, July 31, in the afternoon, explaining the workshop procedure be given to incoming workshop group next year by members of previous year's group. It would be most valuable, I think, in helping inexperienced ones to get the feeling.

I suggest large groups of pupils should be enrolled in the laboratory school as well as pupils from our own schools. A course should be worked out by which the children brought in from outside districts could learn to play together in a variety of recreational activities.

The present theme of health education should be continued. I would like to see more practical theories in operation, such as municipal departments, and hear the man-on-the-street's reaction to health projects.

I think the weather should be considered in the length of the day and that there should be fewer general meetings and more individual work.

It would be nice to change the themes of the different workshops, thus giving a teacher a chance to broaden his thinking in all fields.

17. *Complaints.*—In answer to the question, "In what respects have you disliked the workshop?" there were forty-three comments, which included the following:

Sitting too long. Too much stress on rural schools—not as much time given to graded schools. We need it too. We are dealing with more children and larger range of ages.

My criticisms seem petty, but since you asked for them, I'll state them again. (1) The day seemed too long—I was often completely fatigued and past the saturation point. (2) Occasionally I felt I dared not voice a suggestion for fear I'd be given another job where I already felt loaded. (3) We needed more frequent relaxation periods. (4) A week of observation, at three-hour sittings, seemed tiring. (5) The schedule seemed too crowded the last two weeks.

I have in no respect disliked the workshop. After getting it straight as to the problem on which I wished to work, I can say it has been an enjoyable experience to me.

None. I have not only enjoyed my summer, and learned so many things, but it has been one of the most profitable summers in which I have ever participated.

None whatsoever. I have liked it the most of any course I have ever taken and learned the most, I believe!

18. *Praise.*—In answer to the question, "What aspects of this workshop have you liked particularly well?" there were forty-eight comments, including the following:

The fine staff. They have been so human, not placing themselves on a pedestal above the pupil teachers.

The informality and friendliness of the workshoppers. You could work on the things in which you were most interested.

The sharing of ideas and problems. The democratic attitude of instructors. The set-up seemed to be for *everybody*—no one special. The opening of avenues to *use* to enrich the life of the community when we return. The value set on personalities—after all, we each *deeply* respect our *self*.

Informality—friendliness—free interchange of ideas—atmosphere conducive to persistent effort—the leadership—availability of materials—concern of the leaders about progress of each person—inspiration of leaders.

I have especially liked the idea of having an adviser, the informality, the subjects of discussion, the work on our own problems, the freedom to participate in discussions and activities, the idea that this workshop was in the community and that I could commute, thus enjoying the inspiration of summer school and still being able to enjoy my home in the evening.

I liked the informality, the sharing of experiences, large and small group conferences, freedom allowed to work out our own problems, needs and interests, the evaluating of each day's work.

The way the discussion groups have been carried on and the emphasis on health that I *needed* were most important to me.

*The Report of Student Opinion.*—Another appraisal of the workshop was made through the "Report of Student Opinion" given to all University of Michigan campus students enrolled in education courses. The form used is reproduced below, along with a tabulation of the responses obtained in the workshop.

## REPORT OF STUDENT OPINION

### SCHOOL OF EDUCATION—SUMMER SESSION 1941

*To the Student:*—In order that the staff members of the School of Education may modify their policies and courses in terms of the judgments of students, the Administrative Committee desires that you furnish the information requested. A report should be made for each of your courses in Education. Do not sign your name. The report should be prepared during the class period and placed in the ballot box that is supplied for each classroom.

A summary of the reports will be prepared under my direction and a confidential account of the returns will be given to the instructor some weeks after the close of the session. Fairness and frankness on your part will be highly appreciated.          J. B. EDMONSON, *Dean*

1. Give the information requested here by checking the appropriate answers:
(*a*) First summer **11**, Second summer **8**, Third summer or more **33**.
(*b*) Man **8**, Woman **40**; Graduate **14**, Undergraduate **33**.

2. To what extent have you been satisfied with your total program of summer work:
Little satisfaction...., Fair **1**, Average **3**, High Degree **24**, Unusually High **14**.

3. Appraisal of course in Education. (Give number) **Workshop**, Instructor. **staff**

Directions: Place a mark on each scale at the point which expresses your judgment. Use your present and past experience in University courses as a guide for determining your judgments. **Comments: Unusually high, good, high degree, high, average, very good, excellent, above average, especially good, fine.**

PREVIOUS PREPARATION. *Rate your own previous preparation for the course in terms of adequacy.*

| 6 | | | 34 | 4 | | 6 | |
|---|---|---|----|---|---|---|---|
| Much too little | | | Satisfactory | | | Entirely adequate | |

LOAD. *Rate the course on the total amount of work involved in it.*

| | | | 42 | 7 | | 1 | |
|---|---|---|----|---|---|---|---|
| Much too little | | | Average | | | Much too heavy | |

VALUE OF ASSIGNMENTS. *Rate on the educational value of assigned tasks.*

| | | | 14 | | 1 | | 34 | |
|---|---|---|---|---|---|---|---|---|

Merely            Average           Highly
busy work                            Valuable

APPRAISAL OF THE COURSE. *Rate the entire course on its value to you.*

| | | | 6 | | 1 | | 43 | |
|---|---|---|---|---|---|---|---|---|

A waste of           Average           Splendid
time                                 Course

4. Would you recommend this course next summer to one of your associates who had your background of training and experience? Yes **47**, No....., Doubtful **3**.

Use the reverse side for any suggestions relating to the work of the course or relating to general practices or policies of the School of Education that should be continued or that should be changed. **Comments: More workshops. It's a question in my mind if the staff can evaluate at this time just what the individual has gotten from the course. Just how much of the summer's work we make use of in our school program remains to be seen. There is no learning unless our learning is assimilated and put into practice. Then how can you staff members know how to mark A, B or C?**

### PROGRESS MADE IN SOLVING PROBLEMS

The progress that was made in working on the special interests or problems which teachers selected was most satisfying. Rather spectacular progress was made, particularly when one considers the many activities in which everyone participated. Half of the group, twenty-six, reported that their problems changed as they worked on them. Although most of the members had plans well under way at the end of the workshop, solving their problems required further work during the school year. Progress on their problems in the workshop is summarized generally and briefly.

Four principals of small elementary schools studied problems of grade children and developed plans for meeting these problems through a health education program. Seventeen rural teachers developed rather specific and detailed plans for such units of work as a school lunch program, communicable disease control, and safety. In addition, they worked out more general plans for solving other school problems. Twelve teachers who worked in the field of parent and community education studied their problem, developed new techniques of working with community groups, planned specifically for kinds of working meetings, and in many instances were able to get such a program under way.

Eight teachers of elementary school children worked on many such health problems as the evaluation of a health program and the development of activities for children with handicaps. They prepared materials for use in their teaching program during the coming year. Six members of the high school group made significant progress in planning to meet health needs of high school students and developed specific materials from the health science field to be incorporated into their own teaching.

Two junior high school teachers worked on guidance and prepared a cumulative record for guidance uses in their school systems. One junior high school teacher developed material from the health sciences to be incorporated in a core curriculum. A commissioner of schools secured the help of other participants in preparing a teachers' self-appraisal check list for use in his program of visits to schools.

In view of their accomplishments it is not surprising that these teachers looked forward with pleasure to the coming school year. They were eager to continue their work and to put plans into action.

# CHAPTER III

# COMMUNITY WORKSHOP DEALING WITH PROBLEMS IN SCIENCE EDUCATION[1]

*Initiation of the Workshop in Science Education.*—Early in the fall of 1940 the Barry County teacher education committee[2] conducted a survey to determine the professional needs of teachers in Barry County, Michigan. In this survey many teachers indicated that they wanted help in improving the science programs in their schools, and that they would like to visit outstanding teachers and to observe the work of these teachers with children in classroom situations.

On the basis of these two general needs the teacher education committee recommended a summer workshop in science education which would provide opportunity for teachers to develop their own backgrounds in science, to organize science programs for their schools, and to observe exceptional teachers working with children in a laboratory school. These recommendations were presented at a meeting of the seven-county committee on teacher education with the deans of the departments of education from the University of Michigan and the University of Chicago. This group approved the recommendation that one of the five proposed community workshops be organized with special emphasis on science, and designated Barry County as the location for it if some community in that county could provide adequate accommodation for the program. Dr. J. Darrell Barnard, whose field of special competence was science education and who had been working with many of these teachers as a consultant during the school year, was appointed director of the proposed workshop. It was decided by the deans that the University of Chicago would sponsor this workshop in science education.

Since most of the teachers wanted course credit for their participation in the workshop and stated that they would like to receive that credit in subject areas other than education, Dr. Tyler made arrangements with various departments at the University of Chicago

---

[1] Mr. J. Darrell Barnard is the author of this chapter. He was director of the workshop at Hastings during the Summer Session of 1941. He served as consultant in the Michigan Community Health Project from August, 1940, to September, 1941, during which time he was on leave of absence from Colorado State College of Education at Greeley.

[2] The Teacher Education Committee in Barry County was made up of Mr. E. L. Taylor, principal of Hastings High School, Mrs. Maude W. Smith, county school commissioner, Miss Helen Wade, elementary school supervisor in the Hastings schools, and Mr. Arthur Kays, Miss Marjorie Spitler, and Mr. Henry Cunningham, teachers.

to provide such courses in biological science, physical science, sociology, and library science. The subsequent announcement to teachers contained the following general description of the science education workshop for Barry County:

This workshop is being planned for elementary (both rural and village) and high school teachers. Science will be given special emphasis in the program with consideration for both the science and the nonscience major. Teachers who have majored in science and who would like additional work in the functional subject matter of science can obtain such work under the direction of staff members who have had special training in science. All participants who desire a better understanding of the important principles of biological and physical science will be provided this opportunity through a study of the function of science in everyday life adjustments. All participants will be given an opportunity to observe science classes and to organize learning activities suitable for the development of science concepts at various grade levels.

In planning the program, consideration has been given those teachers and school librarians who are confronted with the problem of organizing and administering a school library. A competent staff member will be available to assist participants in their work on such problems related to school libraries.[1]

The following areas of registration were described in the bulletin:

### A. *Science*

1. Biological Science, General Course
2. Physical Science 294, Survey Course in Physical Science for experienced teachers

### B. *Education*

1. Education 381, The Science Curriculum
2. Education 367A, Current Problems in Elementary Education
3. Education 367B, Current Problems in Secondary Education
4. Education 320B, Foundations of Good Adjustment; Methods and Goals in Personality Study and Guidance of Children

### C. *Sociology*

1. Sociology 201, Introduction to Sociology
2. Sociology 329, Methods for Studying the Modern Community

### D. *Library Science*

1. Graduate Library School 325, Objectives and Administration of Secondary School Libraries
2. Graduate Library School 326, The Book Collection of Secondary School Libraries
3. Graduate Library School 327, The Elementary School Library

---

[1] A project in the development of book and library resources had contributed generously to the schools during the preceding year, and this sudden growth brought a special request from many teachers for assistance on library problems.

This bulletin was distributed among the teachers in Barry County and other teachers within the area of the Michigan Community Health Project.

### HELPING TEACHERS PREPARE FOR THE WORKSHOP

Since the request for a workshop in science education had originated with the teachers in Barry County, it was natural that the largest number of applicants for this workshop should be from Barry

*Local teachers and school administrators were responsible for getting a community workshop in Hastings and arranging the local facilities for handling the program.*

County. The procedures used to help teachers prepare themselves for most effective participation in the workshop were in accordance with the description presented in Chapter I.

### COMMUNITY PREPARATION FOR THE WORKSHOP

*Selection of a Community.*—In the original request the teacher education committee recommended that this workshop be located in the W. K. Kellogg Rural Agricultural School, but they found that it would be impossible for the rural community in which this school was located to accommodate the number of teachers who would be enrolled in the program. Two other schools then asked that the workshop be located in their respective communities. One of these schools, Hastings, was located in the county seat, and Middleville, the other school, was in a smaller town located in the northwestern part of the county. The director was invited to assist the committee in choosing the location of the workshop, and each of these communities was examined in terms of the criteria for selecting a local community that are outlined in Chapter I.

After comparing the two communities with regard to these seven conditions, the teacher education committee decided that Hastings would be the better location. Upon the recommendation of the superintendent of schools, the Hastings board of education provided a large modernly equipped elementary school building with full-time janitorial service for the workshop. This building, the Central School, included twenty well-equipped classrooms, four offices, and a large auditorium.

*Arranging for the Laboratory School.*—In a survey of teacher needs and interests, the teacher education committee had found that most of the teachers were interested in visiting outstanding teachers to observe them work with children. Hence, the committee recommended that a laboratory school be maintained as an important part of the workshop. The rural teachers on the committee urged that one division of the laboratory school be located in a typical rural school, attended by rural children, and taught by a person experienced in rural education. Since this group were so definite in their request, the director asked them to take the responsibility for locating the school and selecting the teacher they felt would work best with those children. They chose the Altoft School, three miles from Hastings, met with the local board, parents, and even the children themselves, and got these rural people so interested in the possibilities of a summer program for their children that the parents asked that one section of the laboratory school be located in their community. This section was to enroll children from the first eight grades.

The four other sections of the laboratory school were located in the Central School building in Hastings. One section was to enroll a group of early elementary school children; the second, an intermediate elementary group; the third, a later elementary group; and the fourth, a high school group.

In order to enroll enough children to maintain the laboratory school, the director of the workshop and some members of the teacher education committee met with the teachers in Hastings and discussed ways in which parents and children could be acquainted with the nature of the summer program. It was suggested that a committee of local teachers work with the director in planning a way for making these contacts. This committee made arrangements to discuss the laboratory school in three different meetings of parents and prepared a mimeographed announcement of the laboratory school. This announcement contained a description of the program and an application blank which could be used by any child interested in attending.

Teachers in the Hastings schools and the teacher in the Altoft school distributed these announcements among their children after talking with them about the possibilities of attending a summer program. The director of the workshop and the committee of local teachers assisting with the laboratory school met with high school students in personal conferences and in groups, to discuss the summer program, since it became evident that fewer of them were interested.

Seventeen high school students and 178 elementary school children applied for admission to the laboratory school. Since more elementary children had applied than could possibly be accommodated, it became necessary to make selections. This again was done by the local teacher committee after deciding what criteria should be used in making the selection. These criteria included the following:

1. Children selected for any one section should in general represent children of that age group in an actual public school situation.
2. Children should be selected who give reasonable assurance of regular attendance.
3. Where several children from one family apply for admission, all or none should be selected.
4. Children should not be admitted with the idea of making up school work or advancing beyond their normal progress in school.
5. There should be reasonable assurance that the parents of children selected will cooperate in carrying out the summer program.
6. In selecting children, those attending parochial schools should be given the same consideration as those attending public schools.

After selections had been made, a letter was written to the parents of each child who had applied. The letters to parents of children who had not been selected stated that, since it was impossible to make provision for all who applied, their child's name had been placed on a waiting list. The local teacher committee felt that these letters to parents should go out on University stationery and should be signed by the director of the workshop. This, they felt, would eliminate a possible cause of ill feeling between local teachers and these parents.

*Developing the Participation of Community Groups.*—The director was in Hastings for some time before the workshop opened, and he sought opportunities to inform various community groups about the workshop. He met with the Hastings Chamber of Commerce and discussed the purpose of the summer program, the staff and teacher-participant personnel, and the ways in which the Hastings community might make use of these resources. The officials of this group offered to write a letter of welcome to each person from outside the Hastings community who was planning to participate in the workshop and to send a mimeographed list of living accommodations which was prepared with the cooperation of a group of high school students.

The secretary of the Barry County Y.M.C.A. became interested in the program and the director had several conferences with him regarding local situations which should be taken into account in the planning. Mr. Taylor, the principal of Hastings High School, assumed the responsibility for writing news stories concerning the workshop for the local paper, and cooperated with a local reporter for out-of-town dailies who had offered her services in preparing news stories concerning the workshop for those papers. Two months before the workshop opened, Mr. Taylor started a series of weekly articles in the Hastings paper on the plans and the staff of the workshop.

Mr. Van Buskirk, superintendent of the Hastings schools, was consulted frequently regarding plans for the summer. Through these conferences, an understanding was reached regarding the use of buildings, school equipment, and other facilities. Mr. Van Buskirk was most cooperative and was a source of valuable advice in making preparations for the summer program.

Some of the local teachers corresponded with staff members who were not able to visit Hastings before the workshop opened, providing them in advance with information about the community. This correspondence was effective in causing the local teacher to feel a greater responsibility for the program, aside from its value in acquainting the staff member with the setting of the workshop.

*Coordinating the Workshop with the City Recreation Program.*—For several years, Hastings had maintained a summer recreational program for young people. Such a program had been planned for the summer of 1941, with the high school physical education teacher in charge. The director of the workshop had several talks with this teacher about the advisability of coordinating the recreational program and the workshop activities. They agreed that the playground activities would be scheduled so there would be little or no conflict with the laboratory school hours, and the supervisor of these activities soon afterward enrolled in the workshop to study problems related to the summer recreational program in Hastings.

The week before the workshop opened the sociologist of the staff and the director of the workshop were invited to attend a meeting of the city recreation committee, to consider problems in connection with the recreation program. One of the main problems was that of obtaining the support of parents in local play areas. The various aspects of this problem were discussed and it was decided that a parent committee should be formed in each of these areas to assist the playground leaders with the play program. This decision was reached after an analysis of the problem in terms of several questions: Whose children are these?' Whose playground program is this? Who should be concerned about the problem?

After the meeting the chairman of the city recreation committee said, "If this is the kind of help we are going to be able to get from the workshop staff this summer it looks to me like it's going to be a practical program for teaching." It is interesting to note here that the director of the Hastings recreational program and the workshop sociologist had begun to attack a community problem before the workshop had officially opened. This meeting began the development of community conciousness and confidence concerning the way in which the resources of the workshop could be used in attacking community problems.

*Organizing the Library Service.*—The director visited the local library and talked with the librarian concerning the possibility of using certain library materials. She offered staff and workshop participants the use of any materials in the library and even offered to transfer some things temporarily to the workshop library.

*Making Friends with the Janitors.*—An incident illustrated the desirability of seeing beforehand that the janitors knew of the workshop program. The director had made arrangements with the superintendent of schools to move into an office in the Central School building on the Monday following the close of school, but when he attempted to gain admission to the building on that day, the janitor who came to the door refused to let him enter without a written permit. The director had done nothing to acquaint the janitors with the summer program and with the ways in which their cooperation would be needed. This incident was taken as an opportunity to explain the arrangements, and the janitors were most helpful throughout the summer. At the close of the program one of them said, "I have certainly enjoyed working with these fine people this summer, and I'm going to miss them."

*Securing Lunch Facilities.*—Before the opening of the workshop, arrangements were made to use the high school cafeteria for the noon lunches, with the woman who operated the cafeteria during the school year in charge. She took over the complete responsibility for purchasing food, planning menus, preparing and serving the food, and managing the cafeteria so that it was self-supporting.

*Rooming Accommodations.*—The housing of teacher-participants and staff in Hastings presented no problem, since there were more places available than could possibly be used. In fact, the campaign which had been conducted in an attempt to locate living accommodations had left an idea with some local people that it was going to be comparatively easy to rent their places. When it was finally discovered that many more places were going to be available than could be used, some of them felt that they had been slighted. Although this did not present a serious problem, it is a matter that should be given consideration in future programs of this kind.

### TEACHING PROBLEMS AND SPECIAL INTERESTS

Seventy-two teachers finally enrolled in the workshop: 63 women and 9 men. There were 12 high school teachers, 23 village elementary school teachers, 36 rural elementary school teachers, and one county school commissioner. Twenty-nine of these teachers were graduate students, 37 were working toward the bachelor's degree, and 20 were working on the master's degree. It is interesting to note that 29 of the 63 women were married and maintaining their homes in addition to participating in the workshop. Fifty-three of the teachers came from Barry County, 5 from Eaton County, 4 from Allegan County, 2 from Calhoun County, 3 from Van Buren County, and

5 from outside the area of the Michigan Community Health Project.

As has been previously stated, the principal purpose in conducting interviews with teachers in their own schools was to help them define the teaching problems or projects they would like to work on during the summer. Since very few of the teachers had ever participated in a workshop, many of them did not appreciate the importance of having such a definite purpose for attending the workshop, and few of them had defined problems before the interview. During the interview the director helped each teacher to analyze her own teaching situation and to define those teaching problems which she considered important to her. The resources of the workshop were then explained and, in terms of these resources, the problems which it seemed most reasonable for her to take to the workshop were determined.

*Basic Teaching Problems.*—The problems or purposes these teachers eventually identified as being those which they would like to consider in the workshop can be organized into four groups, dealing with science teaching, use of books, community study, and parent-school relations.

These are listed as topical problems under each of the following headings, and the number of teachers listing each problem is indicated before each.

### A. *Problems related to science teaching*

22 To develop background in biological science
15 To organize a science course for a rural school
15 To organize a science program for the early elementary grades
14 To work out methods for using local environment in teaching science
3 To develop usable science demonstrations for the elementary grades
3 To make science of more practical value to all high school students
2 To develop a topical file of source materials in science
1 To select a general science textbook
1 To develop supplementary laboratory activities in high school physics

### B. *Problems related to the use of library books*

3 To organize a library for a rural school
2 To organize a library for a consolidated school
2 To develop techniques for making better use of children's books in a rural school
2 To develop techniques for making better use of children's books in the elementary grades
1 To plan a program of student participation in the administration of the school library

1 To work out a plan for interchange of library books in rural schools of the county

1 To learn to locate literature related to the science program

### C. *Problems related to community study*

4 To study problems in my local community

1 To study my local community from the standpoint of recreational needs

1 To study ways by which parents can obtain recognition through participation in the school program

1 To develop closer relationship between the village high school and the rural area which it serves

### D. *Problems related to parent-school relations*

5 To survey parents' reactions to parent-teacher conferences

2 To work out a program which will develop greater harmony in my school among parents and children.

*Special Interests.*—In the preworkshop interviews, teachers were asked about special interests which they would like an opportunity to pursue during the summer. Only 43 out of the 72 teachers felt that their interests were definite enough to be stated. The following list is a frequency distribution of special interests which teachers mentioned:

| | | |
|---|---|---|
| 21 Arts and crafts | 3 Outdoor recreation | 2 Dramatics |
| 11 Music | 3 Golf | 1 Movies |
| 5 Trips or travel | 2 Nature study | 1 Tennis |
| 4 Picnics | 2 Reading | 1 Riding |
| 4 Swimming | 2 Dancing | |
| 4 Fishing | 2 Bridge | |

### STAFF PREPARATION FOR THE WORKSHOP

Since the principal aim of the community workshop is to exploit local community resources in carrying out a functional program of community education, it was quite important that the staff become acquainted with Barry County, its resources, the kinds of schools located in the county, the teachers in those schools, and the kinds of problems which concerned these teachers. In some cases it was possible for staff members to spend several days in the area visiting teachers in their schools. The expense of such visits was paid by the W. K. Kellogg Foundation. Since only four of the staff of the Barry County workshop had an opportunity to visit this area before the opening of the workshop, the others were introduced to the community, as indicated previously, through correspondence. The director wrote detailed letters to each of these staff members describing the local situation and the nature of the workshop program. He sent copies of all materials which had been prepared in planning the workshop. He also asked local teachers to write different staff members so as to help acquaint them with the local scene.

When staff members visited the area before the opening of the workshop, they were encouraged to visit a rural school, a typical village school, the county school commissioner, the chairman of the teacher education committee, and any other teachers with whom that staff member might be working during the summer. All of those who had an opportunity to make this preliminary visit to Barry County have stated that it was a valuable experience in orienting them to the kind of thing that needed to be done in terms of the interests and needs of teachers in their local communities.

Illustrative of the effectiveness of a preworkshop visit to the area in which the community workshop is to be held, was the experience of Dr. Buchsbaum, whose special field was biology. Before he came to the county for a three day visit, Dr. Buchsbaum had a pretty definite idea as to the nature of the content material he would present in the biological science course. This arrangement of content was patterned very much after the course which was taught on campus, and Dr. Buchsbaum expected to give examinations of the type used on campus. In fact, the course was to differ very little from the campus course in general biological science. After he had had an opportunity to talk with local teachers who were interested in biological science, he found that they had, for the most part, some definite purposes in taking this work. They wanted to learn more about birds, plants, insects, and other biological organisms, how to identify them, and how to display and use these organisms in science activities when they were brought in by children. Although it did not seem that these were the most important kinds of things for these teachers to do in biological science, Dr. Buchsbaum modified his original plan to include among his assistants men who could work with teachers in these kinds of activities.

*Staff Sessions.*—All members of the workshop staff were asked to meet in a series of planning sessions in Hastings on Thursday and Friday of the week preceding the formal opening of the workshop. Representatives of the Barry County teacher education committee and the local superintendent of schools were invited to participate in these sessions.

Most of the time during the first day's meeting was spent by the staff in getting acquainted with each other and with the local people who attended this meeting. During the morning of the first session various persons representing local teacher groups told how the workshop idea had developed in Barry County and what they considered the important purposes of such a workshop program to be. They emphasized the importance of the library program in the workshop, since some 22,000 new books had been secured in the county within

*Representatives of the Barry County teacher education committee participated in the preworkshop staff conference at Central School in Hastings. Mr. Edwin Taylor (center), chairman of the committee, reviewed the activities of the committee in getting a workshop for the teachers of Barry County. Mr. Winch (left), staff sociologist, and Mr. Van Buskirk (right), superintendent of Hastings schools, listen as Mr. Taylor tells the workshop staff that the teachers of Barry County requested that a laboratory school be maintained as an important part of the workshop.*

the preceding year through a project sponsored by the W. K. Kellogg Foundation. They pointed out to the staff that very few of the teachers felt qualified to make best use of these books and had on repeated occasions asked the teacher education committee to provide some kind of service on this problem.

The chairman of the teacher education committee reviewed the manner in which a survey of the educational needs of teachers had been conducted the preceding fall and reported that teachers in general wanted an opportunity to improve their science programs and to observe good teachers at work with children. He pointed out that the teacher education committee, in planning a workshop in science education, had felt that if a laboratory school could be maintained as a part of the workshop, both these general needs of teachers could be met. One of the group representing rural teachers explained that there had been considerable disharmony between rural and village elementary school teachers, and that she would expect a good social-recreational program during the summer to help a great deal in reducing this apparent cleavage between the two groups of teachers. Another of the local teachers said that she felt the workshop could do a good deal for teachers in helping them learn more about the democratic process and how it could be applied to teaching situations.

Questions came from the staff concerning the contact which the director had had with teachers who were planning to enroll in the workshop. The procedure on teacher interviews was reviewed, and the records of information obtained from these interviews were made available to all members of the staff.

During the discussion on the first morning, the group identified a number of problems which they felt it was important to discuss before the opening of the workshop on Monday. These were listed and given consideration in later meetings.

The group decided that it was important for participants to be given an opportunity to plan the program with the staff. It was agreed that a meeting with a representative group of participants and staff should be held on Monday afternoon to plan a general schedule of workshop activities which would make it possible for each of them to get most out of the summer program.

The functions of various staff members were discussed and a number of questions concerning interrelationship of functions were brought out. This gave the staff an opportunity to express their own concepts of what they considered their function to be in this program, and to help clarify the interrelationship of staff functions. This gave each staff member an opportunity to begin thinking about the way in which he, in working with his particular group, might use other members of the staff. This development was evidenced by the number of times certain members of the staff asked other members to assist them in one way or another.

The importance of keeping some kind of record of workshop activities was discussed. Some felt that a very detailed record should be kept, while others did not foresee much value in such an undertaking. Staff members representing the subject-matter areas of biology, sociology, and library science brought out the point that the departments they represented would want some account of what took place in the workshop, and said that it was going to be necessary for them to keep a rather complete record of group activities for which they were responsible. The importance of keeping a photographic record of the workshop was mentioned, and a member of the staff, Mr. Johnson, was chosen to serve as the staff photographer. He, it was understood, was to be available whenever any staff member or group felt that the thing they were doing was worth recording by photograph. The staff reached no general decision concerning the manner in which records of the workshop would be kept, although they felt that it was important to keep some kind of record, that the type of record which would be kept would depend on the nature of the various kinds of activities, and that the situations could not be anticipated at this early time.

Since teacher-participants in the workshop were to receive credit in various subject fields other than education, the danger of departmentalizing the program was discussed. It was generally agreed that those who would receive credit in a particular course for which one of the staff was responsible should meet at specified times during the week with that staff member. There was no general agreement as to the time of day or frequency of such meetings. The danger of departmentalization from the standpoint of differences between secondary school teachers and village and rural elementary school teachers was discussed, and it was decided that staff members should use every available opportunity to bring these groups closer together.

The minimum requirements for credit in the various courses were considered by the staff. Dr. Buchsbaum had worked out a very specific schedule of activities which he was planning to require of participants who would receive credit in general biological science. This schedule was so definitely worked out that he could tell members of the group just what was going to happen on any one day during the next six weeks. He said that he was obligated to his department to see that a certain minimum of activities was scheduled, and that he saw no other way of meeting that obligation.

Mr. Winch stated that he planned to give the participants working with him in sociology the background of sociological principles which were covered in corresponding sociology courses on campus at the University of Chicago. Although this plan, so far as the possibility of working on real problems in a community is concerned, was challenged by some of the staff, Mr. Winch felt that teachers working on sociological problems should have a thorough understanding of the principles of sociology before they attacked the problems.

Miss Hunt, staff member in library science, felt there were certain basic concepts concerning the organization and administration of a library which all teachers receiving credit in library science should have, but that it would be possible to develop these concepts through a direct approach to the teacher's literature and library problems. She wanted definite times set aside each week to meet the group with which she would be working, although she had no outline to be assimilated during the summer.

The staff members responsible for courses in education agreed that although there were basic concepts which teachers working with them should develop during the summer, the best way to develop these concepts was through an organized attack on the teaching problems which the participants would bring to them.

All this discussion of the minimum requirements for credit in various courses led into a discussion of "What do we as a staff conceive as our purposes in working with these teachers?" After spending some time considering this question it was agreed that there were several purposes which the staff should keep in mind in working with these teachers. These purposes were stated as follows:

1. The staff should assist each participant with whom they work to define and clarify the problem which he brings into the program.

2. The staff should help him explore all the resources in the workshop community which could be used in attacking the problem.

3. The staff should help each participant learn how to use these resources more effectively.

4. The staff should give the participants assistance in the interpretation of evidence, information, and materials which he obtains from these various sources and in terms of the problem on which he is working.

5. The staff should help each participant leave the workshop at the end of the six weeks with definite ideas concerning the ways in which he is going to improve his teaching situations.

Another problem which was brought up for discussion during the preworkshop conference was the way in which the laboratory school would be used in the program. It was generally agreed that the laboratory school would be used in the program and that it was one of the most significant resources available in the workshop, if staff and participants would make adequate use of it. It was also considered inadvisable for the staff to set up a schedule by which the laboratory school should be used, but that the participants should make this decision. It was decided that, since the laboratory school was not to officially open until the second week of the workshop, it would be well for laboratory school teachers to be available to participants from 10:00 to 12:00 each morning during the first week. At this time they could talk with teacher-participants about the organization of each of the laboratory school groups and about the ways in which this program could be used to greatest advantage by all concerned.

The staff discussed the use of local resources. It was recognized that one of the principal advantages of a community workshop was the opportunity to help teachers learn how to use local resources in their teaching. The group encouraged those staff members who had not had an opportunity to explore Barry County or the city of Hastings to spend some time before Monday in getting acquainted with the resources of the area. One of the teacher-participants suggested that local teachers would be very happy to help the staff in this orientation. The way in which the local faculty and parents of children who were planning to attend the laboratory school might be used as resource people was also given consideration.

Toward the close of the second day of the preworkshop conference it became evident that it would be advisable to work out some kind of organization which would make it possible to give individual teachers adequate advice and counselling in planning their workshop participation. It was agreed that the most immediate way of handling this situation would be for each staff member to be responsible for advising a group of participants. These groups would be known as advisory groups and the membership would be determined by the major interest of the adviser and the advisee. The advisory groups which were to function during the first week of the workshop were set up by considering the information which the staff had concerning participants and assigning each participant to a staff member who would be likely to give him the best help during the first week.

Since few of the staff had had an opportunity to familiarize themselves with the Central School building in which the workshop was to be housed, a member of the group made floor plans of the building for use in planning the allocation of rooms. A committee assumed the responsibility for selecting the rooms in which workshop library materials would be located. After the library had been definitely located, the staff working individually and in smaller groups made room selections for the various other kinds of group activities.

During the two-day planning session the director intentionally avoided letting the staff work out a definite schedule of workshop activities, because he felt that a schedule should not be developed until all of them, participants and staff, had had an opportunity to recognize the significance of a schedule in such a program. The staff did decide that it would be well to have some kind of schedule for Monday, since the participants were going to be in the building at 9:30 and somebody should know where they were to go and what they were to do at that time. The following schedule for the first Monday of the workshop was finally approved by the staff:

| | |
|---|---|
| 9:00–10:30 | General meeting |
| | *a.* Introduction of the staff |
| | *b.* General announcements |
| | *c.* Discussion of questions concerning workshop procedure |
| 10:30–12:00 | Registration and opportunity for individuals to meet their advisers |
| 12:00– 1:30 | Lunch |
| 1:30– 3:00 | Advisory group meetings |
| 3:00 | Barry County teacher education committee's reception for workshop participants |

On Saturday afternoon the staff of the Barry County workshop met in Battle Creek with the staff members from the other three workshops. Dr. Henry J. Otto, of the W. K. Kellogg Foundation, reviewed the purposes of the Foundation and the various activities which comprise the Michigan Community Health Project. The discussion which followed the presentation helped a great deal in orienting staff members with regard to the relationship of the workshops to the total program of improving community living. This meeting and the picnic that followed helped staff members from the four workshops to get better acquainted, and thus facilitated a more adequate use of staff resources through an interchange of personnel during the summer.

### WORKSHOP RESOURCES

In planning the workshop at Hastings, a variety of resources were planned in cooperation with representative groups of county teachers and were selected in terms of the problems which teachers were bringing to the workshop.

*The Staff.*—Dr. Ralph Buchsbaum, Assistant Professor of Zoology at the University of Chicago, worked with teachers in the general course in biological science. Mr. Robert Winch, M.A., an instructor in the Department of Sociology at the University of Chicago, directed the activities of teachers working on problems of community study. Miss Mate Graye Hunt, M.A., Children's Librarian of the

*Teachers' problems, purposes and organization of workshop activities, and the use of local facilities were among the topics discussed by the teacher education committee and the workshop staff during the two-day preworkshop conference. Here the director is recording the group's suggestions for uses of various rooms in the Central School building.*

W. E. Griener High School, Dallas, Texas, worked with the teachers who were concerned with library problems and wished to obtain credit in the library courses.

Since forty-six students enrolled for credit in the biological science course, Dr. Buchsbaum arranged to obtain the assistance of four other men in biological science. Dr. George Neville Jones, Professor of Botany at the University of Illinois, worked with teachers for six days in making plant collections as a part of their work in biological science. Dr. Victor Dropkin, a zoologist from the University of

Chicago, was obtained for the last four weeks of the workshop to assist teachers in making their collections of animals. Dr. Arthur Hasler, a limnologist from the University of Wisconsin, worked with teachers for three days in the study of lakes. Dr. Jones Schreider, a physiologist from the University of Chicago, also assisted in this area by performing demonstrations in mammalian physiology during the last week of the workshop.

Miss Catharine M. Bergen, M.A., Consultant and Teacher of

*The 1941 community workshops were only one phase of an ongoing program of education in the Michigan Community Health Project. Dr. Henry J. Otto, of the Kellogg Foundation, reviews this program for staff members of the four workshops and points out the significance of these workshops in the education of teachers in this area.*

elementary science in the Lincoln School of Teachers College, Columbia University, was employed to assist teachers in problems dealing with the elementary science curriculum. Dr. Gertha Williams, Professor of Psychology at Wayne University, was asked to work with teachers in problems of child guidance. Mr. Carl Johnson, A.B., a high school principal from Irvine, Kentucky, was employed as the laboratory school teacher for the junior high school group. Miss Jennie Kaufman, A.B., Rural School Consultant in Ottowa County, Michigan, was employed to teach the rural laboratory group in the Altoft School.  Mr. W. E. Martin, M.A., Supervising Teacher of biological science in the University High School, University of Michigan, was invited to serve as the laboratory school teacher for the high school group.  Mrs. Marion Wanless, A.B., Supervising Teacher of elementary science at Wayne University, was employed as teacher of the intermediate elementary laboratory school group. Miss Vesta Watson, M.A., Demonstration Teacher in State Teachers College, East Stroudsburg, Pennsylvania, took charge of the early elementary laboratory school group.  Dr. J. Darrell Barnard, the director, worked with high school teachers on problems in the general field of secondary education as well as in science education at the secondary level.

Members of the staff were selected in terms of a personnel who could provide the most adequate assistance to teachers on their various teaching problems.  In some cases local teachers even participated in the selection of laboratory school teachers who, in their opinion, could do the kind of teaching they wanted to observe.

*The Library.*—Library materials were selected from the most recent publications on subjects related to the problems teachers were bringing to the workshop.  A professional library of about five hundred volumes was made available.  A group of teacher-participants, with the assistance of one of the staff, prepared these books and other materials for use.  This provided the teachers an opportunity to learn the mechanics involved, and to have a first-hand acquaintance with the variety of materials which had been brought together for their use.

*The Laboratory School.*—The laboratory school, as one of the resources of the workshop, resulted from the requests of teachers for such a program.  A committee of local teachers worked with the director in planning a laboratory-school that would meet the needs and interests of teachers for observation.  Since the teachers themselves requested the laboratory school and helped to organize it, they understood its function and used it as a resource.

*Building Facilities.*—The selection of school buildings to house the workshop activities was made by a representative group of teachers after considering ways in which the arrangement of rooms and available physical equipment could be used in such an educational program.

*Local Communities.*—The local communities which employed these teachers were considered important resources.  Before the official opening of the workshop, teachers were encouraged to study their own communities to determine how people, institutions, agencies, and the natural environment of that community could be used as resources in attacking their teaching problems.

*Visual Aids.*—Visual materials such as movie films, pictures, exhibits, and charts were selected by staff and participants. Some of these aids were obtained free, and others were made available through a special fund provided for this purpose.

*Up-to-date pamphlets and bulletins relating to the problems which teachers brought to the workshop were an important part of the library resources. The above materials on sociological problems are illustrative.*

*Secretarial Aid.*—Secretarial assistance was provided for both staff and participants. Two well-qualified local girls were obtained to provide this service. These girls took care of all the routine clerical work in the general office and prepared typewritten and mimeographed materials needed in the program.

*Travel Fund.*—A special fund was provided to cover the automobile expense of staff members for field trips and visits to local schools. It was thus possible for each staff member to work with teachers in areas of the county where the problem under consideration actually existed without involving additional costs to individuals.

## ORGANIZATION OF GROUPS

In order that the resources of the workshop could be used most effectively by staff and teacher participants, it was necessary to develop an organization of work groups. The nature of the teacher's problems as well as the course credit which the teacher desired were used as bases for organizing the original work groups.

Since an attempt had been made to prevent the staff from planning a schedule beyond the first Monday, so that participants might have some part in the planning, a representative group of participants met with a committee of the staff on the first afternoon to plan a general weekly schedule by which the work groups would operate. The following schedule was developed as a result of this meeting:

| | |
|---|---|
| 8:00–10:00 | Work-group meetings and individual conferences |
| | 1. Biological science, Dr. Buchsbaum |
| | 2. Library problems, Miss Hunt |
| | 3. Science curriculum problems, Miss Bergen and Dr. Barnard |
| | 4. Guidance problems, Dr. Williams |
| | 5. Problems of community study, Mr. Winch |
| 10:00–12:00 | Observation in the laboratory school |
| 12:00–12:30 | Lunch |
| 12:30– 1:30 | Open for general meetings, social, and recreational activities |
| 1 30– 3:30 | Work-group meetings and individual conferences |
| | 1. Biological science, Dr. Buchsbaum |
| | 2. Library problems, Miss Hunt |
| | 3. Science curriculum problems, Miss Bergen and Dr. Barnard |
| | 4. Guidance problems, Dr. Williams |
| | 5. Problems of community study, Mr. Winch |
| | 6. Arts and crafts activities |
| | 7. Special committee meetings |

In general this schedule was followed throughout the six-week period, although there were some variations from day to day. Not all of the work-groups met regularly at the time scheduled nor were individual conferences with staff members always held at the designated periods. Frequently staff members went with teacher-participants to their local schools to study the various problems confronting the teacher in these school situations. Field trips were sometimes scheduled for a half-day or an entire day, which made it necessary to modify the proposed schedule. On some occasions general meetings extended beyond the one-hour scheduled period in the afternoon.

Different work-groups occasionally met together to work on some problem of common interest. Most of the teachers in the biological science group were also regular participants in the science curriculum group, although occasionally the two groups met together with the staff leaders of both groups to discuss the relationship of their respective activities. The child guidance group and the group working on problems related to community study met several times to consider the place of the child in general community activities. The science curriculum group and the guidance group had several joint sessions on such problems as the place of student needs in developing a science program for the elementary and secondary schools.

Staff members other than the regular group leader, were often called on for assistance with some phase of a problem, and the laboratory-school teachers were frequently asked to give such assistance. This practice helped to identify the laboratory school as a resource which could be used by various work-groups.

An effort was made by both staff and participants to reserve the period from 10:00 to 12:00 each morning for observation in the laboratory school and for discussion of observations with the laboratory-school teachers. Since the laboratory school was in session from 9:30 to 11:30, the following half-hour was free for the laboratory-school teachers and the participants to discuss the morning's observation. Other members of the staff also participated in these discussions and helped bring out the significance of the observation from various points of view.

A number of committees were selected to consider common problems or interest, and to plan special events. These groups met at various times during the day whenever it was convenient for members of the respective committees. Social and recreational activities were generally scheduled in the afternoon or evening, depending on the nature of the activity.

### ACTIVITIES OF THE BIOLOGICAL SCIENCE GROUP

*Lectures.*—The program of activities in the biological sciences consisted of (1) a theoretical part and (2) a series of special activities. The theoretical part, by far the most important in the opinion of the instructor, consisted of lecture-discussions extending over four two-hour periods a week for six weeks. During this time the following topics were taken up:

A. *Plant Kingdom:* (1) survey of main forms of algae, fungi, moss, fern, and seed plant with descriptions of structure and life history, (2) photosynthesis and respiration, (3) plant growth.

B. *Animal Kingdom:* Survey of body plans of animals from protozoa to mammals, with emphasis on how each solves the main life problems and what each contributes toward the evolution of the higher forms. Economic and medical aspects such as food and parasitic organisms were considered in each group.

C. *Machinery of the human body in health and disease:* The human organism as a living machine and how it carries on its life activities. Physiology of blood, heart and circulation, respiration, reproduction, and pathology emphasized.

*Discussions.*—In the discussions greater emphasis was placed on the basic ideas of biology than technical terms or details. Wherever possible, illustrative examples from the local situation were chosen and in discussions the points raised by participants were used to bring out biological concepts. The staff member in charge of this group felt that the use of illustrative examples from a local environment with which all participants were familiar was a technique which could not be used so effectively on campus where students are drawn from varied backgrounds.

*Readings and Films.*—Reading in biological science was provided from a set of five books.[1] Ten sets of these books were rented from the University of Chicago Bookstore and the copies placed on shelves in the classroom. Judging by the demand, reading was very extensive, although the pressure of examinations in this group may have accounted for such extensive reading in these five books. A number of special references were available in the workshop library and were used for additional reading by some of the group. A number of sound films[2] dealing with various topics covered in the work were used.

*Field Trips and Collections.*—Special activities were carried out to illustrate some of the biological concepts, and to supply additional instruction in subjects of special interest in Barry County. In connection with each of the four such activities, a "specialist" was called in to assist.

Dr. George Neville Jones of the department of botany, University of Illinois, spent three days during the first week of the program taking participants on field trips, identifying plants, and showing par-

---

[1] Coulter, *The Plant Kingdom;* Buchsbaum, *Animals without Backbones;* Romer, *Man and the Vertebrates;* Carlson and Johnson, *Machinery of the Human Body;* and Buchsbaum, *Readings in Ecology.*

[2] *Respiration, Digestion, Mammalian Reproduction, Tiny Water Animals, The Nervous System, From Flower to Fruit,* and *The Carbon Oxygen Cycle.*

ticipants how to use keys to identify plants. Two weeks later he returned to give participants further assistance with the plant collections which they had made. Participants learned how to make standard herbarium specimens and, with a few exceptions, collected and identified a hundred or more different kinds of local plants.

Dr. Victor Dropkin of the department of zoology, University of Chicago, was in the workshop for four weeks assisting participants in collecting, describing, and classifying various types of animals.

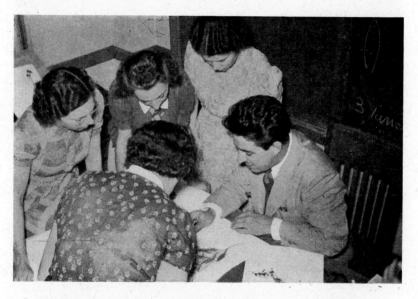

*"What's the name of this plant?" was a question which children frequently asked teachers. These teachers wanted to learn how to identify common plants in their own school community. Dr. George Neville Jones of the botany department, University of Illinois, spent several days working in the field with teachers on this project. Here he is shown checking the work which four rural-school teachers had done.*

Methods of keeping animals alive for exhibit were demonstrated and an exhibit of local animals, including worms, insects, crustaceans, amphibians, and reptiles, was prepared. Dr. Dropkin also took major charge of the three students who were registered for credit in an advanced field zoology course. These students made a more complete collection of the animal life found in the local environment.

Since there are about two hundred lakes in Barry County, fishing,

boating, and swimming play a large part in the lives of the people
in this area.  Dr. Arthur Hasler of the department of biology, University of Wisconsin, was brought into the workshop to work with
some of the participants in developing the major concepts of lim-
nology.  He demonstrated, on Middle Lake near Hastings, the use
of apparatus for studying lakes.  This included thermometers to
measure temperatures at various depths, dredges for sampling bot-

*An important part of the work in science, since Barry County has over*
*two hundred lakes, consisted of activities dealing with an understanding of*
*nature life in these lakes and a study of the ways in which man can make*
*better use of it.  Here Dr. Dropkin of the University of Chicago assists in*
*the identification of tiny water animals which are used by fish as food.*

tom mud for organisms, water samplers, oxygen determination, and
plankton nets.

Dr. Jonas Schredider of the department of physiology, University
of Chicago, worked two days in the program using special apparatus
to demonstrate some of the machinery of the body.  He used such
animals as dog, frog, turtle, and snake in performing these demonstrations.  Blood clotting, blood pressure, vasomotor changes in response to adrenalin, nervous control, heart cycle, control of heart
action, and respiration were demonstrated.  A number of demonstra-

tions were conducted without special apparatus to help teachers see how these could be used in their own classrooms.

The major emphasis in the biological science group was on the development of a theoretical understanding of certain concepts in biological science, with less time spent on the practical application of those concepts in community living. The field trips which this group took dealt primarily with collecting and identifying plants and animals.

*Hastings public school busses were used in transporting teachers to local areas where they would study the natural environment and learn how it could be used more effectively in science activities with children. This group is leaving for an all day trip to the sand dunes near Hastings.*

### ACTIVITIES OF THE ELEMENTARY SCIENCE CURRICULUM GROUP

The twenty-nine participants who were concerned about problems dealing with the organization of elementary science programs frequently worked as a group. Their problems fell into several general classifications. Some wished to develop a course of study in elementary science which they could use in their schools the next year. Others desired to work out a list of demonstrations suitable for the science work in the elementary grades. A few were interested in developing a bibliography of science materials which could be used in improving their own backgrounds in science, as well as materials which could be used with children. Still others had the problem of determining what resources were available in the local community and how these resources could be used in their science teaching.

*Science Background.*—Several kinds of activities were planned by the group in attacking these teaching problems. Some felt that, in view of their lack of subject-matter background, they would like

*Collecting, mounting, and labeling plant specimens for future reference in elementary science classes were activities in which a number of teachers participated. This rural teacher is learning to mount plant specimens so that she can assist her children in such activities.*

an opportunity to work with their staff leader on some of the subject matter in physical science which they could use in their science teaching. This subject matter was presented by using materials, demonstration, and other activities which were suitable for use in the elementary school. An attempt was made to use only inexpensive equipment which could be obtained in any small community. Since there was not enough time to cover the entire field, this phase of the work was limited to activities in units on astronomy, weather, electricity, geology, machines, and pressure. The elementary science materials in the workshop library were used extensively by these teachers, and were supplemented by field trips.

*Demonstration Materials.*—Teacher-participants who were interested in science demonstrations that could be used in their own school situations were assisted by their staff leader in locating the materials, performing the demonstrations, and preparing written descriptions of them. Each teacher kept these descriptions in the form of a card file and the teachers from one school system kept a common file to which all contributed. A county school commissioner, interested in the use which rural teachers might make of these demonstrations, prepared a description of a large number of demonstrations, had them mimeographed, and distributed them among rural teachers.

*Methods of Teaching.*—There were many group discussions on the techniques for teaching science to elementary school children and the values which might be derived from these techniques. Collections, identification, a study of principles of science, and the development of enriched concepts of such things as space and time were among the topics included in these discussions.

On several occasions the staff leader in child guidance discussed the function of elementary science in a good elementary school program. The staff leader in biological science participated in meetings with this group and made his contribution from the point of view of a subject-matter specialist. Participants working on bibliographies of science materials did a good deal of their individual work with the library specialist.

*Use of Community Resources.*—This group made extensive use of community resources. One group visited Clear Lake Camp, near Hastings, and observed sun spots through the telescope located at the camp. Ways in which the teachers could make use of this telescope with their own students were discussed. Since a number of the teachers wanted to learn more about birds, several bird walks were scheduled with Dr. Dropkin.

A conservation study was conducted in the yard of one of the local Hastings residents. An exhibit of the State Conservation Department at the Bluegill Festival in Hastings was visited and discussed by a number of participants in this group.

Since Barry County has no exposed bedrock, an all-day trip was made to study the rock formations which the group had observed in neighboring counties. They visited the Marshall sandstone quarries near Battle Creek, the Bayport limestone quarry near Bellevue, the sandstone ledges along the Grand River at Grand Ledge, and the clay factory at Grand Ledge.

Some members of the group visited the local water works in Hastings. They studied the source of water supply, the use of pumps, and the distribution of water over the city.

Some of the members of this group prepared an exhibit of materials donated in reply to requests written to publishers, commercial companies, agencies, and organizations providing services to schools.

*To understand and use local resources was a major objective of the community workshop. Teacher participants and staff visited the Government Recreation Project at Yankee Springs, and are here shown discussing the purposes and nature of the recreational project with a government representative in the Park.*

This material was arranged in convenient display and was available for all to use. Plans were made during the last week of the workshop for these materials to be kept in Barry County as a part of a curriculum library which the local teacher education committee was sponsoring.

*Use of the Laboratory School.*—The activities of this work group were closely coordinated with the laboratory school, since one of the laboratory-school teachers developed with her children the same units that this group of teachers was working on. This made it possible for them to observe the procedure used in developing learning activities for children and to discuss these activities with the laboratory-school teacher at a time when they themselves were concerned about the subject matter of the units. These teachers observed in other divisions of the laboratory school, and made frequent use of laboratory-school teachers on problems dealing with the organization and administration of learning activities in elementary science.

*Other Group Interests.*—Several subsidiary groups, in the area of elementary science curriculum, developed during the six-week period. One group of elementary school teachers from Hastings worked together in developing a science program for the elementary grades in Hastings. A group of rural teachers worked cooperatively in the development of a program of science for the rural schools of Barry County. At the close of the workshop, neither of these two groups had entirely accomplished the purpose for which they originally organized, although they had gone far enough on their project to continue this activity throughout the coming school year.

*The Park Improvement Project.*—A discussion of the educational values of the park improvement project that was carried out by the laboratory school provided opportunity for this group to integrate its thinking with respect to the place of science in such a general activity. Several meetings were held in discussing this problem, and a number of values were identified which helped this group to see that an activity program should be designed to contribute more than mere activity. The understandings, attitudes, skills, and appreciations of science involved in such a project were listed, and the techniques teachers could use in order to accomplish these outcomes of such an activity were discussed.

### ACTIVITIES OF THE COMMUNITY STUDY GROUP

Seven participants worked together as a group interested in studying community problems. Two of these people had registered for credit in the introductory sociology course and five had registered for credit in an advanced sociology course. The activities of these people were organized so as to retain the usual content of sociology which the staff leader regarded as essential and to modify the non-basic materials so they would bear as directly as possible on the problems and interests of the participants.

*Lectures and Readings.*—For the first two and one-half weeks, two-hour sessions were held daily for the purpose of presenting material to the participants which the staff leader considered of such a basic and essential character that he was unwilling to assume that it could be adequately assimilated in any other way. The next week and a half was given over to reading, with only one or two sessions on special problems. The two-hour sessions with participants were resumed during the last two weeks, during which questions concerning

*Discussions of professional problems frequently preceded or followed social activities. Jennie Kaufman, rural school consultant for Ottawa County, is here leading a discussion of the relationship of the village high school to the rural schools from which they obtain their students. This discussion followed a picnic supper held on the lawn of a local teacher's home.*

participants' reading were clarified. In these sessions no attempt was made to distinguish participants registered for the introductory course from those registered for the advanced course, and they met as a single group.

*Conferences.*—Interviews were held with participants every morning and afternoon during periods when no group meetings were scheduled. These interviews for the most part dealt with the formulation and analysis of the participants' problems and, where two or more participants' problems fell into similar areas, they were encouraged to work together.

*Definition of Problems.*—At the opening of the workshop session most of the problems were quite vaguely identified by the participants, and this made it necessary to spend some time in clarifying the problems. The problems which developed could be classified into three types:

1. *Research:* An example of the research type of problem was one which set out to determine the relation between parent's participation and interests in school to their children's emotional maturity and scholastic achievement.

2. *Community action without analysis:* In problems of community action, the value of the purpose was assumed, and defensible means of action were sought. An example was a problem to develop community support for a summer playground program in Hastings.

3. *The conventional term paper:* Projects consisting of term papers were undertaken only after it had been thoroughly established that the participant either did not have a problem or found it inadvisable because of community pressure to study such a problem. A typical term report in this area consisted of a discussion and analysis of the procedures for studying the community, with special reference to the community's definition of the teacher's role and its conception of the educational institution.

Few of the participants in this group got beyond the stage of defining their problems, reading textbooks in sociology, discussing principles of sociology, and writing examination papers. During the last two weeks of the workshop four Hastings teachers worked cooperatively in plotting a sample occupational distribution of Hastings. In the opinion of the staff leader, this was an example of the "drive to bring theory and technique to bear upon the local community and the participants' problems."

*Visual Aids.*—During the six-week session the sociology group exhibited four government documentary films[1] to acquaint participants with the availability of this type of material rather than for any relationship the films might bear to the problems of these teachers. Each of these films had sociological implications and was discussed from the standpoint of the way in which it might be used in high school and adult discussion groups.

*Assisting the Community.*—Representatives of this group met frequently throughout the summer with the Hastings' city committee on the summer recreational program for children. They helped the committee see that as long as they continued to impose a ready-made

[1] *The Farmer in This Changing World, Rural Electrification, The River,* and *The Plow That Broke the Plains.*

recreational program upon various neighborhoods in Hastings, they would continue to have the many problems confronting them. It was decided that parent committees should be organized in each of these neighborhoods and that these parent committees should study the recreational needs in their respective neighborhoods, plan the program to meet those needs, and come to the city committee for help whenever they needed it.

Members of the community study group met with these parent committees on a number of occasions and helped them to study local needs and plan recreational programs to meet those needs. These committees became very active in accomplishing their purposes during the summer and in making plans for a continuation of other projects related to the recreation program. Some of the teacher-participants who worked with parent committees were local Hastings teachers, who planned to continue their work with these groups. Although the other participants would not be able to maintain close relationship to the program, since they teach in other communities, they learned some of the techniques of working with such groups.

*Group Discussions.*—As previously mentioned, the group working on community problems met on several occasions with the child guidance group to clarify their thinking about the place of the child in various kinds of community activities. The staff leader in child guidance assisted members of this group in their work with parent committees on neighborhood recreational problems.

ACTIVITIES OF THE SECONDARY SCHOOL SCIENCE CURRICULUM GROUP

Six of the workshop participants were concerned with problems in the area of the secondary school science curriculum. These problems dealt with the selection of a general science textbook, functionalizing chemistry and biology courses, the use of community resources in the science program, devising supplementary laboratory activities in physics for noncollege students, and pupil-teacher planning in science classes.

*Discussions.*—During the first two weeks these participants met frequently as a group to discuss their individual problems and to identify relationships between problems which would make it possible for them to work cooperatively on various topics. In these discussions questions regarding the philosophy of science teaching at the secondary school level, objectives of science teaching, suitable learning activities, and evaluation were considered. The staff leader referred the group to a variety of reference materials available in the workshop library, including books on secondary education, on the philosophy of education, and on the organization and administration of science teaching in the high school, as well as evaluation materials and curriculum materials which had been prepared by groups of science teachers in various parts of the country.

*Individual Work.*—There was no formal organization for group activities, although a record was kept of topics covered in discussion. At the end of the first two weeks the group decided not to meet regularly as a group, but to work individually or in smaller groups of two or three on the particular problems which concerned them. The staff member then made himself available both mornings and afternoons for individual conferences. In these conferences a plan for attacking the problem was developed and the participant was given assistance in the use of various resources. The staff leader of this group averaged four individual conferences or small group meetings each day.

*Visits to local schools.*—On several occasions the staff member working with this group accompanied teachers on visits to their local schools to observe the physical arrangement of the science rooms and to recommend modifications of the arrangements that would facilitate the kind of science program the teacher was attempting to follow.

*Using a Consultant.*—During the fifth week of the workshop four of these teachers met with the staff leader to plan a program by which they could obtain and make the best use of the services of a consultant in science education during the coming year. They worked out statements of purposes they would want to accomplish through such a service as well as a tentative plan of the way in which that service would be used.

In no case did any one of this group complete his project before the end of the workshop. Three of the group were working on a generalized science program for the high school, based on the adjustment point of view. Although they had not completed this work, they made enough progress to be able to continue the work during the coming year. One of the participants had made a fair start in the organization of a chemistry course for high school students, based on the common life adjustments of man. Another had practically completed the preparation of a series of supplementary laboratory activities for the noncollege physics students in this school. Another one of the group had gone far enough in the reorganization of his biology course so that, with some assistance during next year, he can complete it.

In group conferences these participants made frequent use of a number of other staff people. On several occasions Dr. Williams, in child guidance, was asked to discuss the needs of adolescent boys and girls and the consideration which should be given those needs

*Dr. Williams, whose field was child guidance, and Dr. Barnard, especially interested in science education, discussed with high school science teachers the importance of considering the needs and interests of boys and girls in planning a science program for the high school. Small-group discussions of this type proved valuable in assisting science teachers with their teaching problems.*

in the high school science program. The two laboratory-school teachers working at the junior and senior high school levels participated frequently in all group discussions and helped the participants see how they might make best use of their observation in the laboratory school. The laboratory-school teachers also delegated certain responsibilities for working with children in the laboratory school to these participants.

## ACTIVITIES OF THE CHILD GUIDANCE GROUP

Most of the participants in the child guidance group had registered for credit in the course on "Foundations of Good Adjustment" or in courses on "Current Problems in the Elementary and Secondary School." The activities of this group included:

1. Group meetings to discuss common problems of participants
2. Individual conferences (*a*) on educational problems brought to the workshop by individuals, and (*b*) on personal problems of participants involved in making better adjustments as teachers
3. Observation in the laboratory school and of the summer recreational program
4. Participation in the community park-improvement project
5. Reading in the library

*Individual Problems.*—The method of procedure in this group was to start with the specific problems of participants and go from these back into the general principles of guidance. The problems given consideration during the summer were not only those which participants brought to the workshop but others which arose during the summer or were suggested as a result of group discussions. The following are listed as illustrations of some of these problems which were treated in either individual or group conferences:

1. Reporting to parents
2. Physical needs of children which should be given consideration in a community recreational program
3. Parent-teacher relations
4. Educational values of the community park improvement project
5. Safeguards in pupil-teacher planning
6. Rewards and punishments
7. Individual differences
8. Basic needs of children
9. Growth and development—physical, emotional, social, and mental
10. Learning—its relation to maturation, interests, emotions, attitudes, and their relation to learning
11. Development of meanings and concepts
12. Noon hour recreation
13. Organization of eight grades in a rural school
14. Home calls
15. Teachers clubs

*Visits to Schools.*—The work of this group was not confined to the one building in Hastings. Schools and homes in communities where these participants taught were visited, and an attempt was made to work out problems in the environment in which they occurred.

As an illustration of the purpose and nature of visits to local communities an instance is reviewed. One of the participants planned to teach in a new community during the next year. She had heard that the former teacher had had trouble in getting along with parents in this community and she wanted to avoid a repetition of the difficulty. In conference with her staff adviser it was decided that she should become better acquainted with the people of this community before school started in the fall. It was evident that the teacher was reluctant to visit these people because she did not know how to go about it. Techniques for making home calls were discussed by the group and the staff leader helped the teacher see how various techniques applied to her own situation. After the teacher had completed her plans for making home calls, she and the staff member with whom she had been working spent one afternoon making several calls. The outcomes of these calls were discussed and plans were made for the teacher to continue until every home had been visited.

*Use of the Laboratory School.*—The participants' observations in the laboratory school were related to the problems being considered by the group. Laboratory-school teachers frequently attended the meetings of this group and assisted in the discussion of their problems. On a number of occasions these staff members asked the group to assist them with problems they encountered in their work with children in the laboratory school. Local parents participated in all discussions dealing with home and school relations. At one meeting there were more parents than teacher-participants. On several occasions superintendents of schools were invited to join in the discussion of problems involving superintendent-teacher relationships.

*Using Resource Persons.*—This group was responsible for bringing several outstanding people into the workshop to assist on special problems. Miss Bernice Leland, a consultant in remedial reading from the Psychological Clinic of the Detroit Public Schools, conducted a discussion of problems dealing with reading in elementary and secondary schools. Miss Ruth Murray, an expert in health education from Wayne University, met on several occasions with this group to discuss problems in her field. Mrs. Mildred Stanford, a director of W.P.A. arts projects in Michigan, through the efforts of the child guidance group, spent two days in the workshop. She worked with the teacher-participants and the children in the laboratory school in an attempt to help teachers understand the function of art in a well-rounded educational program.

As a direct result of their participation in this group and of individual work with the staff leader, the participants working in this group achieved satisfactory progress on their problems.  Several of the Hastings teachers developed a procedure for evaluating the teacher-parent conference as a means of reporting to parents.  Before the close of the workshop, they had actually begun their evaluation which was to be completed in the fall.  Several teachers who were concerned about the organization of activities in an eight-grade one-

*Parents, laboratory-school teachers and teacher-participants met on several occasions to discuss the purpose and nature of the activities of children in the laboratory school.  Here they are discussing the educational values of excursions and are making preliminary plans for an all-day excursion.*

room school had worked out a program of activities which were educationally more effective than the organization they had previously followed.  Another participant completed an evaluation of the recreational program for which he was responsible, and worked out recommendations for reorganizing it in terms of the needs and interests of the boys and girls.  These instances are typical of the progress made by participants.

ACTIVITIES OF THE GROUP WORKING ON LIBRARY PROBLEMS

Through discussions and written statements, the staff leader of the library group obtained specific information on the problems which participants in this group had brought to the workshop. Almost without exception these problems related to either (1) learning the technical procedure needed in taking care of the new books obtained through the book project, or (2) learning how to use these books advantageously in school work.

*The books in the workshop library were prepared for circulation by teachers who were interested in learning about these procedures under the supervision of Miss Hunt, staff member in library science.*

The following statement, taken from the report of the staff leader on library problems, gives some indication of the approach which was made to the activities of this group:

As a scheme of attack I formulated my objectives, to myself, along several broad lines, keeping in mind constantly that this was a workshop set-up which was by its nature much more flexible in its requirements and methods than a campus course:

1. To give as much technical training in library science as the existing conditions seemed to justify

2. To find out what books, new and old, were in each participant's individual school
3. To ascertain the need of material in individual cases
4. To institute a plan of procedure on the part of the participant that would enable her to know her material and have it indexed so as to be readily available for her use and the use of her pupils.
5. To lead the participants to a larger and growing appreciation of the advantages to be derived from the use of the varied wealth of printed materials within their schools and easily accessible through a system of local exchange

*Teachers wanted to learn the mechanics of preparing library books for circulation. Miss Hunt is demonstrating the use of the electric stylus in labeling books.*

*Group Meetings.*—The participants working on library problems met frequently with their staff leader. In these meetings an attempt was made to develop through discussion and lecture an understanding of the ideas and procedures relating to the two general problems on which these participants sought help. The technical points given consideration included such things as accessioning, simple cataloging, marking books, making and filing catalog cards, pasting book pockets, making borrower's cards, making simple bibliographies, checking books in and out, methods of calling pupils' attention to new books, student help, sources of materials and supplies, and the arrangement of books on shelves. In order to provide experience with these activities, the group was given the task of preparing all materials in the workshop library for circulation. This took several days but gave the group an opportunity to learn in a practical way some of the activities involved in library work.

*Children's Literature.*—In the area of children's literature, the staff leader made an effort to relieve the evident lack of background among the participants. In the brief time allotted, it was possible

*Miss Hunt, staff librarian, worked with teachers and children in their own schoolrooms. She is assisting a high school teacher and her student librarians to prepare their new books for circulation.*

to give only an overview of the field and to point out ways in which they could continue their work in children's literature. Short lecture periods, discussions, book exhibits, lists of readings, and books on children's literature were used as means of accomplishing this purpose. Readings from magazines and books were available in the room at all times but no required reading list was issued. The staff leader reported that the participants did a great deal of reading on their own account when pertinent material was called to their attention.

*Discussing the Problems "at Home."*—Another feature of the activities of participants working in the library group can best be described by a quotation from a report written by the staff leader of this group:

> In order to see the participant in her own school situation, to ascertain what her equipment was, to learn more of her problems, and to establish her confidence in my sincerity, I made personal visits to three village schools and twenty-five one-room rural schools ranging in distance from two to sixty miles from Hastings. These visits were made with the participants individually or in groups. One participant made this statement in an evaluation paper early in the term, "I feel that the opportunity to have you go with us into our individual situation helped me immensely."

*Library nooks for rural schools were started by a number of rural teachers through the encouragement of Miss Hunt.*

In this group participants were encouraged to hand in weekly written evaluations of their activities, reports on the extent to which their problems were being covered, and suggestions for further discussions. The staff leader said that these evaluations served as a valuable guide to her in planning individual conferences and group discussions.

During the last half of the term very few group meetings were held and the teachers were encouraged to spend that time in their own schools working, with the assistance of some of their pupils, on the new books. Problems that arose from these activities served as a basis for later discussions.

It appeared that, because of the encouragement which participants in this group were given to work in their own school situations during the summer, their activities with regard to the library problems they brought to the workshop had tangible value. The frequency with which teachers referred to the practical value of their participation in this group suggested that working with the teacher in her own school situation is especially effective. At the close of the six-week session, all the participants working in this group had developed plans for using their new books when school opened again. Most of them had unpacked the books in their school during the summer and, with the assistance of the staff librarian, had prepared the books for circulation and arranged them for display. In a number of cases these teachers had worked out plans for exchanging books among different schools of the county so as to increase the number of books available in any one school. The county school commissioner took the leadership in this latter project, hoping that it might be possible to work out such a plan on a county-wide basis.

### ACTIVITIES IN THE LABORATORY SCHOOL

The laboratory school was organized as a part of the workshop program because of a general desire of Barry County teachers to visit outstanding teachers and observe them at work with children. The laboratory school had five groups: a rural school group at Altoft School near Hastings, and the twelve-grade range divided into groups covering three grades each at Central School in Hastings. A full time laboratory school teacher was maintained for each of these groups.

*Principles of Organization.*—The laboratory school was in operation during the last five weeks of the workshop, with sessions from 9:00 to 11:30 each morning. The programs in these groups varied considerably, although the teachers were concerned with two principles in the organization of these programs: (1) the program should develop from the interests and needs of boys and girls enrolled in each section, and (2) science activities would be encouraged because they represented a dominant interest of the teacher-participants. Three of the laboratory school teachers had extensive backgrounds in science and had taught it for a number of years. Two of the laboratory teachers had not had special training in science, but were out-standing teachers with rural and early elementary school children.

*The Rural Group.*—Enrolled in the rural school division were twenty-two boys and girls ranging in age from five to fourteen. These children were divided into three groups: primary, intermediate, and upper grades. These divisions were maintained only for special kinds of activities. Most of the time, all the children met as one group. These children participated in a variety of undertakings, including a study of the farm, gardening, birds of the community, conservation of wild life, understanding Barry County, and the improvement of school grounds. Discussions, reading, art work, writing, interviewing specialists, listening to talks by specialists, and field trips were among the activities of these children. The teacher of this rural group listed the following purposes underlying the program as far as its demonstration values for teacher-participants were concerned:

1. To learn how better to use community resources
2. To demonstrate various kinds of groupings of children in a rural school
3. To help teachers see that children are capable of doing their own research work
4. To demonstrate that the school can be a happy, interesting place to live and learn

*Early-Elementary School Group.*—Enrolled in the early-elementary school group of the laboratory school were thirty-two children ranging in age from five to eight. Since many of these children had not been used to working in a school situation with children of different ages, the point of view underlying the approach which the laboratory school teacher used with this group was, "We are not a 'grade' but a group of boys and girls living together happily each day; learning comes through experiencing; our group is comparable to any social group in a community; social groups have leaders and such leaders are chosen because the community respects them for their abilities."

Since the teacher of this group thought of science as finding out or discovering truths about phenomena of our own environment, she attempted to use discussion, experimentation, observation, and reading as the basic activities of this group. These activities related to several different topics, such as the daytime sky, weather, air, balancing an aquarium, and the uses of milk as a food. Through these activities the teacher attempted to help children develop an understanding of the broad generalizations related to each of the topics.

*The Intermediate Grades.*—In the intermediate elementary group were thirty children ranging in age from eight to twelve. The program for this group was one of elementary science, for a period of two and a half hours each day. Units of activity dealing with the development of an understanding of the following generalizations of science were planned and carried out with these children:

1. Animals protect themselves in various ways.
2. Rocks tell the story of the earth.

*The early-elementary school group learned how physical and biological factors affect the growth and development of living things by preparing a place in the pool for turtles and fish to live.*

3. Man's knowledge of magnetism and electricity has developed slowly through the ages.
4. Many animals live in communities and cooperate for the community's good.

These units were worked out with the children because teacher-participants had asked to see such a program, and the laboratory-school teacher experienced no difficulty in getting these as suggested interests from the students. Since this teacher had had considerable experience in teaching science, she not only made a special effort to help teacher-participants observe good techniques of working with boys and girls, but also demonstrated ways in which materials and biological organisms can be displayed in the schoolroom to stimulate interest among children.

*The Junior High School Group.*—The junior high school division of the laboratory school had an active enrollment of twenty-two boys and girls. The program for this group was planned to provide opportunity for these students to work on individual activities and to work as a group on some general activity of interest to all. The individual activities were based primarily on the personal interest of the indi-

*Children learned the science of their natural environment, and were encouraged to express their ideas in a variety of art activities.*

vidual, and included such activities as collecting insects, culturing bacteria, surveying pond life, growing an ant colony, building simple telegraph sets, building electric motors, building model airplanes and crystal radio sets, and developing and printing pictures. In considering group activity these students decided to engage in an activity or project that would improve Hastings as a place to live. After conferring with various citizens, including the mayor, they decided to clean up a small park area on the outskirts of Hastings near one of the main highways. This project included cutting weeds, trimming shrubbery, mowing and raking the lawn, and hauling away rubbish; and it later developed into a larger park improvement project which involved the entire laboratory school.

*The Senior High School Group.*—The high school group which enrolled seventeen high school boys and girls began its activities with a discussion of "What is science?" This discussion led to the identification of a number of phenomena which could be classified as science and which were interesting to these boys and girls. After they had talked about the kinds of activities in which they might participate during the five-week period, these students were organized in four groups on the basis of the special interests. The students not only worked with the teacher in these smaller groups, but came together frequently as a single group for the discussion of matters of common interest. During the third week of the session, a request to assist a local recreation committee in cleaning one of the parks was submitted to this group of students. After discussing the possibilities of assisting in such an undertaking, they conducted a survey of things which needed to be done to the park area and planned ways in which they might get the cooperation of all the laboratory school groups in completing this project.

*Participation of Parents.*—The laboratory school teachers visited the parents of each laboratory-school child before the summer school opened. The importance of these preliminary contacts with parents was discussed with participants and a number of teacher-participants accompanied the laboratory school teacher to observe the home calls. Parents were encouraged to visit the laboratory school and many of them visited frequently during the five weeks. At the end of the second week a general parents meeting was held, and matters concerning purposes, organization, and activities of the laboratory school were discussed. Teacher-participants were also encouraged to attend this parents meeting to observe how teachers might work with parents on such occasions. On this and other occasions, parents asked the advice of different laboratory school teachers regarding their relationship to children in the home and other such problems.

*Observations by Teachers.*—The observation of participants in the laboratory school was not required nor definitely planned each day. Laboratory school teachers, at the request of participants, posted daily the general program which was being planned by each of their groups. The program for each morning was posted the afternoon before. This made it possible for participants and other staff members to plan observation in the laboratory school at a time and under the conditions when it would be most meaningful to the participant. Frequently laboratory school teachers were called in to teacher-participant work groups to discuss the nature of a program which had been planned with the children and to help observers identify the kinds of things they should look for during their observation the following day.   Each day the half-hour from 11:30 to 12:00 was reserved for participants and laboratory school teachers to discuss the observation of the morning.

Reports from participants at the conclusion of the workshop indicated that their observation averaged 14.8 days out of the 25 days the laboratory school was in operation.

Frequent reference has been made to the "park improvement project" in discussing various activities within the workshop.  This particular project was significant enough to warrant reviewing it as a special group activity, although it cut across the activities of all the organized groups in the workshop.

On Tuesday evening of the third week of the workshop, two of the laboratory-school teachers and several of the workshop staff met with the local recreation committee to discuss the problems which parent committees had encountered in attempting to carry out summer playground programs in their respective neighborhoods.  The playground program was hampered because of its location in a park area that was littered with debris and had insufficient equipment.

In discussing the problem an attempt was made to determine who might do something about these conditions.  It was brought out that the property really belonged to the city, although the school had been using it.  Yet, neither city nor school felt that they should take the responsibility for cleaning up this wooded area covering two square blocks behind the high school building.  The area had become known as "no man's land" since no one had taken the responsibility for its maintenance.

Since the children were making use of this park as a play area, it was decided they should be given an opportunity to do something about cleaning it.  A number of the children attending the playground were also enrolled in the laboratory school, so one of the parents asked whether the high school students in the laboratory school might not not be interested in taking over this problem as a

*Defective drainage was responsible for puddles in the streets adjoining the childrens' playground after every rainfall.*

*Conditions such as these made the park area unsuitable for a playground. Parents asked the children in the laboratory school for help in improving the area.*

special project. The teacher said he did not know how the children would feel about it, but that he would tell them of the proposal on the following morning.

This request for help from the local playground committee was submitted to the high school students the following morning. After some discussion of the possibilities, they spent the rest of the morning making a survey of things that needed to be done in the park to make it suitable for playground activities. They identified some

*Teachers, children, parents, city and public utilities employees worked together on the park improvement project. Tree trimming and stump removing called for adult help, but most of the other projects were completed by the children themselves.*

thirty-seven different kinds of things which needed to be done in the park area. These things were then sorted into two lists; those which they themselves might do, and those which the city or some other group would have to do.

These students realized that it would be necessary to have more children participate in the project if much were to be accomplished before the laboratory school closed. A representative from the high school group met with each of the other laboratory-school groups, presented the problem and asked each group to send a representative to a general planning session. These representatives constituted the planning committee, which set up twelve work committees to deal with the items of the survey made by the high school group.

The clean-up committee had the responsibility for picking up rubbish, raking leaves, collecting tree limbs, cutting wood, and asking the city council for rubbish cans. The fix-up committee was to mix concrete for patching the tennis courts, construct playground

*City employees, working with teachers, removed fallen trees from the play area. These trees were to be trimmed and made into log benches for the proposed amphitheater.*

equipment, paint the present equipment, and clean the baseball diamond and the sand pit in which the smaller children were to play.

The grounds committee was to mow and pull weeds, rake the grounds, make and plant flower beds, hoe shrubbery, trim along the walks, and obtain the city's help in pulling stumps and locating signs necessary for proper use in the area. The landscape and planning committee was to plan locations for trees, shrubs, and flowers for planting, and to plant and seed the area.

The tree-trimming committee was to get in touch with the Consumers Power Company or the city and obtain their assistance in trimming the limbs from the trees which were a hazard to children

playing in the park.  The picnic-ground committee was to see the
city council about getting tables, outlets for running water, and
garbage cans, to build stoves, and to pile wood near the stoves.  An
amphitheater committee was to plan for drainage and the placement
of log seats in a natural amphitheater, and obtain the assistance of
community groups in constructing this amphitheater.  Another committee for making playground equipment was to make contact with

*Dead branches were trimmed from the trees and cut into firewood for
the fireplaces that were built in the park.*

various community groups to obtain materials and to construct
simple playground equipment which could be used.

The labeling committee planned to label all trees and shrubs and
prepare museum specimens of the leaves of trees found in the park.
The bird committee was to build shelters, feeding stations, and houses
for birds, and to locate them in the most suitable places within the
park.  The records committee was to prepare maps of the area with
proposed changes, make a record of the history of the park project,
take pictures before, during, and after the project, and write a complete record of the entire project.  The safety committee was to look
after the physical welfare of all people who were working in the park
area during the time the program was under way.

Children enrolled in the four divisions of the laboratory school located in the Central School in Hastings were encouraged to associate themselves with one of these twelve committees for the duration of the project. The laboratory school teachers and the teacher-participants also worked on one or more of the various committees.

Wednesday, July 23, 1941, was designated as "clean-up day," the day when the work on the project would begin. Laboratory school children, teachers, and a number of teacher-participants spent the

*Replanting was necessary in some sections of the park. These junior high school girls are surveying the area to determine what planting should be done.*

entire morning working at the various tasks which had been assigned to the different committees. A number of local people also assisted in getting the program under way. Linemen from the Consumers Power Company spent one day trimming trees. The county agricultural agent, the county sanitary engineer, and a local person interested in landscaping worked with the landscaping committee in developing their plans. The playground leaders also assisted. City trucks and several employees were made available to assist in hauling rubbish away. The local Junior Chamber of Commerce donated paint; a lumber yard contributed wood for building some playground equipment; and one of the local people contributed two large picnic tables to be placed in the park area. The City Youth Council contributed twenty-five dollars to buy movie film so that a moving picture record could be kept of the project.

Since a number of improvements required adult workers and expenditure of considerable amounts of money, a committee of laboratory school children called on the mayor to talk with him about the possibility of having the city undertake these major

*Pits for horseshoe pitching were established by the cooperative labors of children in the laboratory school and teacher-participants in the workshop.*

projects. The mayor told the children that he did not have the authority to grant such a request but he would like for them to meet with the city council and present their request to that group. In the following week these children met with the city council and presented recommendations that all trees within the park area be carefully trimmed, a project involving an expenditure of about three hundred dollars; that certain areas of the playground be covered with black top soil; that outlets for drinking fountains be provided in various sections of the park; and several other suggestions for the improvement of the park. The council was most enthusiastic about the fact that these children came and talked to them concerning a

*Since the park area really belonged to the city of Hastings, a committee of children presented their plan for improvements to the mayor, who in turn asked them to help him sell the idea to the city council.   In the upper picture, the children are discussing their plans with the mayor.  Below, the plan is presented to the council, which pledged its cooperation*

problem which they had more or less overlooked for some time, and
told the children they would do everything possible to see that these
recommendations were followed.

Many of the jobs involved in the park improvement project had
been completed by the close of the workshop. Mr. Martin, the
laboratory-school teacher who had been directing all these activities,
visited a number of community people and arranged for various
community groups to complete the project. The playground com-

*The junior high school children surveyed the park for gravel walks. Under
the supervision of laboratory-school teachers, activities of this kind provided many learning situations for these children.*

mittee, made up of parents whose children were participating in the
playground program during the summer, met after the workshop
had closed and planned ways to make sure that each one of these
jobs would be completed.

The park improvement project was promoted by members of the
workshop because they believed it had educational value. Rather
than leaving the recognition of these values to chance, a number of
special meetings were held to discuss the possible educational values
of the project and how they might be achieved. The development of
social sensitivity, cooperativeness, and other characteristics of effec-

tive group participation were defined and there was discussion of ways to guide participants in the better realization of these values. An analysis of the specific activities involved in the various jobs was made and the significance of these physical and mental activities in the growth and development of children were pointed out by members of the staff. The attempt to define the science concepts which could reasonably be developed through participation in the various activities involved in the project led to a discussion of the so-called

*The children obtained experts to assist them in planning the park improvements. An expert in landscaping, the county sanitary engineer, and the county agricultural agent are discussing the plans with teachers and children.*

pure and applied science concepts as defensible outcomes of science programs in the public school. There were some who felt there was little or no science involved in the project since its end was not the development of scientific concepts but an application of those concepts. When the development of abilities in problem solving, scientific attitudes and an understanding of major generalizations were accepted as the major objectives of science programs in both the elementary and the secondary school, a number of values related to the science program were recognized.

Each committee was confronted with problems calling for definition and analysis. Sources of information had to be discovered and evaluated. Ideas had to be brought together and conclusions developed. Critical attitudes had to be exercised in planning solutions to problems, in selecting sources of information and evaluating conclusions. Concepts in science were related to conservation of soil and wildlife, construction of bird houses and playground equipment, the ecology of the wooded area involved, the selection of trees and shrubs to be transplanted in the area, the care of plants and animals, the effect of physical factors of the environment on the growth of living things, and the control of pests.

### ACTIVITIES OF PARTICIPANTS IN SPECIAL COMMITTEES

A number of special committees were organized during the six-week session to facilitate certain kinds of activities which participants in the workshop considered desirable. Most committees were organized as a result of the suggestions of participants who appointed all committee members. In some cases the committees served throughout the workshop session and in other cases they were appointed only for a particular job. In the early part of the session, the participants appointed a committee to represent them at staff meetings to consider problems related to scheduling of activities, the time to be spent in various activities, evaluating different workshop activities, planning ways of improving the workshop program, making greater use of the laboratory school, expenses associated with field trips and social activities, and other problems of this nature. It was interesting to note that the participants, in selecting the committee members, were careful to see that secondary, village elementary, and rural school teachers were all represented. This committee met with participants on several occasions to obtain their reactions to the workshop so that the committee could better represent them at staff meetings.

*Arts and Crafts.*—Before the workshop opened twenty-one teachers had indicated a desire to participate in activities related to the arts and crafts. Since there was no staff member to provide guidance and leadership for these teachers, they appointed an arts and crafts committee. This committee made an inventory of materials and equipment available in the local school, in outlying schools, and in possession of individuals. They worked out a plan by which participants who were accomplished in some particular area of art would work with interested groups of teachers during the afternoon. All materials and equipment, as well as samples of types of things that could be made by children and adults, were brought together at Central School in a room designated as the "arts and crafts room." One member of the committee assumed the responsibility for keeping the room open from 2:00 to 4:30 each afternoon and provided assistance to any teacher-participant who cared to work at that time. During the time that Mrs. Stanford, a W.P.A. art director,

*Teacher-participants learn from each other. Since there was no staff member in arts and crafts, teachers interested in such activities organized their own program and pooled their skills. These teachers are receiving instruction in leather work from one of their own group who has had some previous training in the art.*

visited the workshop, the arts and crafts committee arranged a number of meetings at which she discussed the place of art in schools, and exhibited and demonstrated various kinds of inexpensive materials which could be used in art work. The arts and crafts committee arranged several displays of things made by teacher-participants and arranged them in the lighted showcases located along the lower hall of Central School.

*Publicity.*—One of the Hastings teachers had written all the news stories concerning the development of the workshop before its opening. After the workshop was officially opened, one of the staff, the sociologist, and three teacher-participants took over the responsibility for writing news releases each week to be used in the local paper and papers of nearby cities and towns. This group, known as the publicity committee, at some time during each week talked with each of the staff members and group leaders to obtain news concerning recent developments in workshop activities. This committee also arranged,

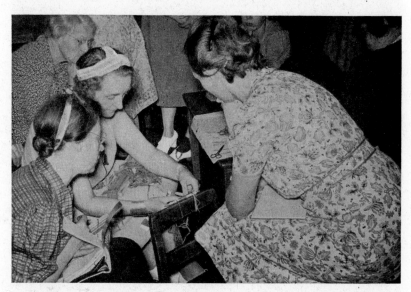

*When Mrs. Stanford, a W.P.A. art supervisor, visited the workshop, she found a number of teacher-participants eager to learn ways of providing creative art experiences for children in their own schools. Here she is demonstrating simple broomstick weaving.*

as a means of publicizing the workshop, a public lecture by Dr. Buchsbaum on plant and animal life of the tropics.

*Socialization.*—The social and recreation committee assumed general responsibility for maintaining a social and recreational program which met the needs of workshop participants. A special committee was appointed to handle the specific details of each social activity. A favorite time for socialization was the noon luncheon period when, in addition to group singing, a special skit was prepared by different members each noon. The social activities included a reception for workshop participants, a reception for educational delegates from

*Many problems were discussed during lunch. Staff members distributed themselves at various tables so that they would be readily available for participation.*

*Singing after the noon lunch was a popular activity. One of the participants is leading the group in a song written by another member of the workshop.*

*The after-luncheon stunts, prepared by different groups of participants, were planned to include both staff and participants. Since Dr. Dropkin was to be married soon after the workshop, the group presented a rehearsal for his benefit.*

*A reception, planned by the Barry County teacher education committee on the opening day, provided teacher-participants an opportunity to become better acquainted with each other.*

Mexico, a dinner and social evening in honor of the educational delegates from South America, three picnics, and a lawn party given by the participants for the staff at the close of the workshop.

*Noon Meals.*—At one time it seemed that it might be necessary to close the cafeteria, and an announcement to this effect was made to the participants. They agreed that if the cafeteria were closed one of the most effective socializing agencies in the program would be eliminated. Since the cost of maintaining the cafeteria was the

*Mr. Van Buskirk, superintendent of the Hastings schools, and Dr. Barnard, director of the workshop, talk over the program as they take refreshments during the reception which the teacher education committee gave the workshop enrollees.*

principal factor involved, three participants volunteered to form a committee to study the solution of this problem. The committee met on several occasions, and worked out a plan which enabled the cafeteria to maintain itself.

*Exhibits.*—A considerable amount of materials from publishing companies and other organizations producing materials for use in schools had been collected before the workshop opened, and a volunteer committee of participants took the responsibility for arranging an exhibit of these materials in a room adjoining the workshop library.

The committee worked with two staff members in planning the arrangement of these materials as well as the way in which the exhibit could be changed from week to week so as to make it more attractive to teachers.

*Visitors.*—Some of the scholarships to the workshop had been made available through the county health offices, and a number of participants suggested that the county health directors from the counties represented be invited to visit the workshop. A special

*Mexican delegates learn about the community workshop and the workshop participants learn about teacher education in Mexico. These people from Mexico, who were attending the New Education Fellowship conference in Ann Arbor, were guests at a workshop reception given in their honor.*

committee took the responsibility for inviting each of the county health directors and county school commissioners, and for arranging for the entertainment of visitors during each hour of the day.

The values to teachers of participating in committee work and the activities of other more or less spontaneously organized groups should not be overlooked. Before they enrolled in the workshop, many rural teachers had indicated that they disliked associating with village teachers. The opportunity which rural and village teachers had to work together in smaller groups on various committees helped break down this barrier. Many of them learned how to take responsibility for planning and completing activities ordinarily initiated and carried out for them by someone else. Many of them stated in their evaluation that through observing the initiation of committees and working on some of these committees they had seen possibilities for greater student participation in the affairs of their own school.

*Participants planned a variety of social activities because, as one participant said, "Our workshop parties and picnics have helped me to learn how to coordinate work and play into one grand summer." Staff and participants entered with equal enthusiasm into such games as the one above.*

### ACTIVITIES OF PARTICIPANTS IN GENERAL MEETINGS

During the six-week session there were fourteen general meetings which involved all teacher-participants and, in all but one meeting, the entire staff as well. These general meetings were discussions of educational problems as well as problems dealing with the nature and organization of workshop activities which were of general interest to all participants. Participants, as well as staff members, served as leaders for these discussions. A complete stenographic record was kept of all general meetings so that it would be possible for any one to determine from this record what points were covered in the discussion and what decisions were reached.

The following list of general meetings will give some idea of the nature of subjects covered in these discussions and of their distribution:

June 23. Planning the general organization of workshop activities
June 26. Discussion of the various workshop activities and the way in which a participant can plan his time so as to gain most from these activities

*Planning sessions were frequently held after lunch in the dining room. These teacher-participants are discussing ways in which various workshop activities could be scheduled to eliminate conflicts with other activities.*

June 27. The ways in which observation in the laboratory school might be used most effectively
June 27. The relationship of the rural school to the high school
July  1. Ways in which the workshop staff can be better used by teacher participants in their work upon individual teaching problems.
         A review of workshop activities so that all might be acquainted with the nature of activities in the various groups
July  1. A discussion, "What are the problems of the relationship of the town high school and the rural school community it serves?"
July  9. Ways in which we can provide more time for observation in the laboratory school
         Planning the individual participation in various workshop activities

July 10. Discussion with parents of the purposes and activities of the laboratory school
July 12. A discussion of reading problems in the elementary school
July 14. Participant evaluation of the first half of the park improvement project
July 22. Teacher education in Barry County for the next year
July 24. The educational values which could be derived from the park improvement project
August 1. Participant discussion of gains and projected activities resulting from the workshop experience

### GENERAL STAFF MEETINGS

Whenever a staff meeting was called, it was understood that all staff members, including the laboratory-school teachers, were to attend; and in the meetings no distinctions were made. Since most of the staff had never worked together before, these meetings became quite important in clarifying the thinking of the group concerning various workshop procedures. Two members of the staff, representing the subject-matter fields of biology and sociology, feared that too little time would be allowed for participation in their groups, so that the essential subject matter of those areas might not be covered. The staff experienced confusion over the conflict between qualification for credit in these subject fields and the solution of the individual teacher's problem. No attempt was made by other staff members to force these two people to modify their programs beyond justification in terms of academic respectability.

It is estimated that approximately 50 percent of the time in staff meetings was spent on problems evolving from the conflict between meeting minimum requirements for course credit and working on what appeared to be the individual problems of teachers. It was felt that the staff had an opportunity to make some contribution to other workshops which might be confronted with the same problem by working out a plan to resolve this conflict. From the reactions of staff members to the workshop program it is quite evident that this conflict still exists in the thinking of certain members of the staff.

During the six-week session there were eleven staff meetings dealing with the following subjects:
June 19. Preworkshop planning (two sessions)
June 20. Preworkshop planning (two sessions)
June 23. Discussion of workshop problems which developed through the first day's contact with participants
June 24. A continuation of the discussion of workshop problems which have developed out of getting the workshop organized

June 26. Conflicts in scheduling resulting from the necessity of certain groups having to meet at a definite time in order to meet minimum requirements for course credit

June 30. Discussion of the advisability of encouraging each participant to look to some one staff member as his adviser

July  1. Coordination of participants' activities

July  8. The relationship of the workshop to parents of children in the laboratory school

July 15. Discussion with committee of teachers regarding participants' evaluation of the first half of the workshop

July 21. Evaluation of the park project
Report on the workshop program

July 24. The formation of a staff committee to assume administrative responsibilities in the absence of the director during a portion of the last week

## EVALUATION OF THE WORKSHOP

There were two major purposes for evaluating the workshop: (1) since this program had been planned to help teachers improve programs of instruction in their schools, the workshop should be evaluated from the standpoint of its effectiveness in developing attitudes, abilities, and understandings which would result in the participants' becoming better teachers; and (2) since the value of community workshops has been questioned by some institutions on the grounds that the work is not academically respectable, it should be evaluated from that standpoint. The responsibility for evaluating the workshop rested primarily on those who participated in the program.

*Staff Evaluation.*—In reports of workshop participation which members of the staff submitted at the close of the session, all the staff indicated that these six weeks had been an unusual experience for them and that they considered the community workshop an effective means of teacher education. One staff member stated that

In all, this workshop experience has been a very interesting educational experiment for me and I have thoroughly enjoyed working in such intimate contact with other members of this cooperative staff and with the very ambitious participants.

Another member of the staff wrote that

The workshop idea is a splendid one and I am very grateful for the opportunity to take part in this one. This has indeed been the high peak in my educational experience.

The biologist on the staff reported that

Every participant really participated. I assigned no D or F grades because even the poorest participant met a certain minimum standard of performance.

These quotations are representative of the expressions made by the other members of the staff.

In addition to general comments concerning the value of the workshop, the staff made other statements which indicated some weaknesses in the program. The laboratory-school teachers felt that the laboratory school had not been used as effectively as it might have been for observation by the participants. Some felt that each participant should have been required to observe on a certain number of days as a. part of the requirements for credit in some one of the education courses. It is interesting to note that this matter was discussed by participants and staff before the laboratory school opened and it was decided that there should be no requirements for observation, but that each participant should feel free to observe whenever and wherever he felt the observation would be most meaningful to him.

Most of the staff indicated that the credit feature of the workshop was a limiting factor in developing a program that was as functional as it could have been. In the recommendations, more than half of the staff members stated that in planning another workshop, credit ought to be limited to courses in education or that no credit should be given at all.

A minority of the staff felt that too many activities were planned which resulted in the confusion of the participant. One staff member said,

I felt that there were too many social distractions to the point of fatigue, too many committees, and too much pressure of committees interfering with the total program. While rigidity of schedule has its bad points and certainly unusual opportunities that come up should be made available to all that may benefit, yet there were several times when special events were arranged that seemed to have no special bearing on the total workshop program and cut seriously into the biological science program.

The staff was not in complete agreement with regard to the educational philosophy on which it felt the workshop should be based. The subject-matter specialists believed that subject matter needed to be taught regardless of whether the teacher could find any immediate use for it. This attitude conflicted with the view of other staff members that subject matter should be introduced primarily in relation to a better understanding of a teaching problem. The sociologist on the staff expressed his point of view on this controversy as follows:

While there was a very noticeable difference in educational philosophy among members of the staff which, on occasions, seemed to hamper operations, the writer felt that the representation of divergent views was, for myself, a stimulating experience and I feel that until the educational world is sold upon one or the other brand of pedagogy, it is desirable to have divergent views represented.

The point of view of another member of the staff, the specialist in child guidance, was expressed in this statement:

I am fully in sympathy with spreading the workshop idea to the liberal arts departments and realize that this is necessary if the workshop plan is to survive, but six weeks is a very short time for the success of any such plan and there is danger of too great a price being paid by the participants for the education of the subject-matter specialists.

Two members of the staff, the biologist and the sociologist, felt that it would be impossible to assign grades to participants without giving a final test. One of them wrote:

I believe that in spite of the obvious "drive" on the part of the participants to work, we achieve much more thoroughness of understanding by having a formal test. Also, since we were required to assign grades, a written examination is the best way to get at it.

Examinations were not given to qualify students for credit in the other courses although each staff member who assigned a grade in those courses made a critical evaluation of performance and accomplishment of the participant toward solution of his problem. There were 143 different grades assigned to the 72 participants enrolled in this workshop. All but one of these grades were "C" or above; 13 percent of them were A, 54 percent B, and 32 percent C. From this record it is apparent that those who had the responsibility for assigning grades considered the work done by participants average or above in practically all cases.

All of the staff mentioned the fact that they would like an opportunity to follow the activities of participants with whom they worked to be able to form some judgment of the application of the plans developed in the workshop. This indicated that the staff felt a personal obligation to participants.

*Teacher-Participants' Evaluation.*—The participants on two occasions met as a group for the purpose of evaluating their workshop experience. One of these meetings, which none of the staff members attended, was held on July 14. The participants spent two hours discussing the first three weeks of the workshop and things which might be done to improve the program. Among the significant points brought out at that meeting were the following:

1. The program was so full that they did not have time to do the reading they would have liked to do.

2. The requirements for course credit in biology were not clear, and a number of the participants were confused as to how much they were supposed to do in order to qualify for credit.

3. The main objective of some members in coming to the workshop was to watch expert teachers in the laboratory school, and these members felt that they did not have enough time for observation.

4. Participants felt that all staff members had something valuable to offer and that they would have liked an opportunity to attend more of the different discussions.

5. It was suggested that the workshop, so far, had not been doing anything about the community.

6. One person commented, "We have such a wealth of material and so many valuable things here that we just flounder around, not being able to decide which will benefit us most."

This meeting was followed by a meeting of a representative group of participants and the staff to discuss these matters. Plans were made at that time for improving the program in terms of the participants' suggestions.

During the last week of the workshop a committee of teacher-participants and staff met frequently to develop an instrument which could be used by each teacher in evaluating his participation. The evaluative instrument consisted of ten questions and was to be returned unsigned to the committee. The first question dealt with the nature of the problem which the teacher had brought to the workshop. These problems were reviewed earlier in this report.

The second question was, "Have you changed or modified your original problem as a result of your workshop activities?" Thirty percent stated they had, 61 percent stated they had not, and 9 percent were uncertain as to whether their problems had been changed. Those who had made changes in their problems were asked to specify ways in which those problems had been changed. A number of them said they had narrowed their problem so that it might be studied more thoroughly. Others stated that they had completely changed their problem either because they had become more interested in another problem or because they recognized another problem as being more significant. The following are some of the reasons these teachers gave for changing their problems:

Did not get much help in study of natural resources in my community, since I had to take the general biology course for credit.

Have concentrated upon developing a science background rather than developing a science program for my school.

Other things have been brought to my attention at this workshop which were not noticed before.

The third question was, "Has sufficient progress been made in solving your problem?" Eighty-one percent of the participants said there was, 9 percent said there was not, and 9 percent were uncertain concerning the progress made in solving their problem. They were asked to indicate reasons for insufficient progress, and the following are some of the reasons given:

I took two sociology courses to meet degree requirements. Perhaps it would have been wiser to have taken only one sociology course and one education course, giving me an opportunity to develop problem in a fuller and more balanced procedure.

Couldn't do what I wanted and get credit for it.

No one, unless to have been twins, could have been in two places at the same time.

I don't believe my problem of selecting a general science text can be solved adequately.

The fourth question asked the participants was, "Has your subject-matter background been improved?" Ninety-seven percent of the participants said it had, while only 3 percent were uncertain. They were also asked to make comments concerning the way in which this background had or had not been improved. The following are a few of the comments:

In both my problems I have enriched my background as well as being exposed to material for future use.

I have more of a sociological attitude than before.

The observation classes were certainly object lessons in tying up community resources with science teaching.

I have enriched my knowledge enough to attempt many things in science.

Most of my time has been spent in learning how to use the subject matter I already know.

The fifth question was, "Do you think your teaching will be modified as a result of your participation in the workshop?" Eighty-seven percent said they felt that it would, 5 percent felt it would not, and 8 percent were uncertain. They were also asked in what ways they were planning to change their teaching. The most commonly recurrent statement was, "I plan to teach more science." Some other statements made by these teachers were:

I think I'll be more aware of the things about me and not so afraid to experiment.

Have improved my technique by viewing situations objectively.

Have gained much from the laboratory school.

I plan to work out more projects with pupils and to be less formal in my classes.

Things which were once so commonplace as to be unobserved are being utilized in my teaching to create interest and love for life.

I feel that I have profited by observing the fact that politeness, courtesy, patience, and sympathetic understanding are cardinal virtues in dealing with elementary children.

I'm going to fix a library corner.

My work has opened avenues in everyday living that no text could present.

I will be able to carry out an enriched science curriculum through having observed the various activities in the laboratory school.

More student participation in units in which they are interested and less forcing of units upon children.

The sixth question was, "Have you visited the laboratory school?" All participants indicated that they had. They were asked to indicate the number of days which they had observed and the number ranged from 3 to 25, with a mean of 14.75. They were also asked to state the way in which the laboratory school had contributed to the improvement of their teaching. The following are representative of the many different statements that were made:

I enjoyed watching someone else teach and see how they handled the problems as they came up.

I got many new ideas of things for children to do that will be interesting and worthwhile.

Tactful discipline, group participation, and pupil planning summarize it all.

The laboratory school was an inspiration for progressive teaching.

Better methods of performing demonstrations in order to get the idea across made me keenly aware that science is a vital elementary school subject.

How to plan with pupils and how to evaluate the work.

The participants were also asked to indicate whether they considered the laboratory school an important part of the workshop program. All but two indicated that they did. They were asked to state whether they thought it was absolutely necessary to have a laboratory school. Sixty-eight percent said that they did, 19 percent did not, and 13 percent were not certain.

On the questionnaire they were also asked to make general remarks, comments, and suggestions. Only five participants failed to make a written statement under this heading. The majority of the statements indicated that the workshop had been practical and worthwhile. Other statements referred to staff members who had been especially helpful. Quite a large number of the participants felt that there should have been more time for observation in the laboratory school. Ten of them made some comment about the fact that the workshop was operating at cross purposes; that credit pressure prevented them from participating in many activities which would have had great value for them. Fifteen of them made statements about the friendly, cooperative attitude of the staff. The following are some comments which are representative of statements that cannot be easily classified:

The sociology courses do not lend themselves to a six-weeks program.

Should have more definite understanding concerning the graduate status of courses.

The workshop has broken the barrier of urban and rural feeling.

The workshop has given new life to this community.

There were too many activities—selection was confusing.

This is my third workshop and my most enjoyable.

Laboratory school should be tied up more closely with the rest of the workshop.

We should have had more general discussion meetings.

Participants were asked, "If another workshop were to be organized in this area, should it be on a 'credit' or 'noncredit' basis?" Sixty-one percent said that it should be on a "credit" basis, 36 percent said that it should be on a combination credit and noncredit basis, and only 3 percent felt that no credit should be given.

Another question was, "In what fields do you think another workshop should be organized?" Arts and crafts, science, and educational methods were mentioned most frequently.

The final question was, "Do you want another workshop?" Eighty-three percent reported they did, 16 percent were uncertain, and only one participant reported that he did not care to attend another workshop, primarily because he was planning to retire in a few more years and no longer needed course credit. Over 70 percent felt there should be a workshop again the next year in Hastings.

The last three questions on this questionnaire do not give much evidence by way of evaluating the workshop, although they do indicate the feeling of this group concerning future workshops.

*Community Evaluation.*—Parents serving on recreation committees in the city and parents of children in the laboratory school had most contact with the workshop. In all cases the reaction of these parents to the program was most favorable, and in many cases they asked that another such program be brought to Hastings next summer.

Numerous comments were made by people in the community concerning the way in which the park improvement project was carried on. The following are statements made by some of the people in the community:

> This place will never be the same after the workshop.
>
> This is our city. We are proud of it and we sincerely appreciate the help which you have given us in seeing how we can continue to improve it.
>
> It's very interesting what people can accomplish whenever they are provided the leadership.

Probably the most valid evaluation which community people made of the workshop was the way in which they cooperated in various workshop activities. They attended receptions and other meetings to which they were invited and took an active part. Parents visited the laboratory school and frequently participated in planning various parts of the program. The mayor, the city council, the county agricultural agent, the county health department, the Junior Chamber of Commerce, the Garden Club, and other organizations participated in a number of the workshop activities.

# CHAPTER IV

# DEMOCRATIC CITIZENSHIP AND THE HEALTH OF CHILDREN IN THE COMMUNITY SCHOOL[1]

The community workshop at Grand Ledge differed from the other workshops in the seven-county area in that it was necessary to change its character after the applications had been received by the teacher education committee. The workshop was originally set up as an arts and crafts program. Registration areas for graduate and undergraduate students included such subjects as psychology, sociology, decorative design, and education. About the middle of February, however, it became evident that the program would need to be changed. In a letter sent to the teachers on February 19, this fact was made known to them. There was disappointment, especially in view of the fact that eighty-seven teachers had applied for admission to the arts and crafts workshop.

Along with the letter to the teachers went a description of a new workshop designed (1) to assist teachers to discover and plan solutions to problems which arise in connection with the growth and development of children in the community, (2) to assist teachers to discover their responsibility for and to improve their skill in teaching democratic citizenship in the community, (3) to assist teachers in studying the nature of communities, their problems, and their resources, in relation to the improvement of the community school.

It was planned that the workshop would provide adequate library facilities, special lectures, demonstrations, and exhibits. As planned, it offered an opportunity for school superintendents, principals, and teachers to work together to develop plans for school modernization and improvement, and to work with children and adults in developing community-school programs of health and citizenship education. Definite arrangements had been made so that teachers in the workshop might have the advantage of consultation on individual problems before the course began, during the course, and during the coming school year after the course had been completed.

Registration was open to rural school teachers, village elementary

---

[1] Mr. William G. Woods, the author of this chapter, was director of the workshop at Grand Ledge during the Summer Session of 1941. He served as consultant in the Michigan Community Health Project from January, 1940, to September, 1941, during which time he was on leave of absence from North Texas State Teachers College at Denton.

school teachers, and village high school teachers, at both the graduate and the undergraduate level; and it was stated that those who
completed the work satisfactorily might earn a total of six hours
of credit—two in hygiene, two in sociology, and two in education.
The courses were listed as follows: Physiologic Hygiene, Community
Problems, Modern Social Problems, Theories and Techniques of
Teaching, and Newer Practices in Secondary Schools.

*Community groups in Grand Ledge met to discuss the workshop.*

### PREPARATION BY THE COMMUNITY

The community of Grand Ledge, partly because the Eaton County
workshop was announced before the community was chosen, made
an effort to have the workshop located there. The superintendent
of schools and the board of education asked for the workshop and
meetings were held with a great many such community groups as
the parent-teacher association, chamber of commerce, church circles,
and service clubs. As evidence of their interest, they presented a
petition signed by 250 people. It was apparent that the possibilities
of a workshop program had been widely discussed in the community.
The superintendent of schools and the board of education offered

whatever physical resources of the public schools the workshop group wished to use, and it was decided to use the second floor of the high school building. The large library room was the center of activity, adequate office space and conference rooms were located nearby, and the high school division of the workshop met in a large room opening directly into the library. The classrooms, as well as the library, were equipped with tables and chairs, rather than school desks.

*The Grand Ledge high school building was headquarters for the workshop.*

At a workshop meeting in Grand Ledge, April 1, the director indicated that it seemed feasible, since a large number of the teacher-participants would be rural teachers, to operate a rural school as part of the laboratory school program. A few days later the Aldrich School District, having a small rural school located only a mile and a half from Grand Ledge, petitioned the University of Michigan and the Kellogg Foundation to include that school in the workshop program. The request, signed by nearly a hundred people, was granted; and the Aldrich school became a part of the resources of the workshop.

*The Laboratory School Division.*—The laboratory schools included four groups: lower elementary, upper elementary, high school, and rural school. No special attempt was made to supervise the classification of children into these four divisions, placement being left largely to the superintendent and the teachers. Care was taken to avoid overoptimistic promises regarding the school program, and the preliminary statement suggested that the laboratory school "might offer teachers and parents an opportunity to explore some techniques of working with boys and girls." During the first week of the workshop, before the children arrived, the teachers in the laboratory

*The library was used for larger group meetings.*

school visited parents of children who had evinced an interest in attending, and these teachers reached decisions with parents regarding the things that would be done in the school. This plan proved to be quite satisfactory, except for the fact that the teachers were somewhat surprised to find that the plans for the school had not been completed before they arrived in the community.

*Planning with Local Groups.*—The director purposely avoided making contacts with service groups and committees except through the superintendent of schools. He explained the purposes of the workshop at a meeting with the local parent-teacher association, and discussed the program with the school board from the Aldrich District. It was made clear that the program was not necessarily

concerned with "progressive" or "modern" education, but was rather
an attempt to discover more effective means of providing the kind
of education that has long been desired.

These were the only contacts with official agencies, and the work
with the local teachers consisted largely in helping them to consider
the problems of the school on which they could work most effectively
during the summer session. The superintendent of schools had

*The Aldrich school housed one division of the laboratory school.*

formed committees of the faculty so that this group could be ready
to accommodate the workshop. One of the local faculty members
was the director of the summer recreation program, and another was
the director of the summer music program. Plans were worked out
with these local teachers to give members of the workshop an opportunity to observe the programs in action and to work with the
directors regarding the various problems which arose in connection
with planning and operating such programs.

Since there was no librarian in the Grand Ledge high school, no
attempt was made to plan the library phases of the workshop in
advance. It was decided to use the village library as any other group
might use it, and no contacts beforehand were necessary.

Arrangements with the local school board were all made through the superintendent of schools, and other community preparations were made through the leaders in the community. Work with the newspaper was all done through a teacher in the Grand Ledge high school. A series of weekly articles was outlined for the paper, beginning about six weeks before the opening of the workshop. The first of these news stories, explaining the general nature of workshops and giving the history of the movement, is included as an illustration.

Grand Ledge is one of Michigan's favored communities this summer. On the 23rd of June, teachers from all parts of the seven counties in the Kellogg Area will gather here for a period of six weeks to participate in a new kind of cooperative experiment in education.

Teachers whose homes are near will drive back and forth each day but many plan to make Grand Ledge their home for the summer and Superintendent Sawdon is already receiving requests for lists of furnished rooms and houses which will be available.

The idea of a Summer Workshop for teachers is relatively new. It grew out of a need felt and recognized by teachers themselves. The traditional type of summer school with its more or less arbitrary division into "courses" did not offer what they wanted. These teachers had specific problems—problems of classroom techniques, problems of administration, problems pertaining to their own local communities. They wanted an opportunity to work out answers to these problems with the assistance of other teachers and a group of professional experts. The Summer Workshop is the answer to this need.

An essential part of every good Summer Workshop is the laboratory school composed of students from the community who would like to participate in work offered during the summer. Grand Ledge will have these laboratory schools if the young people of the community and their parents recognize the value of the opportunity which is open and rise to the occasion.

Strange as it now seems, the first Summer Workshop ever offered was open only to teachers of science and mathematics. That was in 1936. It grew out of a suggestion made by a group of people who were studying the relationship of college entrance requirements to the curriculum of the secondary schools. Thirty-five teachers from a selected list of schools responded and came together at Ohio State University for a six-week period that first summer.

In spite of its obvious limitations, this first workshop brought marked changes in the idea and practice of those who took part in it with the result that during the following summer a second workshop with a wider range of subject fields and a hundred and twenty-six teachers participating was held on the campus of Sarah Lawrence College, Bronxville, New York. City school systems, awakening to the value of this kind of educational experience for their teachers began sending delegations of teachers with part of their expenses paid from school funds to participate in the workshop and bring back helpful suggestions for making changes in the programs of their own schools.

For the summer of 1938, four workshops were set up and more than five hundred teachers were in attendance. A feature of the 1937 workshop which had impressed everyone was retained and emphasized—namely, the opportunities afforded for enrichment of personality through social and recreational contacts. These 1938 workshops also admitted for the first time an entirely new group—college and university faculty members from sixteen different institutions of higher learning. Gradually it was coming to be recognized that workshops were an invaluable part of the graduate programs of our leading universities. And about this same time another angle of the whole problem presented itself.

Up to this time, workshops for teachers had all been established on the campus of some college or university. A demand now arose for local workshops, each serving a single large school district and within a short time a number of these were set up under the direction of leading universities throughout the country.

This newest type of workshop has a number of advantages, among which is the fact that they make possible a year-round cooperation between university faculties and local school authorities.

Thus, from modest beginning, has this movement grown. It has grown because the breath of life was in it. It represented a vital response to a real need.

Another article named the staff and gave their background; and another explained the nature of the work to be carried on in the various school divisions. News articles continued to appear during the workshop.

The matter of preparing the janitors was also left largely in the hands of the school superintendent. However, the director did take occasion early in the program to sit down and have a long talk with them. At this time the attempt was made to find just exactly what the janitors thought about the whole idea, to gain their sympathy, and to make friends with them. They proved to be most cooperative during the summer program.

It was at first thought that some planning should be done with regard to the matter of the noon lunch. However, in this matter as in others, the director felt that the problem of the noon lunch concerned all the members and therefore should be considered by all of them. Possibilities were explored in advance so as to have pertinent facts when the time came to discuss this problem.

The housing problem was handled by a local committee consisting of teachers and members of the chamber of commerce. This committee located available places to live and made mimeographed lists which they mailed in advance to all staff members and applicants who had indicated a desire to move into Grand Ledge for the summer. Housing the staff was difficult because of the defense activity in Lansing, only twelve miles away. Although there were enough rooms, none of the staff members was able to secure a house. This circumstance was considered unfortunate because, aside from personal inconveniences, it placed some limitations on social life.

### PREPARATION BY THE STAFF

During the spring months the directors of the four workshops met often for consideration of their common problems. Also, they attended two meetings of large groups of people who served as staff members of various workshops. One of these meetings, attended by about 150 directors and staff members, was held in Chicago, and the other, attended by the directors and staff people of the fifteen Michigan workshops, was held in Jackson during the summer of 1941.

*The Selection of Staff Members.*—The task of selecting a staff was the joint responsibility of the director and the dean of the institution sponsoring the workshop.

Dr. John Cuber, Associate Professor of Sociology at Kent State University, was a practical sociologist and an expert in the field of guidance. He had come up through the rural schools in the seven-county area and was a graduate of the University of Michigan. His broad training and his experience in the public schools in the seven-county area gave him a valuable background for his position on the workshop staff.

Dr. Lloyd Florio came to the workshop from the Division of Public Health and Laboratory Diagnosis of the School of Medicine at the University of Colorado. He had also worked previously in the seven-county area, and his knowledge of local conditions, coupled with his intensive interest and experience in the field of public health, made him an exceptionally desirable choice. Dr. Florio holds degrees in medicine and in public health from Harvard University.

Dr. Walter H. Gaumnitz, Senior Specialist in Rural Education in the U.S. Office of Education, was able to serve for four weeks. Because of his wealth of information regarding rural school problems, he contributed richly to the success of the workshop.

Miss Loretta Locher was selected to teach the rural division of the laboratory school. She had served previously as a critic teacher, had been charged with responsibility for elementary school supervision, and had previous experience in a workshop.

Mrs. Mary Frances Williams, demonstration school teacher at North Texas State Teachers College, and summer-school teacher in the laboratory school at the University of Michigan, was chosen to teach the lower-elementary school group. Her experience included one summer in a campus workshop.

Mr. Julian Smith, principal of the Lakeview high school at Battle

Creek, was selected to teach the high school division. He had participated in an earlier workshop as a student.

There were many disappointments in the search for a suitable teacher for the upper-elementary school group. Several excellent teachers, for one reason or another, were unable to accept the position, and the last invitation was declined so late that the students were already in school—and still there was no teacher for them! This was a typical workshop problem, however, and it was turned over to the group of teacher-participants who were especially interested in developing a program with the upper-elementary school children.

Since all the staff members, except one, had worked in Michigan before, it was considered unnecessary to have the staff visit the county before workshop opened. Four staff members had worked previously in the seven-county area. An attempt was made to orient them to the local problems by letter, but the plan of the workshop was not explained beyond saying that it would be built around two principles; namely, that teachers should have the opportunity to work on problems which to them were real and vital, and that the work should be planned by all those concerned with it.

*Bibliography of Materials.*—The bibliography of materials to be available for the workshop was compiled by the director, and the necessary purchases were made by the Foundation. Staff members, on invitation to make suggestions regarding materials which they wished to use in the workshop, added a few titles. The bibliography included four hundred items, consisting of books, pamphlets, bulletins, magazine articles, and so on, listed under the following headings: Philosophy of Education; Curriculum Planning; Adolescent Psychology; Student Needs and Counseling; Regional and Community Life, and Techniques for Study of the Community; Literature and Language Arts; Foreign Languages; Consumer Education; Health, Physical, and Safety Education; Mathematics; Science; Evaluation and Research; and Administration of the School. The use of this collection was supplemented from time to time by trips to the W. K. Kellogg Foundation Professional Library, to the State Library and the Curriculum Laboratory in Lansing.

*Preliminary Staff Meetings.*—The staff met for a preliminary conference on Thursday afternoon, June 19, to consider workshop procedure. The questions recorded for further discussion were:

1. What is to be done about registration?

2. What should the staff do about individual guidance of teacher-participants?

3. How can the staff arrange to work with participants on their individual problems, and at the same time meet reasonable academic requirements for two hours of credit in education, two hours in sociology, and two hours in health science?

4. What is to be done about scheduling?

5. What should be done about evaluating (a term which was preferred to "evaluation")?

6. What is to be done on the opening day of the workshop?

*This group is engaged in a preworkshop staff conference.*

7. What should be done about interest groups, their motivation, stimulation, and so on?

8. What plans should be made in organizing the laboratory school?

9. What kind of record of events and happenings should be kept?

The following paragraph, a quotation from the daily record of a member of the staff, indicates the progress of the staff planning session on the second day:

The program seemed to take definite shape. The staff arrived at a number of unanimous decisions and began talking the same language for the first time. The several decisions reached are recorded in the minutes. My reactions at the end of Friday may be summarized under three captions: (1) The *esprit de corps* of the staff is excellent; most of us appear to enjoy the contacts *per se*, not just as a

"responsibility." (2) My faith in democracy in education is buttressed somewhat by having seen a number of diametrically opposite views brought together
in unanimous compromise decisions. (3) I am still a little fearful, but less so,
that what I earlier called anarchy might need to be "adulterated" by a little
gentle, benevolent dictation. In other words, I still wonder if there isn't a
middle ground. I am looking forward to conference sessions on Monday to get
more light on this problem.

By the middle of the second afternoon the staff had begun to see
its way clear. Relationships between problems became apparent,
and methods of attack were developed. Regarding the laboratory
school, the staff was in complete agreement that there should be no
discrimination between the laboratory staff and the so-called "professional" staff; that the professional staff should assume responsibility for planning with the laboratory staff in terms of the needs
of the boys and girls in the particular laboratory group. The laboratory-school teachers, on the other hand, had agreed to share with
the professional staff the responsibility for the individual guidance
of the teacher-participants in the workshop. The staff had agreed
likewise that guidance is an obligation of the individual teacher,
and that some one of the staff members should therefore assume the
responsibility for the guidance of each of the participants.

With regard to schedule, the staff agreed to make a schedule when
there was a need for it; and that the schedule would be made with
the people whom the schedule concerned. The staff also agreed that
evaluating and guidance are dependently related. Staff members
giving individual guidance could also assist each participant to evaluate his progress in terms of the solution of his problem. Programs
were devised for the initial session on Monday and for registration on
Tuesday. Small groups of participants were formed arbitrarily to
meet with various staff members, and staff members who were not
directly engaged in registration were to work with individuals and
small groups on clarifying the problems chosen for workshop study.

One of the questions on which the staff reached no definite agreement concerned the foundation of interest groups in the workshop.
There was uncertainty as to how much stimulation and direction
should be given to small groups of workshop members.

A conviction that workshops have resulted in changed attitudes
on the part of members suggested an attempt to determine what
caused these changed attitudes. The staff decided, therefore, to
record what they did each day and to try to evaluate their activities. The records were to include names of participants engaged in

consultation as well as a summary of discussions, and these records were to be exchanged among staff members. Teacher-participants also were to be asked to record their activities.

The final staff meeting before the workshop opened was a general meeting at W. K. Kellogg Foundation in Battle Creek on Saturday, June 21, attended by staff members from the four workshops.

### PREPARATION OF THE PARTICIPANTS

*Preliminary Meetings with Participants.*—Application blanks sent to teachers were to be returned early in March. All who made application to enroll for the redesigned course were invited by letter to a meeting of the people interested in any one of the four workshops, to be held in the Grand Ledge high school on April 1. About forty teachers attended this meeting, and their questions were numerous and varied.

One of the first questions was, "What is a workshop, and why are we having them?" The general answer was given that teachers had felt a need for other kinds of educational experience, not as a substitute for regular campus courses, but as a supplement to them. It was explained that a workshop is a part of a teacher-education program which is so designed that each teacher might have the opportunity to work on a problem which seems to be real and vital to the individual, and involving cooperation with other people having similar interests. Among the other questions discussed were:

1. Will I have the opportunity to ask questions?
2. Will the staff members be available to us when we want them, either in Grand Ledge or in our individual communities?
3. Will the theory and practice be too far apart for us to see any relationship?
4. Will I have time to work on my own problem or must I take three courses which are already completely planned for me?
5. Will I have time to do some reading concerning my problem? and if so, what about books and materials that I need?
6. Why is a workshop held in a nearby community, rather than on the college campus?
7. May I bring some of my board members, some other teachers, some parents, and some students to visit the workshop?

A mimeographed bulletin explaining the community workshops was distributed. This bulletin was prepared as a guide for teachers in getting ready for the workshop; it contained information regarding conditions for admission, steps in preparing for the workshop, and factors which might serve to make the educational experience more significant. The following items were stressed because they seemed to present some characteristics of a workshop experience:

One of the conditions for admission is: (*a*) the fact that I want to explore with other teachers some more effective techniques of working with boys and girls; (*b*) the fact that I, as a teacher, want to explore with other teachers some techniques of working in a community; (*c*) the fact that I would like to practice using different kinds of resources in my teaching; or (*d*) the fact that I have defined a problem which to me is real, and that I can have the opportunity to work toward its solution.

The teachers were informed that an attempt would be made by the workshop director to visit them in their own schools at a time that would be convenient for them. Since most of the teachers expressed no preference, the schedule of visits could be quite flexible. Of the fifty-two teachers who were admitted to the workshop, twenty-one of them attended this meeting in Grand Ledge. Eleven other Eaton County teachers who attended this meeting applied for admission but did not enroll in the workshop.

It was part of the plan that each of the workshop directors should hold meetings in two counties. The second meeting of similar nature was conducted by the director in Van Buren County, at Bloomingdale. The procedure was very much the same. There were seven teachers present from Van Buren County who came to the workshop in Eaton County (at Grand Ledge). Five other teachers at this meeting applied for admission but later withdrew. Seven members attended similar meetings in other counties.

*Preworkshop Conferences with Teachers.*—Individual conferences held with the teachers who had made application for admission to the workshop consisted largely in going through the mimeographed worksheet with them. Thirty-nine of the fifty-two teachers attending the workshop were visited in their local schools. In addition, twenty teachers who had applied for admission to the workshop, but did not attend, were visited.

A question frequently raised in these individual conferences had to do with the application of credits from the University of Michigan to a program for a degree or a certificate. Other questions concerned transferring credit to some other institution. The mimeographed bulletin on "Getting Ready for the Workshop" was very helpful, but there seemed to be no substitute for the personal interview. Although many of the teachers had already attended one workshop meeting, few of them had done the things suggested at the meeting, and almost none had reached the point of being able to record a statement of the problem to be undertaken. The mimeographed bulletin helped teachers to consider the problem of professional training, to decide whether the workshop would assist them, and to decide how the workshop might be used to best advantage.

*The first group session included a discussion of the purposes that might be accomplished through the workshop.*

### THE BEGINNING OF THE WORKSHOP

*General Meetings during the Opening Week.*—In keeping with the decision of the staff that schedules should be made only when needed, and then by those whom the schedule affects, the preliminary plans made by the staff indicated only the activities for the first two days. The first session of the workshop had been scheduled for ten o'clock on Monday, June 23. The first part of the session was turned over to a group of people from Grand Ledge, including the superintendent of schools, the president-elect of the parent-teacher association, the local newspaper editor, and a representative of the chamber of commerce. The director presented the staff informally, and initiated a discussion of the community workshop and how it might be used. Dr. Cuber led a short discussion centered on the question, "What Are Some Things to Be Considered When Teachers Work in a Community?" Another general session was announced for two o'clock in the afternoon, to consider food, lodging, and recreation for the teacher-participants. These matters had been purposely avoided in the morning because it was felt that after the teachers had explored the community they would be more directly interested in considering the question of a noon lunch. At four o'clock there were meetings for various arbitrary groups formed by taking names at random from the enrollment cards and assigning one staff member to each group. These meetings were get-acquainted sessions, the primary purpose of which was to give the staff an opportunity to help teachers to define their problems.

On the second day graduate students began registering at nine o'clock, and undergraduates at eleven. Before and after registration, members had an opportunity to become acquainted with each other. A staff meeting was held at four o'clock to plan the general session for Wednesday. Since many of the students were still casting about for a problem, it was decided to have students who had selected problems describe their undertakings at this general session. A second item planned for this session was a report from the noon lunch committee.

The general session on Wednesday morning lasted from nine o'clock until noon. The lunch committee made its report, and the ensuing discussion was broadened to include the question of a school lunch program in the seven-county area. At this general session, the students decided to break up into smaller groups. One of the groups, interested in the community survey, met with Dr. Cuber; another group, especially interested in the school lunch, met with Dr. Florio. Mr. Smith met with a group that wanted to study curriculum development. Others of the staff, at various times during the afternoon, met with a group of teachers who had not yet discovered a problem on which they wished to work.

From these group meetings came the request that the staff discuss with them, in general session on Thursday, the ramifications of democracy and education. The groups decided also that on Thursday they wished to continue their deliberations as small committees. The staff purpose for the general session on Thursday was to guide the teacher-participants toward consideration of how they might

plan the workshop with the staff. At the meeting on Thursday the
need developed for all members to consider some workshop problems;
namely, How might the library be used? How could participants
report their activities in the workshop? How could they assist the
staff toward an integrated workshop experience rather than toward
participation in three different courses? Since the four laboratory
school divisions of the workshop were scheduled to begin on the
second Monday, problems of observational activities arose. These

*The planning committee met frequently with the staff to give
direction to the workshop activities.*

matters were all discussed on Friday morning and apparently both
the staff and the participants stood "amazed in the presence of
democracy." All seemed to be surprised that no one told them just
what to do.

*The Formation of the Planning Committee.*—At the close of the
general session on Friday morning, the assembly broke up into
interest groups. From these groups came the decision to hold another
general session, on Friday afternoon, to try to answer the question,
"How do we really organize, now, so that we can get the most out
of this workshop period?" There was much discussion in the after-

noon regarding a planning committee to meet with the staff for cooperative planning of the workshop activities. Such terms as "steering committee" and "governing body" were avoided, and the group was stimulated to think in terms of the real purpose in having a planning committee. It was pointed out that student government, in some schools, had been organized with no thought of what it was to do until finally it folded up from its own inactivity; that such things as coordinating councils had been organized in many of the

*The planning committee served as a representative body to express the needs of teacher-participants in making cooperative arrangements with the staff.*

surrounding communities with nothing to coordinate; that it was a responsibility of the group, to the elected member of a committee, to keep that member informed as to their wishes and decisions; that it was his responsibility, also, not only to represent the group, but to do all that he could to bring enlightenment to the group regarding matters that came up in the planning sessions.

Various plans of representation were suggested, among them one that threatened the development of a unified group: it was suggested that the high school teachers, the rural teachers, and the elementary

school teachers each elect a delegate.   During the preworkshop interviews with rural teachers, it had been discovered that they felt in-
secure in working with town and village teachers.   Certainly, the
workshop ought to help overcome this feeling.   To avoid a planning
committee based on separate group representation, therefore, the
director suggested other possibilities.   It was finally agreed to number
the teacher-participants as they sat around the table and to let them
choose one of the group to represent each seven or eight consecutive

*The larger planning committee was formed of representatives chosen in*
*such a way as to avoid isolation of interests.*

people.   The general session was adjourned so that the teachers who
were to observe in the laboratory school on the following Monday
might have the opportunity to plan in advance with the staff.   The
laboratory school staff and the professional staff collaborated in
preparatory discussions with the participants.

*The Work of the Planning Committee and the General Sessions.*—
After this meeting on Friday afternoon, the staff met with the
planning committee and reached two important decisions: (1) that
the general sessions should relate to the needs of the teachers in the
workshop as far as it was possible to discover them; and (2) that
each general session should make use of at least three members of

the staff, one representing sociology, one education, and one the health sciences. The planning committee agreed to list expressed needs of their constituents, and to report at a planning session to be held on Monday. The committee had been advised at the organization meeting that participants desired to have the general sessions in the afternoons, and to reserve the mornings for observation, interest groups, work on particular problems, library reading, excursions, movies, and so on. Consequently, the general session was called for 1:45 on Monday. The planning committee met for the second time before the opening of the general session. The representative system was not yet entirely satisfactory, but lack of time had been a handicap. One of the committee members had left the workshop early on Friday in order to work in her own community on her problem, and consequently she missed a meeting that afternoon. She returned convinced that a complete six-week schedule should be arranged at once.

The general session on the second Monday afternoon was devoted to a discussion of sex education. Dr. Florio acted as chairman, but was assisted by all the members of the staff. Sex education was discussed from the standpoint of public health, sociology, and education.

The provisions for observational activities apparently left some of the staff members with unexpected and disconcerting freedom. One of them wanted to explore the whole program of the school division in order to see what would happen the first day in each of the various pupil-groups. Two others could find nothing to do on Monday morning, because all the teacher-participants wanted also to observe the first day's work with the children. It was not clear to all that the staff agreement previously reached, to the effect that teaching would be in terms of how theory could be implemented in teaching boys and girls, meant that each member of the professional staff would choose a pupil group and assume part of the responsibility for the observational activities along with the laboratory teacher.

The planning committee met before the general session on Tuesday afternoon to discuss venereal disease, considering the medical and educational aspects and the sociological implications of the topic. The staff agreed that the participants' request for a discussion of sex and sex teaching and venereal disease probably reflected personal interests rather than problem experiences with these matters in school. The success of the committee meeting that day was due, no doubt, to the fact that definite meetings had been held by the planning-committee members with their constituents.

The general session on Wednesday afternoon related to juvenile delinquency, and three or four members of the staff presented different aspects of the program. The teachers did not take much part in the discussions; they explained that they felt they could learn most through listening rather than talking.

The planning group met again Wednesday afternoon for two hours.

*The group interested in arts and crafts developed skill in the activities they wished to provide for children.*

It was decided that general sessions should begin at 1:30 o'clock in the afternoon. It was decided also that an interest group in arts and crafts would meet each Thursday at 1:30. The teachers who were interested planned to meet with Miss Radusch, the arts-crafts teacher for the summer recreation program in Grand Ledge. Another decision reached by the planning committee was that teachers who wished to observe should sign up beforehand and should attend the observation-group discussion on the day preceding the observation. The discussions for the elementary school observation group were scheduled at 1:00 o'clock daily, for the rural group during the lunch hour, and for the high school group at 11:00 o'clock. The staff asked the planning committee members to find out whether the discussions in the general sessions were pitched at the proper experience level for the teachers.

It became apparent by Monday, July 7, that it would be impossible to get the kind of laboratory school teacher that it was desirable to have for the upper-elementary group, and the eleven teachers who were especially interested in techniques of teaching at the upper-elementary grade level were invited to attend a meeting that morning. Several means of solving the problem were discussed. It was suggested that the group might be absorbed into the band, the rural-school group, the recreation group, and the lower-elementary-school group; or that the teachers interested in the work of the upper-elementary grades might use the recreation program and the developing arts-crafts program for observation. The group suggested, however, that they take complete charge of this school division; that they take turns, two at a time, in teaching the children, with the rest of the group serving as critics. They agreed to discuss the matter with others in the workshop and to meet again after the general session afternoon. The plan was adopted, and the following summary of the work with these children is taken from reports of the seven teachers who assumed the joint responsibility:

The students of the later-elementary group of the workshop being without a teacher, the director presented the problem to the later-elementary teachers. After much discussion seven of us, Mrs. Belden, Mrs. Dull, Miss Winfield, Mrs. Miller, Miss Lyon, Miss Hyder, and Miss Pepper, decided to work on the project.

On Tuesday morning we met with the children and the teacher chosen for the day learned that they were interested especially in the following things: arithmetic, cooking, sewing, language, health and citizenship.

The work centered around several projects. The first developed from a buying situation, since materials were needed to carry on the work. Two committees were chosen by the class, one to buy the material available here, the other to go shopping in Lansing. These buying trips furnished arithmetic material for the week.

During the activity periods some children became interested in making aprons and clay figures, which occasioned the discussion of firing the clay. Permission was granted us by the American Vitrified Clay Company to visit the plant. The clay figures which had been made were fired. This trip led to considerable discussion of the other industries, business places, and the park. As a summary to this part of the project, an enjoyable half hour was spent viewing a colored movie.

Another learning project was the serving of a hot lunch. The class created a home situation in which they were the hosts and hostesses. They planned, cooked, and served a balanced meal. They wrote invitations, bought food, figured costs, studied the values of proper food, health, cleanliness, courtesy, good manners, and table etiquette.

The last week was spent in completing projects which had been started, among which was the dramatization of "Merlin's Necklace of Truth."

As one result of the summer work, the children have shown a marked improvement in cooperation and appreciation, and some of them have become more able to assume responsibility. This has been most noticeable in the least prepossessing. Many of the timid ones have developed self-assurance and relia-

*These children made their own costumes for the dramatization of*
*"Merlin's Necklace of Truth."*

bility. The group has worked to discover the needs of each individual and to evaluate progress toward development along lines of health and citizenship.

The topic for discussion at the next general session was juvenile delinquency, a continuation from the general session held the week before. Dr. Cuber assumed chairmanship for the group, but the other staff members participated equally with him in the discussion. The group decided to invite a juvenile court judge to meet with them at a later date, although one of the teacher-participants remarked that she much preferred a discussion led by a trained staff member to one conducted by an elected official without necessary professional qualifications. The superintendent of the Grand Ledge schools suggested that a community meeting be held to discuss juvenile delinquency in that area, since Eaton County has at times had the highest juvenile delinquency rate in Michigan. The community calendar, however, had already become so crowded that it was impossible to schedule such a meeting.

After the general session a meeting of the planning committee was called. It was decided to discuss evaluation in the general session Tuesday, and a date was set for a picnic, with the Grand Ledge

*The problem of evaluating achievement in courses was discussed with the participants at a session early in the summer.*

teachers in charge. With the exception of a movie, for which courtesy tickets were sent to the workshop, this was the first attempt on the part of the members to plan for their own recreation. The following topics were announced for discussion in the remaining general sessions:

1. How can schools serve in a national defense program?
2. What is the place of the federal government in education?
3. How can teachers carry the workshop techniques over into their own school systems?
4. What about contagious and communicable diseases?
5. How can teachers integrate the health program into the total school program?

6. What about ethics?
7. What is the place of case studies in the school program?
8. How can teachers best teach the tool subjects?
9. What are the best techniques to use with the special student?

As chairman of the general session on evaluation, Dr. Gaumnitz presented three or four ideas as to how the work might be evaluated. Among these suggestions were the possibility that each student in

*The school kitchen was available to the teacher-participants for work on practical problems relating to school lunch programs.*

the workshop might receive an incomplete grade which could be removed some time during the next year when the consultant should have had an opportunity to evaluate the things that had actually taken place in the school as a result of the things done in the workshop; that the evaluation be made on the basis of an oral examination; and that a written report be presented, to include the statement of problems, the things which the teachers did this summer, and the ways in which these things contributed toward the solution of the problems.

During the discussion several pertinent questions were raised: Is it necessary to know what the objective is before setting up evaluation procedures? Who should determine the objective or objectives?

In what terms should they be set up? Should they include such things as habits, ideals, appreciations, and skills, as well as knowledges? How can the objectives be set up in terms of the teacher's individual problem situation? What activities are significant as part of evaluation? Is the sole purpose of evaluating to give a grade, or is it to improve the efforts of both teacher and pupil? If there is an examination, when should it come? before, during, or after the course

*Appropriate development of the children in some of the social graces was fostered through experience in the corresponding social situations.*

is over? There was general agreement regarding the following points on evaluation:

1. The staff and the teacher-participants have a joint responsibility in evaluating.

2. Evaluating is a continuous process.

3. Evaluating should be done in terms of work done toward defining ways to solve problems which the teachers have brought into the workshop.

4. A belief in individualizing testing is consistent with a belief in individualized teaching.

5. Both staff and teacher-participants have a joint responsibility to see that teacher-staff contacts are made as frequently as necessary.

6. Permanent and cumulative records of the activities engaged in, both by staff and participants, are a necessary part of evaluating.

7. If personalities differ in their strengths and weaknesses, it follows that some workshop activities should be engaged in to a greater extent by some participants than by others. (Probably more contacts with staff members are needed by some teacher-participants than by others. Likewise, more reading or writing might be needed by some than by others.)

8. Various kinds of tests and examinations might have a place in the process called evaluating.

9. One major purpose for evaluating is that continuous guidance might be provided.

*Both the arrangement of furniture and the activities in the elementary school groups lent an atmosphere of friendliness and informality*

On July 8 a meeting of the planning committee followed discussions in the constituent groups, and decisions were made regarding the nature of the general sessions. Topics for discussion at the general sessions were listed, and posted on the bulletin board by the planning committee. The next meeting was held on July 15. At this meeting these decisions were reached:

1. The laboratory school should run until the last day of the workshop.

2. Arrangements should be made to bring a juvenile judge into the workshop for a discussion on local juvenile delinquency problems.

3. Arrangements should be made to have a tea for one of the staff members who was leaving the workshop at the end of the four-week session.

4. Evaluation data should be collected from workshop participants.

5. Arrangements should be made to send letters of thanks to the W. K. Kellogg Foundation for scholarships.

6. Plans should be made to keep the workshop reference material in the county.

7. The committee should be sure that the problems listed for discussion are the things the teachers want discussed.

8. Special group meetings which are to follow the general session on Wednesday should be posted.

9. The possibilities of a workshop for the following summer should be discussed.

*The high school group was often engaged in roundtable discussions of community problems.*

On July 16 there was a meeting of the planning committee following the constituent group meetings. The schedule for the week of July 21 was set up. No general session was planned for Thursday so that more time might be devoted to group work.

The last planning committee meeting was held on July 23 to discuss the final week's work. Committee reports were given, and a schedule for the week was arranged. It was decided to have no general sessions during the last week, but to save the time for individual conferences with staff members for the purpose of evaluating work on the problems.

The activities of the planning committee were regarded by the staff as one of the most significant parts of the workshop program. It was judged that the committee provided a fine opportunity for leadership development; it was thoroughly democratic; each one of the constituent groups was a cross-section of the workshop; the staff members worked closely with each small planning group; the need for separate staff meetings disappeared; and the planning committee developed enough independence to hold many of the later meetings without the assistance of a staff member.

*These children in the library were surprised at their work
by the ubiquitous photographer.*

### USE OF THE WORKSHOP STAFF

Appointments with staff members, whether for group meetings, for visits to other school districts, or for personal interviews, were arranged in a rather unusual way. All that was necessary was to check the calendar in the office to see whether the persons wanted were free, and to post a notice on the bulletin board. All notices were posted directly from the office by the secretary, and all staff calendars were kept by her.

In guiding the individual teacher-participants toward a better understanding and a workable solution of their problems, and in seeing to it that work in the various courses progressed, the staff in a like manner scheduled appointments. Staff calendars indicate various ways in which the staff was used.

### MISS LOCHER, FIRST WEEK

*Monday*
10:00 General session
2:00 General session
3:00 Discussion groups

*Tuesday*
9:00 Charlotte—
  Surplus foods,
  Mr. Denison
11:00 Home visits
2:00 Home visits
4:00 Staff

*Wednesday*
9:00 General session
11:00 Hot lunch group
2:00 Reading group

*Thursday*
9:00 General session
1:30 Visit to Nixon
  School

*Friday*
9:00 General session
11:00 Meeting of
  Observers—
  Dr. Gaumnitz
1:30 General session
4:00 Planning committee

### DR. CUBER, SECOND WEEK

*Monday*
9:00 Individual
  conferences—
  "Assignments"
  Personality
  problems
  Teaching
  problems
10:00 Library materials
11:00 High school
  lower elementary
  publicity
1:30 Planning committee
2:00 General session—
  Sex education
4:00 Planning committee

*Tuesday*
9:00 High school
10:00 Publicity
11:00 High school
1:30 Planning committee
2:00 General session—
  Venereal disease

*Wednesday*
9:00 Individual
  conference—
  Potterville
  consolidation
10:00 English group—
  Individualized
  instruction
1:30 General session—
  Delinquency
3:00 Planning
  committee

*Thursday*
9:00 Interest group—Sex
  education, venereal
  disease, delinquency
1:30 Rural recreation survey

MRS. WILLIAMS, THIRD WEEK

| *Monday* | *Tuesday* | *Wednesday* |
|---|---|---|
| 9:00 Laboratory school | 9:00 Laboratory school | 9:00 Laboratory school |
| 11:00 Early elementary observers | 11:00 Early elementary observers | 11:00 Early elementary observers |
| 1:00 Later elementary group | 1:00 Later elementary group | 1:00 Later elementary group |
| 1:30 General session— Delinquency | 1:30 General session— Evaluating | 1:30 General session— Education and National Defense |
| 3:00 Visit to Sunfield school | | |

| *Thursday* | *Friday* |
|---|---|
| 9:00 Laboratory school | 9:00 Laboratory school |
| 11:00 Early elementary observers | 11:00 Early elementary observers |
| 12:00 Workshop picnic | 1:00 Later elementary group |
| | 1:30 General session— Federal government and education |

DR. GAUMNITZ, FOURTH WEEK

| *Monday* | *Tuesday* | *Wednesday* |
|---|---|---|
| 9:00 English group | 8:30 Grand Ledge elementary teachers | 8:30 Individual conference |
| 1:30 General session— Practical application of workshop experience | 10:00 Individual conference— Commercial work in high school | 9:00 Dr. Otto and interest group— Teacher education |
| | 11:00 Individual conference— Charlotte survey | 11:00 Ionia—to address civic organizations |
| | 12:00 Luncheon—Mrs. Hammond | |
| | 1:30 General session—, Tool subjects | |
| | Night Hastings picnic | |

| *Thursday* | *Friday* |
|---|---|
| 8:30 Individual conferences | 8:30 Individual conferences |
| 1:30 Potterville group | 1:00 Upper elementary General session— Community resources |
| 3:00 Tea | |
| Night Staff picnic | |

DR. FLORIO, FIFTH WEEK

### Monday

9:00 Hot lunch group
10:00 Hygiene group—
Posture, physical
examinations
11:00 Individual
conferences
1:00 Elementary group
1:30 General session—
Health education
in the curriculum
Night Community meet-
ing at Aldrich—
Skin infections

### Tuesday

9:00 Hygiene group—
General discussion
10:00 Individual
conferences
1:30 Bretton Woods—
School board

### Wednesday

9:00 Individual
conferences
10:00 Hygiene group—
General discussion
1:30 General session—
Health program
in Eaton County
3:00 Planning
committee
Night Coordinating
council of Grand
Ledge

### Thursday

9:00 Hygiene group—
General discussion
10:00 Individual
conferences
1:30 General session—
delinquency
3:00 Rural teachers—
Adult education

### Friday

9:00 Interest group—
Mental hygiene
1:30 General session—
Parent-teacher
relationships
3:00 Grand Ledge
service committee

MR. SMITH, SIXTH WEEK

### Monday

9:00 Laboratory school
1:30 Marshall workshop
Night Sunfield—
Community
meeting

### Tuesday

9:00 Laboratory school
1:30 General session—
P. T. A. problems
Night Workshop party

### Wednesday

9:00 Laboratory school
1:30 Charlotte—
M. E. A. adult
education
committee

### Thursday

9:00 Laboratory school
11:00 Individual
conferences
1:30 Dr. Stucky and
high school
teachers
3:00 P. T. A. President
Night Grand Ledge
improvement
committee

### Friday

9:00 Demonstration
school meeting
10:00 General session

MR. WOODS, SIXTH WEEK

| *Monday* | *Tuesday* | *Wednesday* |
|---|---|---|
| 8:00 Office and individual conferences | 8:00 Office and individual conferences | 8:00 Office and conferences individual |
| 9:00 Individual conferences | 9:00 Individual conferences | 9:00 Individual conferences |
| 10:00 Laboratory schools | 10:00 Interest groups— Hot lunch teacher education | 10:00 English group |
| 1:00 Individual conferences | | 1:30 Office and individual conferences |
| 1:30 Interest group—Eaton County Health program | 1:30 General session— P. T. A. problems | |
| 3:00 Elementary observers | 7:00 Coordinating council | |
| Night Sunfield Community meeting | 8:00 Workshop party | |

| *Thursday* | *Friday* |
|---|---|
| 8:00 Office and individual conferences | 8:00 Office and individual conferences |
| 9:00 Mrs. Jones | 9:00 Demonstration school |
| 10:00 Small group— Teaching of English | 10:00 General session |
| 11:00 Charlotte survey | 1:30 Office |
| 1:30 Office and individual conferences | |
| 3:00 P. T. A. President | |
| Night Grand Ledge improvement committee | |

## USE OF THE COMMUNITY

The following account by a rural school teacher shows how the community was used as a laboratory for teacher education:

When I went to the mail-box one day last January I found an official-looking envelope from the teacher education committee. This envelope contained literature concerning workshops open to teachers in the seven-county area served by the W. K. Kellogg Foundation.

A week before the workshop was to open, I received a card saying that a general session would be held at 10:00 o'clock on June 23. Monday morning arrived and I found as I looked at the clock that I was ready hours before the time to arrive at the first assembly. I watered my plants and did many little chores to help pass away the time. If I had realized the real significance of a workshop, I would have felt free to arrive at an early hour to start work on my problem. As I heard the remark from my fellow teachers as we were becoming oriented, "We must get to work," I thought, "Who is stopping me from getting to work? It is my problem. I must solve it or learn by what means it may be solved."

With a new school came new problems. I should like very much to be a part of a community school. I thought this an opportunity to study the possibilities of such a theme for a rural community. I didn't expect at the end of my six weeks in the workshop to have such a school, but I have learned many angles at which such a school might be built.

I wanted to visit the homes in my new district, but I didn't want to go until I had some reason, so as not to appear "snooping." Before I had thought of any approach I might use to meet my parents and patrons, I was appointed by the chairman of our Eaton County M.E.A. Council to act on the Rural Recreation Committee. This was just the answer for a topic of approach I had been waiting for.

I started work in a community (my new school) where I wasn't known. When I went to the doors of the homes I had to be "on my toes" for their first impression. Remember—I was calling at their homes—it is so different from being a gracious hostess at the school house door the first day of school when the parents feel an obligation to tell you all the "trouble" you will or will not have with Johnnie or Susie.

I had some valuable experiences that will help me next year to understand incidents that may arise. I interviewed seventy-three people and saw forty homes. I would like to tell you about some of the people I met. An elderly lady came to the front door and I didn't think I was going to get much information, when suddenly she said she couldn't open that door, but asked if I would come around to the back door and come in. I visited with (I guess I should say "listened" to her troubles). Some time later another lady (in her fifties) came in and the elderly lady introduced her as her daughter, and made the following remark which told me how I happened to be invited in, "The dog liked her and made friends with her." The daughter talked a while, then she wanted me to see her crocheted bedspread. They offered me green corn when it was ready to pick, which showed their generosity. I stayed two hours. I feel I have a loyal supporter and the school has a resource of beautiful handwork which has never been opened. Maybe in a meager way I have been able to give to that home some moral support.

In contrast I will relate this visit. I called at this modern-looking home and a nice-looking lady in her sixties answered the door bell. She graciously invited me in and for nearly an hour talked about schools. Not much was said about the recreation survey I had called to talk about, as the clubs and organizations she belonged to seemed to take up as much time as she had to spend for out-of-the-home activities. When I was nearly ready to leave, she said, "I don't have children in school any more, you know, but I like to hear about what is going on in schools and am interested in them." I believe she will interpret as well as inform.

The calls I made are just typical of what teachers have done this summer. I heard many, many personal things about my parents and children told to me by themselves, not the gossip of the neighbors, that will be clues to behavior traits I may wish to guide.

Individual conferences straightened out my thinking. In these conferences very definite personal problems were discussed. For instance, I had one interview while working on my survey in which the lady thought the whole community was wrong and that her family was always right. I needed advice as to how I should bring out the apparent leadership present and help the community to understand them. Here I would like to add that in these conferences the individuals' ideas were developed and not entirely replaced, but if we were heading in the wrong direction we were brought back in form by careful deductions.

*The Nickle School, which was only a mile and a half from the workshop headquarters, was the location of the rural division of the laboratory schools.*

I saw a demonstration of an effective way a district might work when the board members, teachers, and interested community people of a certain district invited the workshop staff and other resource people in to discuss a program for next year. I came home impressed with this idea—"Plan *with* them, but not for them."

There is no limit to the number of people wanting to help us and all we have to do is to ask their assistance. Our health departments are a good example. They have so much to offer and service seems to be a motto of theirs. The resources will vary in each community.

Friendships have been cultivated this summer that will never cease to influence the lives of the people concerned. One must be a member of a workshop with a definite problem or problems to be solved to fully appreciate all the opportunities this summer offered.

## USE OF THE SCHOOL DIVISION

The following report by a teacher in the workshop indicates how the program with the high school group was developed and what uses were made of the activities of the students as a basis for observation:

Monday I observed the high school group under the direction of Mr. Smith to discover things which will help solve my problems of directing and making a course of study in social problems or citizenship called "Community Living." A general discussion of the purpose of a workshop followed a brief "get-together" period. The discussion, which was not clearly understood, was finally clarified with a statement from one of the participants—"A workshop is doing and learning at the same time."

Following the discussion, the class divided into groups to discuss their interests. These groups, after a short time, reported their interests: swimming, Girl and Boy Scouts, art, reading, photography, leisure time in the evenings, student government, personal and public health, home economics, and printing. It was interesting to see that they were much concerned with the problem of swimming. The reason was that there are no swimming places within an area of eighteen miles.

I experienced the handling of a group of young boys and girls the first day of school. Homeroom technique was the chief outcome. I saw how a group could be handled under natural circumstances, which helped solve my problem. These pupils could have been mine or those of any other teacher.

In a meeting of the observation group, we discussed the actions of the youngsters, and whether they participated freely. We agreed that the free participation was very good after the discussion got under way. Our teachers contributed some interesting information concerning the students of the high school division.

On Tuesday morning several teachers met to observe the high school group. The discussion opened with the problem of swimming. This led to consideration of community sanitation and health, with emphasis on reasons for the undesirability of the river and sand pit as places for swimming. Recreation for young people in the evenings was also discussed. Investigation of community facilities was suggested and discussed by participants. At this time one boy, who was much concerned with the problem of delinquency, brought out, "Our community has the highest rate in the state of Michigan for its size."

The group then laid plans for the following day. They decided to begin an investigation of the city's sanitation problem and to visit, if time permitted, the sewage disposal plant, the land quarry or pit, and the water supply sources. The students were to meet at 9:30 the next morning to begin their tour.

In the observation-group discussion, most of the time was taken up with the problem of "How to Correct Language or English in the Regular Classroom." No definite conclusions were reached. I would like to have this discussed in a group with the English teachers, or even as a general session problem.

After discussing our problem, we proceeded Wednesday to the sewage disposal plant. The engineer explained how the plant operated. Many questions were asked and much information received. The purpose of the visit was to learn how the sewage was disposed of without contaminating the river. After an hour and thirty minutes at the plant, we returned to the school to discuss our findings. In interviewing the engineer, we discovered that this was the first class from the schools of our community to use the plant as a study. The students discussed its possible future use to classes in chemistry, biology, health, economics, citizenship, and home economics. We considered why the plant was built and brought up questions of diseases caused by sewage in the water. Dr. Florio was called in to discuss these with us.

An interest in agencies of community health was shown, and a committee was formed to find out more about the city and county health departments and their relations to the Kellogg Foundation. Plans were also made to get the sanitary engineer from the county to talk to the group.

I value this experience a great deal, since I am working out a problem of this sort, and it gives me an opportunity to work first-hand with a group of youngsters. They are helping me solve my problem. I am quite impressed with the procedure and technique being demonstrated by Mr. Smith. So far, it has been more valuable to me than any information received from a textbook, or lectures on the subject.

Thursday morning I went to a nearby lake with the community swimming groups. This trip was valuable to me because of the individual contacts I made, and because I am interested in problems of city recreation. Here was a chance for a valuable comparison with our own city program.

I also spent much time in developing a unit of "Community Health." I have this pretty well worked out and am in search of some good source books which boys and girls of ninth grade level could read. My experiences with the high school group in the workshop have been very valuable in helping me with this work. I read several chapters in *Personal and Community Health* by C. E. Turner, which dealt with water supply and waste disposal. This was a follow-up of our sewage disposal and water supply.

Monday morning the group went to the milk-processing company. The results were very beneficial. The procedure before they went, while they were there, and the follow-up discussions were all tied up with community health and sanitation.

Tuesday the group spent in testing water and viewing places used for swimming—the river and the sand pit. We discussed ways of using the test results. Today's activities were also tied up with health and sanitation.

There was a personal health discussion on Wednesday. Problems of individuals were considered freely. This led to talk of the next day's work, when Dr. Florio was to discuss personal health problems with the students. There were also some suggestions for a workshop newspaper. Several boys are carrying on an experiment in the distillation of river water.

On Thursday, the discussion concerning personal health problems took place. This is the first time I have witnessed such an approach in health discussions, and I was quite impressed. The observers met later in the day to talk over this method of presentation, and many conclusions were reached. I think much can be done with this type of procedure.

Friday we were given an opportunity to see how a group organized to make a workshop newspaper.

The group is now working in a democratic way on these projects: (1) community health as brought out through a discussion on the need of swimming facilities in the community, (2) recreation of high school level for boys and girls in our community.

The community health problem has been held up a little. Our county health engineer is scheduled to meet with the group next Tuesday morning. They are also awaiting the results of a test of water taken from the sand pit and the river. Consideration of this problem will continue after the engineer's visit.

The recreation committee is busy now making preliminary plans for a survey of recreational facilities for high school youngsters. They met with the workshop group to gain more information. The superintendent of schools was consulted also. One of the parents explained the community survey which is now going on. Many discussions were also carried on pertaining to the need for recreation for this group.

This observation concerns me vitally because of the procedure used in making a survey with a group like this, and it gives me an opportunity to work out my own similar problems which will arise in a class in social problems that I plan to teach this fall.

On Monday the students discussed the meeting of last week, at which Dr. Florio considered with them questions of personal hygiene. They also made further plans for the workshop newspaper. There was a review of what had been done and plans were made for questioning our county health engineer. I also met with the high school committee to help plan for the survey of recreation for the high school students.

The high school division started to plan Tuesday morning for student government. The type which we have used was discussed, as were several others. Student reaction to student government was very well brought out. Plans for organization of government were to be continued.

On Wednesday there was a presentation of plans for student government by several members of the class. The critical analysis by the students was very good. I discussed with several members of the class the possibility of having a community festival in our town.

The high school group continued with their discussion of student government on Thursday morning. There was a short meeting with Mr. Smith and the curriculum group, at which time a visit to another community was proposed.

On Friday the student government discussion of the high school group was again continued. The staff helped to set up charts for tabulating our community survey, and the tabulation began. There was much interest on the part of the group. Later in the morning the high school observation group met with Mr. Smith to discuss the carry-over of what we observed and learned to our own school situation. This discussion was very profitable. The discussion of procedure will be continued on Monday at 3:00.

On Monday morning I worked with the high school group on our community survey. In the afternoon a group visited a workshop similar to our own. After lunching with our hosts, we attended a general session from 1:15 to 2:30. It seemed to me that much time was wasted in reports and announcements. I liked our system of planning sessions much better. At 3:30 we met with their high school group, interchanged ideas, and talked about the values received from workshops.

The high school group made plans for a picnic Tuesday morning. The discussion was pertaining to student government. Some good conclusions were reached and our school should be able to set up a better functioning student government as a result.

On Wednesday I drove a group of high school workshop students to a nearby lake for a swim.

Thursday morning the sanitary engineer reported to the high school group on tests of water and gave suggestions on how to use these. He also answered questions about health in the county and community.

*A special committee volunteered to keep fresh flowers*
*on the tables of the conference room.*

The high school observation group met with Mr. Smith, Dr. Stucky, and Dr. Cuber. Good advice was given on how to use the workshop in our own situation, and we received good ideas on how to use the county health department.

### OTHER COMMITTEES

It will be seen that the work done by the planning committee made customary committee organization almost unnecessary. When problems were encountered, committees formed themselves. For instance, a group of the teachers volunteered to keep fresh flowers on the workshop tables from day to day. The local superintendent of schools

had organized other committees, one on housing, one on the laboratory school, and one on newspaper publicity, to do some work before the workshop opened. There was another working committee
which met several times and considered possibilities for a noon lunch
period. Temporary committees were organized to work out details
of a workshop picnic, a tea, and a party. During the entire workshop
period, a committee was at work on problems of teacher education,

*The picnic helped participants and staff to acquire a feeling of social unity.*

especially for the rural teachers in Eaton County. The work of this
committee is illustrated by the following report:

> Grand Ledge Community Workshop
> Grand Ledge, Michigan
> July 30, 1941

Chairman, M.E.A.
Committee Adult and Special Education
Dear Sir:

From time to time groups of rural teachers in the workshop have concerned
themselves with the problems of teacher and special education in Eaton County.
During the last week a proposal was specifically made that a systematic attempt
to secure representative opinion be undertaken. Accordingly, a questionnaire
was constructed and circulated among all the rural teachers in the workshop.
The first part of the questionnaire contained a number of statements which had

been made by one or more persons and concerning which each teacher was asked to indicate either a "yes," or "no," or "uncertain" reaction. Following are eleven such statements and the number of "yes," "no," and "uncertain" responses which were secured:

| | Yes | No | Uncertain |
|---|---|---|---|
| 1. Consultant service has not been 100 percent effective partly because the consultant has had too many schools to cover. | 16 | o | 3 |
| 2. Teacher visitation has not been 100 percent effective partly because the best techniques have not been employed to plan the visit in view of a teacher's individual problem, and to include a follow-up after the visit. | 16 | o | 3 |
| 3. Teachers in workshops have felt that they were being helped greatly by observational activities. | 17 | 2 | o |
| 4. There is a need for seeing new curriculum materials developed and tried out in circumstances similar to their own. | 19 | o | o |
| 5. There is a need for observing a good school lunch program in action, and for help in setting up one in their individual communities. | 19 | o | o |
| 6. I believe that there exists a need for a helping teacher. | 19 | o | o |
| 7. There is a need for a center in which could be located a professional library for teachers. | 19 | o | o |
| 8. Teachers have expressed the need for a place where they can work in small groups or committees as part of their Teacher Club activity, rather than to listen to speeches; where the workshop might continue with laboratory teacher, visiting teacher, special consultant, and others available from time to time when needed. | 18 | o | 1 |
| 9. Teachers and community people have expressed the need for a place in which a program of recreation might be set up as an integral part of community school life. | 18 | o | 1 |
| 10. There is a need to demonstrate to communities that they can work together to build for themselves the kind of school they want. | 19 | o | o |
| 11. It is desirable that educational efforts in the county be integrated into one program. | 19 | o | o |

At a group meeting held yesterday morning an integrated program of rural education was suggested by the teachers. It was thought, however, that it was best not to assume that that proposal had the complete endorsement of the group, so it was written and included in the questionnaire as follows:

It seems quite possible that the county school commissioner, along with representatives of the University of Michigan and/or Chicago could work with the people of some rural school district in Eaton County to establish a Rural Education Center.

The center might start with the idea that all people concerned would work to develop the best rural school possible. It is recognized that this will be a slow, continuous process and will never be completely finished. It is recognized also that the project should *not* propose to develop a "model" school with all the answers to all the questions about education.

The Rural Education Center could provide:

1. A building adequately equipped to provide the facilities necessary to the purposes of the Center
2. The best rural teacher that could be found
3. A "helping teacher" to work with the teacher closely enough that the two would know exactly what the other was doing. It is conceivable that these two people could serve the Center in either capacity as occasion demanded.

*In several instances the games at the picnic revealed unsuspected prowess in ancient sports.*

4. A place where a professional library could be located, serving as a curriculum laboratory
5. A center from which audio-visual equipment and materials might be circulated
6. Space and facilities, so that committees from Teachers Clubs, etc., might continuously work with the commissioner on problems which confront them
7. The best school lunch program that could be developed
8. A school-community recreation program which might serve to demonstrate the possibilities to others
9. The kind of adult education program which will meet the needs of rural communities
10. The best accepted practices as far as the local school board is concerned

11. The best program of health education that can be developed
12. The most effective achievement tests and other evaluation instruments so that constant check could be kept on the progress of the children and of the school

Each teacher was then requested to make any additions to this outline which she might deem desirable, and to indicate any omissions which she thought might be made. Finally, she was asked to indicate her preference for one of three positions: (*a*) favorable to the program as outlined by the group, (*b*) favorable to the program with any additions which she desired to indicate, or (*c*) opposed to the program.

*The teachers prepared their own blanks for a survey*
*of recreation in rural areas.*

Fifteen persons favored the program as the group outlined it. Four teachers suggested additions, and no one opposed the program in its entirety or any part of it. The suggested additions were, however, of a minor nature, some of them actually being included in the plan by implication. Specifically the following were mentioned:

1. "Develop the school library to include adult needs."
2. The helping teacher and the rural education center teacher should not interchange duties.
3. The school building should be no more completely equipped than the average rural school in the county.
4. Supervised play facilities should be included.

5. A P.T.A. program should be included.

It is significant to note that only one person made each of these additional suggestions and that none of them in any way conflict with the plan outlined by the group. It appears justified, then, to make the comment that the approval of the Rural Education Center was unanimous.

These data are presented, then, by the rural teachers of the Grand Ledge workshop, with the thought that they might be helpful to the Foundation both as an evaluation of preceding programs and as a guide to programs for the future. This is not to be considered as a counter-proposal to any preceding one, but simply as the result of the work of an interested group of Eaton County teachers. It is thought that this outline of a plan might be useful in developing a more complete program of education in Eaton County.

Another working committee was composed of teachers especially interested in the problem of recreation for the rural area. This committee decided to make a comprehensive survey of the recreational needs and resources of the various school districts which they represented. Under the direction of a staff member, about twenty teachers devised blanks and interviewed about two thousand people. It was explained that

This study is being made with the hope of establishing a recreational program in our community if we want one. If we are to interest the W. K. Kellogg Foundation in our program it is important that all of these blanks be filled out completely and returned to the County School Commissioner's office *or* to the Grand Ledge Community Workshop (high school building) by July 12, 1941.

The directions to those who interviewed people were:

1. Account for every person (this may mean more than one call). List age and sex for all you are unable to interview.

2. Page 2 of **Form A** is to be marked only by checks; page 1 by appropriate answers.

3. Estimate age of adults but give exact age of children.

4. "Recreational Inventory" (Form B) is to be filled in by two or more people besides yourself.

5. Make a separate sheet of Form A for each family in the school district. (These will be returned to the teacher for future reference if desired.)

The questions on Form A were:

1. What recreational activities do you participate in within our school district?

2. Are these existing recreational opportunities adequate?

3. What recreational activities do you participate in outside our school district?

4. Where? (city, town)

The people interviewed were also asked to indicate which of the following recreational activities they would take part in if the activities were made available in the school district:

| *Clubs* | Swings | Skating |
|---|---|---|
| Sewing | See-saw | Tobogganing |
| Hand craft | Others | Archery |
| Cooking | | Horse shoes |
| Garden | *Sports* | Others |
| Livestock | Watch soft ball | |
| Child Study | Play soft ball | *Miscellaneous* |
| Scouts | Watch baseball | Dancing |
| Camp Fire Girls | Play baseball | Dramatics |
| Others | Watch volley ball | Library |
| | Play volley ball | Movie projector |
| *Playground* | Play darts | Roller skating |
| Slides | Play croquet | Discussion groups |
| Sand box | Skiing | Others |

*Teachers, parents, and school board members collaborated in studying the results of the recreation survey.*

School board members, service groups, and parents from each district assisted the teachers in this survey, and the high school students assisted in the tabulation. The results were used in a formal application to the W. K. Kellogg Foundation for assistance in developing a program of community recreation.

### INTEREST GROUPS

Interest groups in the workshop usually originated with an announcement that people interested in some particular problem, specified, should sign their names and arrange to meet with one or more of the staff members at a designated time and place. When the information desired by these people had been secured, through various means, the group dissolved itself. No attempt was made

*One corner of the library was arranged for the use of teachers who wished to study problems of reading.*

on the part of the staff to prolong these groups beyond their own inclinations, and often one session was all that was held. Some groups, however, met more or less regularly throughout the workshop period.

Teachers interested in handicraft arranged to meet with the recreation teacher in Grand Ledge once a week during afternoon periods, when no sessions were scheduled, to pursue their interests in the handicraft shop. Another group that was maintained throughout the summer consisted of teachers interested in health and hygiene. Their daily meetings of from one to three hours were usually directed by Dr. Florio, with the assistance of other staff members.

Several meetings were held by the group interested in personality problems. With the advice of various members of the staff, they considered these problems from the standpoint of health, sociology, and education. Teachers brought children from their own school districts for enrollment in the school division to provide direct observation of behavior problems and for which remedial measures could be suggested. Closely related to the personality-problem group was a group interested in juvenile delinquency. The rural teachers

*Resource persons were called in to help with problems*
*relating to the school lunch program.*

met as a group on several occasions to consider their special problems, and this group served as hosts at the workshop farewell party.

Teachers concerned with reading problems in their schools met regularly throughout the session, set up their own library corner, and arranged to have various experts in the field of reading meet with them. Other interest groups concentrated on individualized teaching, teaching techniques, the language arts, curriculum building, the community school, recreation, and the school lunch. W.P.A. officials were invited to participate in a conference on lunch problems, and an all-day meeting was held at Bretton Woods School where progress was made toward developing a complete curriculum around the school lunch activities. The board of education, parents, children, workshop staff members, representatives from the state Department of Public Instruction, and interested rural teachers worked intensively on the problem.

The work of the interest group on orientation problems studied the initial adjustment of rural children who came into the high school. The group was composed largely of high school teachers and rural

*Community garden projects were among the enterprises
visited by the workshop group.*

teachers. Much valuable work was done, because the rural teachers who taught the children attending the village high schools were able to discuss these problems with staff members and high school teachers. A group interested in surveys and tabulation techniques drew up survey blanks, gathered data, and tabulated results.

Conferences with staff members, by appointments arranged with the secretary, involved these interest groups as well as individuals, general sessions, and other meetings. A summary of these appointments is given in Table I. This table includes only the individual conferences that were scheduled. Much individual work not scheduled, however, was done with teachers during the lunch hour, the recreation period, and during the time spent in driving from the workshop center to the various rural schools in the county.

TABLE I

STATISTICS ON CONFERENCES HELD BY STAFF MEMBERS

| STAFF MEMBER | INDIVIDUAL CONFERENCES | | GROUP MEETINGS | | GENERAL SESSIONS | | EVENING MEETINGS | | MEETINGS OUTSIDE GRAND LEDGE | |
|---|---|---|---|---|---|---|---|---|---|---|
| | Number | Hours | Number | Hours | Number | Hours | Number | Hours | Number | Hours |
| Mr. Woods | 46 | 24 | 46 | 36 | 25 | 36 | 9 | 21 | 4 | 11 |
| Dr. Gaumnitz | 51 | 15 | 31 | 37 | 14 | 23 | 2 | 6 | 3 | 7 |
| Dr. Cuber | 62 | 24 | 43 | 56 | 21 | 33 | 7 | 17 | 5 | 13 |
| Dr. Florio | 40 | 18 | 36 | 44 | 22 | 34 | 11 | 27 | 6 | 21 |
| Mr. Smith | 5 | 2 | 17 | 17 | 24 | 40 | 7 | 17 | 8 | 20 |
| Miss Locher | .. | .. | 23 | 20 | 17 | 27 | 3 | 8 | 2 | 5 |
| Mrs. Williams | 7 | 5 | 30 | 22 | 18 | 28 | 2 | 6 | 3 | 8 |
| Total | 211 | 88 | 226 | 232 | 141 | 221 | 41 | 102 | 31 | 85 |

### THE USE OF LIBRARY RESOURCES

Studies made by participants indicate some of the uses of library material. The cards from 168 books bore the names of one or more teachers. Cards from two of the books indicated they had been checked out by eleven different teachers during the six weeks. Fifty-eight books had been checked out by only one teacher or staff member. The fifty books most widely circulated were checked out a total of three hundred times, an average of once a week per book. In addition, many of the books were used during the day in the various workshop rooms, with no record of this use appearing on the cards.

Twenty-four teachers, who were personally interviewed with regard to the reading they had done, listed and commented on 267 books, about eleven books for each teacher. Some reading was done by the members of the workshop in other libraries, and the workshop library was widely used by visitors from the various communities.

The teachers had agreed that books should be kept only one night and should be returned at the beginning of the session of the next day. During the first day or two, no attempt had been made to set up rules for the use of library material. It was felt that the teachers would be in a better position to make library rules for themselves after they had some experience with the problem.

Dr. Gaumnitz rendered a special service to the workshop by bringing a wealth of printed material from the U.S. Office of Education. The teachers considered it a valuable experience to browse through these materials under his guidance and to make selections which they could use next year in their own teaching.

*In the development of a school lunch program, the workshop group had the assistance of a two-room school and its entire community.*

### EVALUATION

*Group Life.*—It has been suggested that the enthusiastic support participants give to the workshop as a technique in teacher education is due largely to an *espirit de corps* developed through close association. It has been customary for workshop groups to take their meals and seek their recreation together. To a certain extent this factor was minimized in the Grand Ledge community workshop. Of the fifty-two teachers in the workshop, ten regularly made their homes in the community and ten others moved into Grand Ledge for the summer, while thirty commuted from their homes. Even the noon lunch was left to the individual, and, while various small groups did eat together on numerous occasions, no special attempt was made to develop this activity as part of the program. Recreational and social activities for the whole group were limited to two teas, a picnic, a theater party, and a farewell party.

*The supervised play activities of children on a nearby playground suggested new games to teachers for increasing the variety of recreations they could promote in their schools.*

*Problems Solved.*—The problems brought to the workshop were grouped under the following headings:

1. Improving of school and community relations
2. Planning and building a community school
3. Reviewing and improving of methods
4. Improving the teaching of tool subjects.
5. Developing recreation and leisure-time programs
6. Developing a school lunch program
7. Teaching the exceptional child
8. Minimizing delinquency
9. Studying of high school graduates to discover most useful and least useful subjects in curriculum

Statements of the individual. problems are not included because, in most cases, the teachers discovered that their real problems were not the ones they had originally indicated. The extent to which problems changed is indicated by examining statements made by one of the participants, a school superintendent, before, during, and after the workshop. In response to the question, "What is my specific problem?" he wrote:

April 1. To correlate the work of four of my teachers in attendance at the workshop to the end that we might investigate our school needs and draw up proposals to meet these needs.

April 17. To develop a school improvement program.

July 7. To bring together material and techniques for a functional education program and lay plans for physical improvements.

July 14. To improve the instructional program and make plans for introducing the improvements.

August 1. To make innovations or improvement of old practices, to bring about the best means of development of the whole child, and to utilize whatever physical means necessary to make the practices worthwhile to the child. It has been clearly evidenced that to bring about a more healthful, helpful, and useful program, some improvements should be made. Some of these include: (1) incorporating the teaching of functional health throughout the school; (2) developing better everyday citizenship; (3) giving individuals a wider opportunity to study fields more to their liking and needs, including hobbies for all ages; (4) providing more opportunities for social development; and (5) developing leadership.

The statement of decisions reached by this participant does not imply that he solved his problem in the workshop. Another school superintendent who worked six weeks on the problem of "planning and building a community school" did not complete the job; nor is there evidence to show that delinquency has been minimized in the community from which came two teachers who worked on the problem during the summer. Valid evidence that teachers got the answers to their problems will have to be gathered in terms of later results in the various communities.

*Responses on the Appraisal Blank.*—Tabulation of data reveals the following composite opinion of forty-six participants:

1. To what extent have you been satisfied with your total program of summer work? Little satisfaction, o; Fair, o; Average, 1; High Degree, 9; Unusually High, 36.

2. Appraisal of course, Grand Ledge Community Workshop. *Directions:* Place a mark on each scale at the point which expresses your judgment. Use your present and past experience in university courses as a guide for determining your judgments.

*Previous Preparation* (Rate your own previous preparation for the course in terms of adequacy):

| 7 | 1 | 18 | 5 | 14 |
|---|---|---|---|---|
| Much too little | | Satis- factory | | Entirely adequate |

*Load* (Rate the course on the total amount of work involved in it):

| | | 34 | 12 | |
|---|---|---|---|---|
| Much too little | | Average | | Much too heavy |

*Value of Assignments* (Rate on the educational value of assigned tasks):

| | | 2 | 3 | 41 |
|---|---|---|---|---|
| Merely busy work | | Average | | Highly Valuable |

*Appraisal of the Course* (Rate the entire course on its value to you):

| | | | 1 | 44 |
|---|---|---|---|---|
| A waste of time | | Average | | Splendid Course |

3. Would you recommend this course next summer to one of your associates who had your background of training and experience? Yes, 45; No, 0; Doubtful, 0.

Statements from teachers, regarding their workshop experience included the following:

The workshop was the most profitable summer school experience I have ever had. It taught principles of democratic teaching by being consistent in its democratic operation.

This workshop to me, and I believe to every person in the county has been most valuable for the following reasons:

1. It has brought many teachers together where we have had an opportunity to discuss and work on our individual problems, getting each other's reactions.

2. We have been given the opportunity to go out in our communities where our problems exist and work toward the solution of them.

3. We have gained a better understanding of the machinery by which planning has been done in our county. We have, through this workshop, been given an opportunity to participate in committee planning for next year's program with the Kellogg Foundation.

4. We have been made to realize some problems we were not before conscious of.

5. We have seen democracy in action with a group of teachers which we realize can be carried over into our classrooms with our children, communities, and teachers.

6. We have become more conscious of the sociological, hygienic, and educational relationships existing between problems.

7. I have been given proof of the value in calling a meeting of the Board of

Education, members of the community, and consultants to discuss a particular problem of our school. I received this proof from a meeting we held during this summer with our Board of Education, members of the community, staff members, teachers, and consultants in discussing the problem of correlation of the curriculum with our hot lunch program next year.

8. I feel we have done a great deal of planning to carry on a recreation program in our district another year and in other districts of our county.

9. Teachers should realize from the Recreational Survey the value of a thorough study of a problem before attempting to make a plan for its solution.

10. We do not plan *for* people, but plan *with* people.

11. The workshop has been a challenge to me of the opportunity of enriching the curriculum in the small rural schools to serve boys and girls through a program suited to local conditions and needs.

12. I have been given proof of the value of individual conferences.

The workshop plan of education, as we have experienced it, appeals to me as being particularly well adapted to use in a one-room school of a rural community.

We feel that the interest group meetings have encouraged more individual participation in the discussions of pertinent problems of hygiene, sociology, and education. The opportunity for observations in the various groups has been most satisfactory. Conferences and discussions with staff members have revealed and clarified existing problems and situations.

I have learned to find out at what I am aiming before I begin to teach a course.

I am convinced that I have learned to do individualized teaching even in a large class.

I feel that I shall return to my community with a wealth of material to share.

The workshop has been an experience with the breath of life in it. I know because of the eagerness I feel in looking forward to September with its chance to try out some new things. No traditionally-organized summer school course has made me feel that way.

The chance to work intensively on a problem of our selection, where it actually exists, the availability of the staff at all times, the carefully selected reference material, the observational experience, have put the community workshop at the very top of the list of things I value in my professional training.

Often have I heard democratic procedure loudly praised in college classes but this has been my first experience with the actual use of it.

I feel that I have gained more practical knowledge of skills and techniques for working with boys and girls than I have gotten from campus classes.

The Eaton County workshop has provided one of the best situations for achieving professional growth which I have ever had the opportunity to experience.

Together with the school board and patrons of my community I have been able to work on many problems and to make definite plans with them for another year.

The summer's experience has been like the actual schoolroom situation and has itself been an example of the kinds of procedure so often talked about.

I have received much more personal help than I did in the usual college class.

One of my strongest reactions is that the workshop plan or method seems to be the one which more nearly meets my need for advanced professional study and guidance.

## The following statements were written by staff members:

There was clear evidence that as the weeks passed, the students (teacher-participants) not only grew, but their growth became more rapid as they became more familiar with the whole workshop idea.

Now that I am several days removed from my first workshop experience, I shall attempt to evaluate it and to make some suggestions regarding future policy. You already have my daily records and reactions; this is an over-all view.

It would be both impossible and deceiving to conceal my enthusiasm for the workshop. To me it was the most gratifying educational experience I have ever witnessed or participated in. Notably these things are apparent:

1. The volume of work done was tremendous—far in excess of the amount ordinarily done in a six-weeks session. This is true for both students and staff.

2. The capacity of students for self-direction was very gratifying and not a little bit surprising. It is almost literally true that the staff never made an assignment, or a schedule, or required anyone to do anything specifically. Yet the students made a schedule more exacting and confining than the staff would have felt justified in making; they gave themselves and each other assignments greater in scope and difficulty than the staff would have made. How much this is due to indirect suggestion and other types of guidance by the staff is, of course, indeterminable.

3. The spirit and cooperation of the staff was perfect. I have never been associated with a more cooperative, capable, and mutually respected professional group. There were differences of opinion, to be sure, but the spirit of and for resolving them was incredibly fine.

4. The educational experience was functional. Tasks accomplished were for the most part vital to the teachers who did them. I think that this is largely responsible for item (1) and (2) above. Each student could easily see why he was doing what he was doing. Many of the projects begun this summer will be carried out over a period of months or years.

5. The workshop staff made a very practical contribution to the community in which the workshop was held and others nearby. Consultations with school boards, P.T.A. groups, health department officials, etc. were almost daily occurrences. The staff singly and as a group appeared before numerous civic groups and community meetings. Though always theoretically possible, practically, educators rarely do this on the scale which we did.

6. The project included boys and girls along with teachers and staff. Many opportunities for better teaching were thus made use of or made more concrete. The boys and girls also contributed much to the adults and were fine interpreters of the workshop to the community.

Among the limitations I would cite the following:

1. Lack of adequate library materials and an established policy for securing them. For three weeks we did not know how, when, and if books available in the Foundation Library would be made available to us. Likewise some arrangement with the University Library should be possible. It is inherent, also I suppose, that periodical materials are almost impossible to secure.

2. One member of the staff came two days after the staff first assembled and left at the end of the fourth week. Though he contributed greatly to the success of the project, certainly it would have been better to have had him begin with the rest of us and carry through.

3. I fear that we sometimes permitted our staff and our facilities to be spread too thinly by agreeing to deal with any and every problem which arose. Perhaps it would have been better to have limited the scope of the problems more than we did. For example, was it a wise use of an M.D. and a Ph.D. in sociology to spend five hours discussing individualized reading problems with a group of high school teachers of English?

So far as policy for the future, if the project is to be continued, I would suggest these things: (*a*) as few changes in staff as possible; (*b*) continuation of the same general philosophy; (*c*) the same students and community (at least the same county); (*d*) a better *plan* for library materials; and (*e*) devote the workshop to a more integral objective. I would suggest "community organization" as the next logical step, especially if the project were to be located in Grand Ledge or somewhere near there.

The library, coupled with the large and small group discussions, has led to some definite research right now; but, more than this, I have been able to compile a bibliography of professional material I will read during the coming year.

I have found more inspiration and belief that the democratic way of life can be made to function in the school-room from my own observation of the children thus at work, than I ever obtained from any other source.

This workshop has given us an opportunity to really work on a problem where the problem exists. I, together with members of the staff, have been out and really worked in a situation. To me this is far more beneficial than a campus course. This democratic procedure has proven to me that it will work in the class-room.

The workshop gives teachers an excellent opportunity to work out their individual problems, to express their educational desires as individuals as well as in groups, and to see for themselves how schools can be organized and operated along democratic principles.

The workshop is a challenge to the individual teacher to clarify her thinking, to crystallize her educational philosophy.

This is my first experience in a workshop; I entered skeptical; I leave enthusiastic.

In view of the objectives set up for the workshop, the staff was expertly chosen. It was a most competent and congenial group of people, and the various members joined into a working unit in assisting in the solution of real problems. The location was excellently chosen because the people in the community had put forth united effort to get the workshop. It was held in the area and in a situation which more nearly resembles the one where the teachers teach during the school year.

The location was near the community in which the teacher lives or teaches so that she can actually work on very real problems in that community and in some instances it served as the laboratory for the workshop.

The workshop was a laboratory where professional problems were studied, surveys made and analyzed, and where existing state and local educational committees actually put plans into operation. An example of this would be the working of the M.E.A. Recreation Committee on a proposal to be submitted to the County Health Department and reports from other similar committees which were prepared.

One of the most far-reaching results of an interested group of rural teachers was a proposal to the County Health Department that a rural education center be established. The proposal was no sooner made when a large delegation of community people asked that the center might be established in their community. If this plan should materialize, it would, in my judgment, be a natural contribution to rural education, and I am convinced that the workshop is the kind of a situation that produces the stimuli for projects like these.

The workshop was a media through which better understanding between teachers and agencies could be brought about, such as the County Health Department, the W. K. Kellogg Foundation, the Eaton County M.E.A. Committees, the school commissioner's office, and many others. It really served as a laboratory for some of these agencies. For example, the County School Commissioner of Eaton County was able to contact groups of teachers and work with them on vital problems and the County Health Department made contacts with teachers that had not been done during the school year. There is no doubt but that the working relationship of these agencies and the teachers will be more effective than it has ever been before as a result of this workshop.

The workshop was a place where teachers worked on individual problems that have arisen through teaching experience. The solution of these problems was made easier by the association of other teachers, the staff, boys and girls, community groups, and an adequate library. It was possible for the teachers, along with the members of the staff, to actually go to their own communities and start work on problems that will be vital to them next year. A good example of this was a very effective session with community people at the Bretton Woods School on the hot lunch program.

The workshop provided for the improvement of teaching by a realistic situation where boys and girls are participants in the program and where teaching actually takes place. The program was so well united that staff members, teachers, and students became an integral part of the whole program. For example, a teacher might go from a discussion of problems directly into the teaching situation where something was being done about the problem—which, in turn, would be followed up by a discussion with staff members.

The workshop can actually serve needs of the local community where it is located and thus illustrate the kinds of things that can be done in a union of the school and community. For example, community groups, such as the coordinating council, township service committees, and the parent-teacher association discussed problems with the staff, teachers, and boys and girls. A community survey of Grand Ledge sponsored by the coordinating council was made more useful by getting the help of high school students in the workshop and by having assistance in the use and the interpretation of data by members of the staff.

Another example was a union of the parent-teacher association and the school staff in a cooperative program of community education for Grand Ledge next year. Through help found in various ways at the workshop a real program of action has already been planned. A third example was a meeting of a committee of civic-minded people to think through a long-time program of education for the community. This large group actually examined proposed blueprints of a new school building and land plans, gathering evidence to determine building needs. While these things may have been done without the workshop in some communities, it certainly hastens the day when the school will become a real community school.

The workshop was a place where the democratic process actually worked and teachers could see how it could be applied to their own situations by having actually lived it. The director did a masterful job in allowing the process to grow and not once resort to a dictatorial technique. It was a good example of the teacher as a guide and one who plans with students. The whole program took form by group decision which resulted in a more complete use of staff and other available resources than any previously scheduled program I have ever observed. The slogan was "Do things *with* people and not *for* them."

The workshop provided an opportunity for teachers and staff to live together and develop a better understanding of common problems.

There was less emphasis on grades, examinations, and administrative detail, which made the summer experience much happier, and teachers seemed to really enjoy the summer experience.

The staff brought together three broad fields of learning—health, sociology, and education. This provided a very real and practical integration of these areas and should assist teachers in seeing the possibilities of a well-integrated program in their own schools. For example, a discussion of health in the workshop always involved the sociological and educational implications. A good illustration was a discussion of public health problems by a group of community people under the trees in a farmer's yard.

The workshop provided a better system of evaluating the improvement of teaching by placing the teacher in a more natural situation, and in addition to seeing her reactions resulting from discussion and reading, showed how she actually attacked and, in some cases, completed an actual problem. For example, some teachers actually completed a survey of their own community that was needed in order to set up objectives for the community program of education.

The workshop provided an opportunity for individual teachers to get more personal help from staff members. While it may have meant more hours for the members of the staff, the time not used for general sessions and discussion groups was taken by individual conferences or small group conferences with staff members. However, members of the staff felt that this was not a burden but an interesting part of the work.

*Achievement of Objectives.*—Evaluation of a program in teacher education can best be done in terms of its stated purposes. The purposes of the Grand Ledge community workshop were (1) to help teachers discover and plan solutions to problems which arise in connection with the growth and development of children in the community, (2) to help teachers discover their responsibility for and to improve their skills in teaching democratic citizenship in the community, and (3) to help teachers in studying the nature of communities, their problems, and their resources in relation to the improvement of the community school. The real extent to which these purposes were realized can only be determined from a close examination of the actual changes made in education in the communities from which the teacher-participants came.

# CHAPTER V

# ATTACKING PROBLEMS IN SOCIAL SCIENCE, LIBRARY SCIENCE, AND THE LANGUAGE ARTS[1]

The community workshop in Hillsdale was the outgrowth of planning which occurred during the school year of 1939–40. During that year the committees on teacher education in Branch and Hillsdale counties studied the problems of their teacher groups and made joint plans to meet their needs. These plans included: (1) a curriculum workshop in elementary education, sponsored at Coldwater by the Department of Education of the University of Chicago in the summer of 1940; (2) consultative service to be available to teachers who made a small financial contribution during the school year 1940–41; and (3) a workshop to be sponsored at Hillsdale by the Department of Education of the University of Chicago during the summer of 1941.

The committees from the two counties worked together from time to time throughout this period on plans dealing with matters which were of mutual concern. Each committee worked separately while dealing with problems within its own county. This arrangement resulted in a division of responsibility in which the Branch County committee took the major responsibility for planning the workshop in Coldwater, and the Hillsdale County committee took the major responsibility for planning the workshop in Hillsdale.

## COMMUNITY PREPARATION FOR THE WORKSHOP

*Selection of the Community.*—In 1940 there had been an understanding between the Branch and Hillsdale County teachers that the 1941 workshop would be held in the city of Hillsdale. The Hillsdale County teacher education committee discussed the possibility of its being located elsewhere but there seemed to be no logical reason for changing the location to Branch County or to one of the villages in Hillsdale County. Characteristics of Hillsdale gave evidence of many factors that would be helpful to the successful operation of a community workshop. It was a city of about 7,000 people and had

---

[1] This chapter was prepared by Mr. Fred Miller, who had charge of the workshop at Hillsdale. Mr. Miller has been engaged in work in the Michigan Community Health Project since 1937, and has served as a consultant since 1939.

both agricultural and manufacturing interests. It was centrally located not only for the teachers of Hillsdale County but also for those that might enroll from adjacent counties. The city had adequate housing facilities, and the board of education volunteered the use of the school properties. A fairly large group of children were interested in a summer school experience. The three libraries contained adequate supplies of books, and the three cooperative librarians offered their services whenever they might be needed.

*The workshop participants found frequent relaxation and interesting social contacts in the city's parks.*

Hillsdale is the site of Hillsdale College, which offered some resources of books, equipment, space, and personnel. It is also the county seat of government, and thus afforded further opportunities for study to those interested in sociology and in the teaching of social studies. Further possibilities for study were offered by the city's public utilities, its industries, its institutional organization, and its sociological structure.

The city had a number of parks available to workshop participants for recreation. The participants were invited to observe or to take an active part in the operation of the summer recreational program for children whenever they desired. The recreational leaders of this program made themselves available for conferences and assistance whenever possible.

*Participation of Community Groups.*—The people of the city exhibited cooperative attitudes in connection with the workshop. The parent-teacher association organized committees which assisted with publicity, hospitality, and housing of participants. Other parent-teacher association representatives worked with a committee of teachers to inform parents and children of the laboratory school possibilities, to receive applications, and to select the laboratory school group. The garden club planned to furnish flowers for the building and to organize a garden tour for the workshop participants. The literary groups planned to entertain staff members and workshop participants. The churches extended special invitations to those who were to be in town over the weekends.

The chamber of commerce made plans to entertain all the workshop participants at the country club, which in turn offered reduced rates for participants' recreation. Industrial management and labor organizations alike expressed their willingness to contribute to the participants' understanding of industries, facilities, and problems. The health department, the hospital, and other institutions cooperated in planning observational excursions. A service club made arrangements to acquaint participants with the work it was doing in eliminating an area of poor housing. The mayor, the superintendent of schools, the county school commissioner, the county service committee chairman, the probate judge, members of the health department, college faculty members, the city recreational director, and others made themselves available to various workshop groups for discussions of their problems, and invited cooperation in their solution. In short, the people and the agencies and institutions of Hillsdale were very generous in making their resources available to the participants and in cooperating with the program of the workshop.

In addition to these local resources there were evidences of interest in nearby communities which expressed their desire to cooperate and to participate in the workshop program. Two rural districts requested that laboratory school programs be established in their schools.

*Arrangements for the Laboratory School.*—In making its plans for the resources of the workshop, the committee outlined the following conditions which could be met by a well-planned laboratory school: (1) a number of children would enjoy a wholesome, pleasurable school experience; (2) this experience would differ from their regular school programs and would therefore afford a new set of learning activities; (3) a group of parents would have unusual opportunities for observing the activities of their children and for receiving help with problems of child growth and development; (4) the workshop participants would have an opportunity to observe, and to share in, a series of child activities more closely related to children's basic interest and needs than some regular school programs; and (5) through such observation and sharing, and with the guidance and help of the laboratory school teachers as added resource people, the workshop participants would be able to find solutions for specific problems which they were trying to solve through their workshop experience.

With these circumstances in mind, plans were made for three laboratory school groups: an early elementary grade group, an upper elementary grade group, and a junior high school group.

A committee from the parent teacher association worked with a committee of teachers to acquaint parents and children with the possibilities of the laboratory school, to receive applications for attendance, and to select the children who would participate. This joint committee arranged for the discussion of the possibilities of the laboratory school in teachers meetings and in parent-teacher association meetings, and sent letters of notification and application forms to each home represented in the Hillsdale elementary and junior high schools.

When the applications were made, the committee studied them carefully in terms of what other summer educational plans parents had for their children. These plans included such activities as participation in the city playground, arts and crafts, library, and swimming programs; part-time attendance in private or organizational camps; participation in short-term church schools; and travel and part-time residence at lakes or with relatives and friends. It was the judgment of the committee that all these plans involved regular opportunities presented through the efforts and plans of the families or by organized agencies in the community, while the laboratory school experience was to be an added educational opportunity which might or might not become a permanent community resource. The committee decided, therefore, to use the laboratory school to afford special opportunities to those who did not have other educational plans, and as a supplement to the planned programs of others. Hence, they accepted all applications and invited the parents of the children to come to the laboratory school for interviews with staff members concerning the children's individual programs of educational activities throughout the summer. They also recommended to the workshop staff that the program be kept flexible enough to allow for participation by children who had planned for other part-time educational experiences.

*The Selection of Workshop Headquarters.*—Hillsdale has two elementary schools, a junior high school, and a senior high school. The board of education, through the superintendent, offered the teacher education committee the use of as much building space and

*The city's playground recreation program gave the children in the laboratory school opportunities for enjoying new play experiences.*

as many facilities as would be needed in any of the buildings. During the consideration of the various possibilities it was decided that an elementary school would be more suitable for the workshop because: (1) most of the participants were elementary school teachers and could gain much by daily contact with elementary school materials; (2) the facilities of the elementary school would be more suitable for the laboratory school group; (3) a recreational program was being conducted on the playground of each elementary school and would be available for both observation and participation; and

(4) each elementary school was provided with an extension library of children's books which would be available without being moved.

The selection of the Mauck School was indicated by several factors: (1) more requests of children for participation in the laboratory school program came from the area served by this school than from the other, (2) more housing facilities for staff and participants were available in the neighborhood of this school, and (3) the board of

*The Joseph T. Mauck School was an attractive modern building that provided excellent facilities for the workshop group.*

education had planned less summer maintenance work at the Mauck School than at the other elementary school.

*Plans for Library Facilities.*—Hillsdale had three good libraries: the Mitchell Library which was the city public library, the Hillsdale College library, and the Hillsdale high school library. The committee made arrangements with Mrs. Leithel P. Ford, who was librarian both at the Mitchell Library and at the high school, to have the workshop's bibliographical lists checked so that participants would know which materials were available at each of the libraries. Mrs. Ford also made arrangements to have a number of items placed in the workshop library on loan from each of the two libraries under her control.

Hillsdale College cooperated by checking its library resources and making available its library schedule. It cooperated further by loans of many books and encyclopedic materials from its sociology department library.

Local bookshops agreed to lend displays of materials for study in connection with specific teaching areas, such as reading and social studies. The county school commissioner's collections of books were made available, as were the children's books from the elementary schools.

*Lunch Facilities.*—It was the opinion of the committee that it would be desirable for the workshop participants to have noon lunches available at the school building. They arranged with the superintendent of schools, therefore, for the use of the kitchen and cafeteria facilities, and identified a competent woman who could be available to prepare and serve the lunches; but they made no arrangements for her employment, since the decision on whether lunch would be served at school was to be made by the participants.

*The Lists of Rooming Accommodations.*—The local committee secured lists of available rooms through the offices of the county health department and the high school, and these lists were sent to all applicants who desired to secure rooms in Hillsdale.

### TEACHER PREPARATION FOR THE WORKSHOP

*Potential Participants.*—One of the agreements reached by the teacher education committees of the seven counties was that summer workshops should be planned to assist teachers with their own problems as well as to permit the earning of credit toward certificate and degree requirements. The teacher education committees of Branch and Hillsdale counties therefore analyzed the expressed needs of the teachers of their counties and planned the tentative program of the Hillsdale community workshop on the basis of these needs.

The extent of the interest of the teachers was evidenced by the fact that as a result of the distribution of the brochure describing the proposed workshops, 54 teachers from Hillsdale County, 18 from Branch County, and 18 from other counties indicated an interest in the workshop at Hillsdale. Of this group, fifty made arrangements to attend.

*Selection of Course-Credit Areas.*—The course-credit areas which the workshop provided were selected on the basis of teacher interest and needs. The courses, amounts of credit, and enrollments[1] are indicated in the following list.

### A. *Sociology*

1. Sociology 201.  Introduction to Sociology.  ½ C (3) or 1 C (15)
2. Sociology 329.  Methods for the Study of the Modern Community.  ½ C (3) or 1 C (4)

### B. *English and Library Science*

1. English 101.  English Composition.  ½ C (1) or 1 C (6)
2. Graduate Library Science 327.  The Elementary School Library.  ½ C (26)
3. Graduate Library Science 326.  The Book Collection of Secondary School Libraries.  ½ C (11)
4. Graduate Library Science 325.  The Objectives and Administration of Secondary School Libraries.  ½ C (10)

### C. *Education*

1. Education 320B.  Foundations of Good Adjustment:  Methods and Goals in Personality Study and Guidance of Children.  ½ C (3)
2. Education 367A.  Current Problems in Elementary Education.  ½ C (3) or 1 C (7)
3. Education 367B.  Current Problems in Secondary Education.  ½ C (1) or 1 C (4)
4. Education 382.  The Social Studies Curriculum.  ½ C (5) or 1 C (6)

*Preparatory Helps to Teachers.*—Several avenues of interpretation were used to explain what possibilities the workshops might offer teachers for their professional growth.  The procedures included distribution of descriptive brochures and mimeographed guide sheets, discussion meetings in each county, individual conferences with each interested teacher, filling out interview cards, follow-up letters to give further help in securing admission to the workshop, and meetings with teachers clubs and village school staffs.  The educational consultant for Branch and Hillsdale counties arranged for a conference with each individual teacher.  During these conferences special attention was given to helping the teacher identify her major problem or problems, and helping her begin specific plans to solve them.  When groups of teachers from the same school expected to attend the workshop, attention was given not only to their individual problems, but to a program of action for the group as well.  The superintendents of schools and the county school commissioners gave additional assistance to some teachers with their plans.

The teachers needed considerable help in completing the arrange-

---

[1] 1 C indicates 1 course credit of 3 1/3 semester hours.  ½ C indicates ½ course credit of 1 2/3 semester hours.  The number in parentheses following the credit allotment indicates the number of students enrolled.

ments for their enrollment in the workshop. Among their problems were those of securing admission to the University of Chicago and to the workshop, selecting the courses in which they wished to secure credit, and securing acceptance of these credits at the higher institution to which their transfer was desired. The workshop administration made every effort possible to assist teachers with these problems, and cooperated with the educational institutions so that the workshop courses might receive valid credit.

*Teaching Problems Brought to the Workshop.*—The problems which the teachers were interested in solving included the following:

1. Problems relating to the physical set-up of the classroom and its utilization
2. Problems relating to the physical development of children
3. Problems dealing with the emotional adjustment of children
4. Problems of adjusting the daily program and the curriculum program to the needs of individual children
5. Problems in working with parents and community members
6. Problems of planning for improving school lunch programs

*Special Preparations by Teachers.*—A number of the teachers did excellent preparatory work before coming to the workshop. One planned to develop materials on the history of Branch County for children in intermediate grades, and secured much material both from books and through interviews. Three rural teachers made broad plans for community participation of children and adults in planning a program of community integration. Two kept extensive case records on some of their children as aids in meeting specific needs of these children. Three superintendents asked teachers to work on problems of the school lunch program, and each member of this group did some preliminary planning with regard to the needs of his school. Other cases show similar preparation along various lines.

## STAFF PREPARATION FOR THE WORKSHOP

*Selection of the Staff.*—The staff was selected in terms of the requirements for assistance to the workshop participants, in the study of their problems and in the integration of their course work for credit. The following brief notes identify the members of the instructional staff.

Leland DeVinney, Ph.D., Instructor in Sociology at the University of Chicago, had a broad knowledge of community problems and excellent ability in helping students understand them. His educational background was of great value in staff planning conferences.

Joseph Lohman, M.A., Instructor in Sociology at the University of Chicago, had held similar responsibilities at the workshop in Coldwater in 1940 and so brought a helpful knowledge of this general community to the workshop. Mr. DeVinney and Mr. Lohman shared the responsibility for work in sociology.

Enid Chamberlin, M.A., Assistant Professor of Education at the University of Chicago, received valuable experience in the Eight-Year Study of the Progressive Education Association, in which she helped to evaluate private schools for women, and she had served in P.E.A. workshops. She had responsibility for assistance on problems relating to English.

Rosemary Livsey, Teachers' and Children's Department Librarian, Los Angeles Public Library, and Teacher of Children's Literature in the Graduate Library School, University of Southern California, was the specialist in problems of library science.

Dean Chamberlin, M.A., Assistant Dean of Men and Professor of English in Dartmouth College, participated in the evaluation of private schools for men in the Eight-Year Study, and had been a staff member in P.E.A. workshops. Mr. Chamberlin divided his time between the Hillsdale workshop and the Marshall workshop, assisting in arts and crafts.

Fred A. Miller, M.A., Instructor in Education at the University of Chicago, had directed a workshop at the University of Minnesota in 1940 and had been serving as Consultant in Education to Branch and Hillsdale counties. He was appointed director of the workshop, and assumed responsibility for assistance with problems relating to the elementary school curriculum and to child adjustment.

Mariann Marshall, M.A., psychologist in the Francis W. Parker School, Chicago, had been enrolled in the University of Chicago workshop in 1940. She was appointed laboratory-school teacher for the early elementary grade group.

Alex Tudyman, M.A., teaching principal in the public schools of Westchester, Illinois, had previous experience as a staff assistant in workshops at Northwestern University. He was appointed laboratory-school teacher for the middle elementary grade group.

Loren Woolston, M.A., teacher in the public schools of Rochester, New York, and chairman of the Rochester social studies curriculum committee, had been a staff member in the workshop at Syracuse

University. He served as specialist in secondary education and the social studies curriculum.

Robert Bullock, M.A., chairman of the social studies area and dean of boys in the public high schools of Greeley, Colorado, had been a staff member in Greeley workshops. He was appointed laboratory-school teacher in the junior high school group.

In addition to the instructional staff, two local girls were employed to provide secretarial and stenographic assistance. They worked full-time during the workshop, and part-time the week before and the week after the workshop.

*Staff Visits to the Community.*—The process of integrating the staff began as soon as the individual members were employed. The committee felt that it was important for each staff member, in his preparation for participation in the workshop, to spend some time in the community as early as possible. The director and two secretaries, working there, had daily opportunities to study the community's resources. Each of the other staff members was invited to spend a day or two in the area to acquaint himself with the community, its members, their problems, and the potentialities of the community's resources.[1]

*Further Staff Planning.*—Correspondence, conferences, and exchange of plans and materials among the various staff members helped to increase the understanding of problems and the planning of the program between the time of these individual visits and the first meeting of the staff as a unit. Individual staff members also assumed responsibilities for planning for specific group needs and for securing resources in advance of the opening of the workshop. To assure the availability of visual education materials one staff member arranged for an advance order of film materials for the first three weeks of the workshop program. The staff members responsible for the laboratory school collaborated in planning the basic organization of that unit.

*Staff Meetings.*—The staff had its first meeting on Thursday, June 19, although some members were unable to be present. There was a realization of the need for rapid progress in planning the organization of the workshop, and in assuming individual responsibilities for its operation. By Saturday noon the basic organization had been

[1] The expenses of these visits were met through the W. K. Kellogg Foundation Fellowship Program. All but two staff members visited; the other two would have had to come such great distances that it seemed inadvisable for them to make the trip.

planned and the staff members had become acquainted. Committees had been organized and had made reports on plans to the group as a whole. The discussion of the use and integration of resources had brought out interesting differences in viewpoints and plans for workshop procedure. The philosophy of the workshop had been discussed and basic agreement had been reached concerning its applications.

A meeting at Battle Creek, with the staff members of the other

*Staff members discovered a new game, box hockey, at Gull Lake. Details of the equipment were noted and a set was constructed at the workshop to furnish exercise and amusement for the participants and for the children in the laboratory school.*

workshops, and a picnic at Gull Lake tended to develop a spirit of unity among the staff members of all four workshops.

Some time was given on Sunday to a consideration of the specific details of the beginning program for the first workshop sessions; to the discussion of the problems of participants and the acceptance by staff members of the responsibility for the initial guidance and counseling of participants; to the records and reports that might be used to aid the staff members in counseling and guiding the participants; and to the tentative allocation of each participant to a staff member for initial counsel and guidance.

Some attention was given to the problem of a time schedule for the workshop. The plans made for the first few meetings of the participants were not intended to be the pattern on which the workshop would operate continuously. It seemed expedient, however, to incorporate the following kinds of activities into the planned program of the first few days: (1) meetings of the entire group to disseminate information of general interest and to plan for those things which

*The attractive halls were very appropriate for small group discussions.*
*Their cork-panelled walls gave ample space for bulletin board materials.*

affected the group as a whole—this included the designation of those problems which the group decided could be dealt with more advantageously by committees, as well as the appointment of the committees to deal with them; (2) meetings of smaller groups, on the basis of registrations for course credit, to allow staff members to assist registrants in completing their registration and to provide an opportunity to consider the major needs and activities of the group interested in each particular course; (3) meetings of each group for which a staff member had accepted the responsibility of guidance; and (4) individual conferences of the participants with their advisers, as well as with the staff members responsible for other courses they were taking.

*Administrative Preparations.*—While these plans were being formulated, the physical setting of the workshop was being prepared. The city superintendent of schools had instructed members of his janitorial and engineering staff to have the building ready for the workshop; and all the necessary furniture, supplies, and equipment were

*The cafeteria, which serves children's lunches during the school year, was used for more varied purposes by the adults in the workshop.*

made available. The library books had been collected, but were left uncataloged so that the workshop participants might share in the experience of cataloging them.

### ADDITIONAL WORKSHOP RESOURCES

*The Mauck School.*—The workshop was housed in the Mauck School, a fine modern building which made an excellent setting for the workshop. On the first floor it provided an office for the director and the secretaries, and four classrooms. The kindergarten room was used for general meetings, as a library, and for discussion groups.

The other three classrooms were used for the three groups of the laboratory school, and for conferences and observation. The halls and alcoves provided for displays, discussion groups, conferences, publicity, and social conversation.

The classrooms on the second floor were used for meetings of interest groups and for such other purposes as special reading, display, conference, and discussion. Two rooms with adjoining office

*The gymnasium had wide utility for the workshop group. During the forenoons the children used it, and in the afternoons and evenings the adults found it a pleasant place for social gatherings and for folk dancing.*

were assigned to sociology, with two staff members; two rooms and two staff members were assigned to education; and one room and one staff member were assigned to English. An extra room was used for conferences as occasions demanded.

The basement included a cafeteria, a kitchen, a gymnasium, and several small classrooms. The cafeteria was equipped with tables, steel chairs, a work bench, and a piano, and was used for noon lunches, social hour, song sessions, ping pong, and crafts. The small classrooms were used for arts and crafts, woodwork, painting, and finishing. The gymnasium was used jointly by the city recreation program, the laboratory school children, and workshop participants and staff. It was the workshop auditorium for moving pictures, adult meetings, folk dancing, social gatherings, and children's plays.

The building was equipped with individual tables and chairs in sufficient quantity to supply the needs of the workshop group, and the rooms and the halls had ample bulletin board space and display cabinets. There were also a public address system and record playing equipment which were used occasionally for social gatherings.

*The tables and chairs with which the building was equipped provided opportunities for both individual and group work by the children.*

*The Library.*—The method of obtaining necessary bibliographies through the cooperation of the director and the various staff members, and the ordering of these books through the library facilities of the W. K. Kellogg Foundation has been described in Chapter 1.

Through these services the Hillsdale workshop had available about five hundred professional books for teachers selected to meet educational needs in social studies, child development, elementary education, library science, English, and recreation. In addition to these there were about two hundred books for children suitable for all ages from kindergarten to high school.

This library was augmented by the resources of the three local libraries, as previously indicated. Many parents and children contributed books, and the staff members brought their own books in considerable numbers.

*Supplies and Equipment.*—The Board of Education furnished two typewriters, some school supplies, duplicating machines, tools for use in arts and crafts, light, heat, and janitorial services, and met the expenses of telephone service.

*The display cabinets and bulletin board space were in constant use to stimulate children's interests, and to suggest ideas for study.*

University funds provided office supplies and postage, supplies used by the laboratory school group, arts and crafts supplies, part-time service of the cook in preparing noon lunches, travel allowances for staff members to facilitate their working with the teachers in their own schools and communities, part-time services rendered by a few staff members in other workshops in the area, and rental of films and other visual materials.

*Visual and Auditory Aids.*—Moving picture projectors were made available by Hillsdale College and by the W. K. Kellogg Foundation.

Projectors for showing slides and transparencies were obtained on loan from the Hillsdale County Health Department. Some slides and transparencies were supplied by the Hillsdale County Health Department. Three staff members assumed the responsibility for securing such materials.

Other visual aids were contributed by children, participants, community members, and staff members. Aside from the displays of books, encyclopedias, and teaching materials, they included such items as exhibits of toys, Indian paraphernalia, historical collections, flowers, science materials, testing materials, pictures of Guatemala, and child development pictures.

### ORGANIZATION OF THE WORKSHOP

*First Meetings.*—As a result of the planning sessions held by the staff, the general program for the first two days of the workshop was prearranged in some detail. When the participants arrived on Monday morning, June 23, they were met by staff members acting as "receptionists" and were directed to the kindergarten room, where a brief informational meeting was held. The plan for meeting with staff members for counseling and guidance was discussed briefly. The staff members were introduced and there were announcements concerning meeting places of the various groups, plans for noonday lunches, and for the afternoon meeting. The participants then met in groups with the various staff members, who arranged for a series of individual interviews during the rest of the forenoon, the afternoon, and the next forenoon.

The afternoon session served to acquaint the group with the planning which had preceded the workshop. The mayor of Hillsdale welcomed the members of the workshop and discussed briefly the facilities which the city officials, the junior and senior chambers of commerce, and other local organizations wished to make available for the use of the participants. The city superintendent of schools likewise presented the compliments of the Board of Education and expressed their desire to serve the group in whatever manner they could. Further discussion dealt with resources of the workshop, such as the staff and the library; with the philosophy of workshop procedure; with the personal values that might evolve from a workshop experience; and with the various techniques that might be employed to achieve the maximum professional progress. Volunteers were obtained to serve on a committee to study the needs for, and problems incident to, a program of noon lunches. This committee began its work immediately after the general meeting.

Late Tuesday morning there was a general meeting at which the participants began their formal registration, later completed under the guidance of individual staff members. The afternoon general meeting was concerned with problems affecting the whole group. The lunch committee made a progress report and announced arrangements for serving lunch the next day. Interest in other areas resulted in the election of committees to be responsible for (1) showing films and slides, (2) publicity, (3) music, (4) recreation, (5) general meetings and discussions, and (6) integration of program.

At this meeting the general time schedules for the workshop were planned. After a cursory examination of the registration cards, most of which were completed, a time was set for each interest group to plan its first meeting the next day. There were questions and further discussion dealing with the philosophy of workshops, and with some of the specific purposes that might be attained in this workshop. Such purposes included the solving of individual problems, the broadening of professional backgrounds, and the increasing of articulation and coordination between rural and village schools. Considerable interest developed in current educational problems and in teachers' obligation to maintain personal idealism and to improve professional services.

A period late Tuesday afternoon was set aside for the completion of registrations and of the initial conferences, the beginning of individual library work, and attention to the many details of personal and group adjustment. On Wednesday morning the participants met in their respective major interest groups.

*Major Interest Groups.*—The major interest groups were concerned with library, English, sociology, social studies curriculum, and child development. Some participants had major interests in two of these groups; but most of them concentrated on one, giving minor attention to the other. Various members of each group formed committees for the study of special interests within these general fields. Participants also served as active members of the entire workshop group, or as committee members serving the entire group. Some individuals sought solutions for their problems outside the field of their major interest, but in most cases the interest group held the greatest share of the individual's attention.

*Program of Meetings.*—Because of this organization of interest groups it became evident that the operation of the workshop would revolve around them rather than around the group as a whole. As a result the time schedule that was evolved made primary allowance for the activities of these groups and secondary allowance for other meetings. Each major interest group selected and reserved a time when the majority of its members could work on their similar interests. The staff members who held the major responsibility for the guidance of the respective groups attempted to keep these specified times free for work with the groups. There was no high degree of rigidity about engaging in the activities which held the interest of most of the group, but individuals knew when certain resources and activities would be available.

*Resources and Techniques.*—The major resources available often consisted of various staff members, local people, or workshop participants. At other times no special personnel resources were needed and group members worked on individual problems, in committees, or in informal groups.

The information-gaining techniques which were most commonly used included lectures, informal discussions, panel and roundtable discussions, questions and answers, questionnaires, assigned or voluntary reading, personal interviews, conferences with staff members and other participants, committee planning, compilation of bibliographies and lists of source materials, preparation of oral and written reports, planned observation trips, map study, demonstrations of procedures and materials, observation and critical analysis of visual education materials, and observation in laboratory school situations. Various combinations of these techniques were used, and there was free interchange of experiences among the various groups.

*Conferences with Staff Members.*—Most of the initial conferences between workshop participants and the staff members were held Monday afternoon and Tuesday morning. After these first two days each staff member was available for conferences requested by any workshop participant. Forms were drafted listing half-hour intervals for each staff member, and a participant had only to sign his name opposite the time at which he wished a conference to have that time reserved for him.

*Progress in Group Discussion.*—At the first discussion meeting, participants were quite reserved. The discussion leader purposely delayed going to the meeting, and busied himself where he could listen to the tone and volume of conversation in the group. After a time a few could be heard talking, but it was nearly twenty minutes before a "normal" volume and tone of conversation arose. A few minutes later the discussion leader quietly entered the room and sat at one of the tables. Almost immediately there was complete silence, and everyone waited "for the meeting to begin." During the meeting most of the contributions came from the staff members, and the participants asked only a few questions. The Tuesday morning meeting showed considerable progress over that of the preceding day, with discussion less strained but not yet spontaneous. One report said: "Discussion is by no means easy. The attitude of these people is still a little stiff, but there is beginning to be more discussion, some of it 'sotto voce' in the back rows. Not much laughter yet. The demeanor was pretty serious until toward the very end." The questions were more numerous and varied. Particular interest was displayed concerning the laboratory school and its use.

This progress continued more or less steadily throughout the workshop, but much greater freedom of expression was developed in the smaller group meetings than in the larger general meetings.

### ACTIVITIES OF THE LIBRARY SCIENCE GROUP

*General Activities.*—The library science group held an interest for forty-six of the fifty members of the workshop. Most of them classified library science as a minor interest, but eight adopted it as a major interest. The entire group worked on such problems as organizing the workshop library, securing additional books from local library sources, investigating county library services with especial emphasis on rural bookmobile service, organizing books and library records for village and rural schools, compiling a list of book resources for teachers in this area, demonstrating bookmending, compiling bibliographies, and studying such matters as children's use of comics and enjoyment of poetry.

A committee from the entire group developed a booklet of suggestions for organizing village and rural libraries. Organization and planning visits were made in small groups to three high school libraries, two village elementary school libraries, and three rural school libraries in the communities nearby.

*Activities of Smaller Groups.*—The members of the library science group formed three smaller groups to be more closely concerned with the specific interests and needs of the individual participants.

1. A group of twenty-five was interested in the selection of books for the elementary school. This group gave its major attention to the principles of book selection, a study of the development of reading interests in children, and books for children of different ages and interests. They also participated in the community recreation program by assuming responsibility for a story hour at the Mitchell Library each week day morning for a period of four weeks. Each member of the group had ample opportunity for observation,

*Organizing the workshop library provided practical experience for the group interested in library science. They not only learned library techniques which they later used in their own schools, but they also became thoroughly acquainted with the library resources of the workshop.*

participation, leadership, and organizing materials to arouse children's interest.

2. A group of eleven was interested in the selection of books for high school libraries. This group worked on such problems as an understanding of adolescent needs and interests with special emphasis on the interests of nonreaders; the selection of special types of books such as social studies materials, personality development materials, career books, and problem novels; the use and care of magazines;

methods of stimulating reading by use of informal reports; and free reading.

3. A group of ten was interested in the organization of high school libraries. This group devised plans for arrangements of their library rooms, studied budgets and sources of revenue, developed library schedules, planned for the use of student assistants, worked on cataloging and classifying books in an actual library reorganization situation, and developed a twelve-page manual of library practice. This manual discussed the purposes of the library, qualifications and activities of student assistants, preparation of books for shelves, classification plans, shelving, library records, rules for filing, general care of the library room, children's use of the library, and a bibliography.

*Special Activities of Individual Participants.*—The following excerpts from the records of six class members indicate typical activities of individuals who were working on their own problems.

She has developed definite plans for putting her school library into working condition. Excellent organization.

P has worked all summer with a group of high school students getting the library organized. She has put each technique into immediate operation. She has found that her week's schedule will not allow any time for library work. It will all have to be done outside of school hours.

W has made a comprehensive list of books, arranged by periods, to be used in his United States history course.

M spent last weekend and two days this week in C examining the library resources in the high school and elementary schools. She has completed plans for the organization of a library committee with representatives of the high school teachers, the elementary teachers, and the village librarian.

E has made good progress in developing a study hall-library in J. Her plans include re-equipping the study hall with library furniture, shelving the room, and establishing a practical outline of library practices.

G is opening her rural school one afternoon a week this summer so that the children and parents can use the books. She made a farm-to-farm visit to tell the people about it.

*Selecting Encyclopedias.*—Another project of the library interest group developed when one rural teacher presented the problem of helping her school board decide whether to purchase a certain encyclopedia. The library group used local resources and collected ten different sets of encyclopedias designed for school use. These sets were put on display for inspection and study. American Library Association criteria for encyclopedia materials were studied. Local resource people were brought in to discuss their use of encyclopedias in schools and homes; the laboratory school children used the various sets and commented on them; representatives of publishing houses contributed their viewpoints; the workshop participants discussed the experiences and the needs of the children in their respective schools; and each teacher was left free to study the needs of her own group and to decide which materials would be most helpful to her school. It was a stimulating experience, and the school board decided not to buy the set first considered.

## ACTIVITIES OF THE SOCIOLOGY GROUP

*Interests of the Group.*—The group of twenty-three people who worked with the staff members in sociology were interested chiefly in gaining a better understanding of (1) the structural organization of their communities, (2) the problems which faced the community members both individually and collectively, and (3) the resources of the community which might be used in connection with the school work of children.

These three general topics were related to the home and school situation of the individual participants. Those from rural areas worked particularly on activities relating to their localities, as did those from villages. One participant, from the South, devoted part of her time to the study of "The Role of Negro Culture in America." In all of these cases, however, the findings of the individual members were made available to the entire group so that all could attain better understandings of the problems.

*Knowing the Community.*—The participants concerned mostly with rural communities developed much interest and gained a fund of knowledge by making maps of their individual school districts. In preparation for work on these maps showing the sociological and economic organization of their communities, the participants consulted the county school commissioner to secure basic information on the geographic limits of the school district, the district's valuation, its school tax rate, and the school census. They interviewed the local township officials to secure other statistical information on the school revenues.

In analyzing the economic conditions of the district they studied detailed maps to determine the exact holdings of each land owner. They then made a careful canvass of the district to secure information concerning the number of homes wired for electricity, the number of telephones and automobiles, the types of farming being practiced on each farm, other kinds of occupations in which the people living in the district were engaged, the number of home owners and tenants, and the kinds of businesses located in the community. In studying the social structure of the community they determined the number of families attending the various churches and the number belonging to the various adult clubs as well as to 4H Clubs. They also investigated the educational progress of young people beyond the

*Making maps of individual school districts was an effective means of organizing facts concerning them. Participants gained first-hand knowledge of sociological and economic trends in their communities. On the basis of this information they planned curricular materials for the children.*

district school. On the basis of all this information the teachers were able to plan for a closer integration of the school and community programs.

The group that was more largely interested in the urban communities made an intensive study of Hillsdale. Their understanding of the operation of city and county government was greatly increased by their interviews with the various officials of the city and the county. Interviews with local merchants contributed to their knowledge of business conditions and the problems of business men.

A group of three teachers from one of the nearby villages made a detailed study of the social and economic organization of their village. They report their work as follows:

> We have planned with our superintendent of schools in terms of the needs of the community and we are making changes in the course of study to place more emphasis on certain phases of health and nutrition education. We have visited the homes of many of the children in the school. Most mothers were very grateful for our visits and many have promised to participate in our school programs in various ways this fall. It has certainly been interesting, and makes us anxious to try out some of the things we have planned.

*Other Community Problems.*—Two other local problems came to the attention of the sociology group. The first was the problem of eliminating an area of poor housing in Hillsdale. The group, of course, could participate little in the program that was being carried on; but through interviews and discussions they were able to understand how the city government, the health department, the county road commission, a service club, and private individuals were cooperating in an area that needed improvement.

The other local problem was that of adjustment between management and labor. Various factories in Hillsdale were engaged in defense and war industries. Efforts to organize unions in the area had been particularly strong during the winter and spring of 1941. A number of strikes were still unsettled. Again, there was nothing direct that the workshop participants could do, but they were able to obtain the viewpoints of both sides by interviews with the representatives of both labor and the management.

*Using Other Resources.*—To supplement the studies already mentioned, the sociology group had an excellent collection of library materials made available from the regular workshop collection, from the Hillsdale College library, and from government pamphlet materials. The group also cooperated with the social studies group in securing and showing a variety of motion pictures. The films dealing with Latin American relations included "The Continent of South America," "Good Neighbors," and "Uncle Sam, the Good Neighbor." Those dealing with national problems included such films as "The River," "Conservation and Natural Resources," "The City," and "The Plow That Broke the Plains. Those dealing with individual guidance included "Finding Your Life Work," and "Salt of the Earth."

## ACTIVITIES OF THE ENGLISH GROUP

*Special Interests in English.*—While the English group numbered only seven, it presented an inviting array of individual problems. Two participants were primarily interested in improving their expression in written English. They planned their work so that they could write profusely on a variety of subjects. They also devoted considerable time to the fundamentals of English composition and rhetoric.

Another member was interested in improving her critical judgment. To implement the expression of her critical analysis she wrote a number of papers discussing character and personality types, and made many critical appraisals of children's books.

The other four members of the group wished to produce literary compositions of their own. All of them gave evidence of the social-studies viewpoint by dealing with materials relating to personal or community history. One of them, whose teaching experience ranged from frontier conditions in the West to modern schools in large cities, began compiling her experiences to make a volume called *The Autobiography of a Country School Teacher*. Another, whose grandfather had been one of the earliest settlers in Hillsdale County, used the experiences of her childhood as background material for *A History of Hillsdale County—Tales Told by a Pioneer Grandfather.*" A third began a *Simplified History of Branch County*. Her problem was that of reconstructing the available resource material so that it would be suitable as social studies material for her fifth-grade group. And finally, a member of the group was interested in collecting and editing the poems written by her aunt, who had been a contemporary of Will Carleton. These poems were numerous and appeared to have considerable literary value, but they had never been collected.

In addition to these specific interests, every member of the group had more general interests in the use of English in teaching.

*Expressional Developments.*—The progress made on the individual literary compositions varied. The participant who was writing the *Simplified History of Branch County* brought much resource material to the workshop with her. She was able to make rapid progress and by the close of the workshop was able to report, "I expect to have my manuscript of about twelve thousand words completed and typed for use this fall. I expect to place a copy in the Branch County library so that other teachers may use it." Others necessarily progressed more slowly, but each one completed the general plan for her work, and at least a few units that would establish the pattern for completing the task.

The group also worked on improving their skills in some of the more formal activities of the English classroom. Time was spent as needed on such skills as note-taking, developing annotated bibliographies, making outlines, footnotes, paragraph writing, techniques for enlarging vocabularies, figures of speech, oral reading of poetry, choral speaking, and leading discussion groups.

*Workshop Publicity.*—Another interesting part of the program of the group was the reporting of workshop activities to home town papers. About ten of the villages from which workshop participants came had weekly newspapers. The English group had representatives from five different villages, and they requested that they have the opportunity of interviewing the local editors and of submitting materials on workshop activities. The editor of one of the nearby village newspapers conferred with the group on the types of information which would be most interesting to readers, styles of writing, and general length of articles. After the members of the English group had interviewed their local editors and had found them most cooperative, they reported their progress to a general meeting of participants. Teachers from other villages volunteered to interview the editors of their home town papers. Releases of articles were then made each week to those editors who were interested in publishing them.

*Uses of Other Resources.*—The English group planned a program of "guest speakers" to help them with special problems. They invited Miss Livsey to help them with library resource materials. Each of the three laboratory-school teachers was asked to discuss the use of English at the school level of the girls and boys with whom he was working. The workshop director gave help in the understanding of the various psychological approaches to children's interests.

The staff member in charge of arts and crafts was asked to discuss the relationship of English to special areas of school work. An outgrowth of his discussion was recorded in one of the diaries as follows:

When the crafts teacher talked with us, he had occasion to print a poem on the blackboard. A number of us admired the printing and expressed a desire to learn manuscript writing. We found a member of the group who volunteered to teach us, and we have made arrangements to work with her in learning this art.

*Summation Activities.*—In addition to presenting a fine exhibit of writing, the English group closed their work by giving a farewell breakfast to the staff member responsible for the group. They planned the affair as a surprise and invited the crafts teacher and the workshop director as special guests. In addition to the breakfast they staged a "Rhetorical Minstrel Show" with original poems, prose, and choral readings. The entire affair bespoke their enthusiasm and the stimulation which their English expression, both oral and written, had received in the workshop.

### ACTIVITIES OF THE CURRICULUM GROUP

The curriculum group consisted of those workshop participants who elected as their major interests the topics, Current Problems in the Elementary School, Current Problems in the Secondary School, and the Social Studies Curriculum. Because of the similarity in the general types of their interests, and the interrelations of their work, their activities are summarized together.

*Elementary School Subject-Matter Interests.*—The variety of interests and problems with which the elementary school curriculum group began their work is evidenced by the following list compiled at the first meeting of the group.

1. What are some of the more effective methods of teaching reading?
2. What are the criteria for reading readiness?
3. What is the function of the school in helping the parent improve his guidance of children?
4. Should textbooks be owned by the school?
5. What is the effect of readers which show ideal home conditions on children from broken homes?
6. What can we use to supplement the assigned textbooks?
7. How can we arrange rural schoolrooms more effectively?

The group decided to begin with reading, and individual members volunteered to accept the following responsibilities:

1. To compile lists of criteria for reading readiness
2. To secure groups of materials which might stimulate readiness for reading
3. To request the laboratory teacher in charge of the primary group to assist us by discussing reading readiness tests
4. To secure a display of the materials supplementing the basal reading text used in the rural schools
5. To secure and demonstrate special materials used with this set of readers in her school system

6. To bring in a varied display of reading materials used in her school
7. To prepare a bibliography of available materials on recent trends in the teaching of reading

The collections of materials were made available within the next few days and the group proceeded with their study of reading problems. Arrangements were made to observe reading situations in the various laboratory school units, and some of the teachers participated in the programs of helping the boys and girls to improve their reading skills. Members of the group later worked with colleagues in the secondary school curriculum group in further consideration of reading problems. After similar analyses had been made in spelling and science, the group turned to broader curriculum topics: planning units of study, modifying the school program to fit the needs of individual children, and developing programs that would fit the needs and use the resources of their respective school communities. They invited the county school commissioner to meet with them to help them interpret his list of textbooks and study outlines for the rural schools of the county, and he expressed his philosophy with regard to the uses of various types of instructional material.

*Visits to the Individual Schools.*—About half of the group wished to receive help in planning for the utilization of the resources within their own schools. Each village or rural teacher who desired such help listed the items which gave her the most concern, together with tentative ideas for appropriate procedure. She made an age-grade list of the boys and girls who would be in her school or room during the next year, and invited a committee from the workshop to visit her school to help her in planning improvements. This committee usually consisted of the teacher, one or more staff members, and two or three other workshop participants who could make valuable suggestions. In some instances two or three teachers planned a joint tour of their schools, combining their committees to form a larger resource group.

Typical of the contributions of these committees were suggestions for rearranging school furniture, adding materials for the use of beginners in school, improving library conditions and providing more library materials, improving the heating, lighting, and decoration, making better use of playground space, adding recreational equipment for younger children, using more community resources, and planning a daily program in terms of hitherto neglected needs.

*Social Studies Interests.*—The social studies interest group sought to develop materials that could be used at the elementary school level, and to devise an improved organization of social study experiences and materials at the junior and senior high school levels.

The member who chose to work on the elementary school social studies program brought together materials from various courses of study and compiled them by grade levels. The interest in their work spread beyond their immediate group, and led to an open meeting at which they presented their materials to the entire workshop group. The discussion at this meeting resulted in the acceptance of four bases for action:

1. There must be a statement of objectives or ideals toward which the work is directed.

2. There should be a recognition of requirements placed by state or local courses of study.

3. Within the limits determined by these first two principles it should be possible to develop a number of centers of interests at each elementary grade level.

4. Many social studies concepts can readily be developed in informal life situations.

A committee later accepted responsibility for developing a series of suggestions relating to social studies objectives and experiences which might be of interest and help to children at the various age and grade levels.

The group interested in the junior and senior high school levels was smaller, and worked largely on an individual basis. They spent considerable time in working with the junior high school boys and girls in the laboratory school who were learning about the public utilities and other civic enterprises of Hillsdale. Some of the participants made major revisions in the plans for their high school social studies program.

*A Study in Guidance.*—One member of the guidance group arranged with his superintendent to gather data as a basis for modification of the guidance program followed in their junior and senior high school groups. He developed a questionnaire and an interview blank which he used to secure information concerning more than two hundred young people who had been graduated from this high school during the preceding five years. He attempted to secure from these young people candid estimations of the value of the various phases of their high school experience. He then made an occupational survey of Hillsdale. By relating this information to the information obtained in his interviews with the high school graduates, he hopes to be able to give more adequate guidance to high school students.

*Secondary School Curriculum Interests.*—Among the problems presented by the group concerned with the secondary school curriculum were planning a program of remedial reading and library work for a junior high school group, preparing a better program for teaching American History, and planning for the enrichment of the curriculum of a small high school. Most of these undertakings were individual, but some, like the problem of remedial reading, attracted the interest of other participants. They were studied on a committee basis, with adjustments being made to fit individual needs.

*Progress on an Individual Problem.*—Illustrative of individual progress is the workshop program developed by a participant who made plans for curriculum enrichment in a small high school. The participant was about to begin his first year as superintendent of a small school system. One of the teachers from his high school staff, also enrolled in the workshop, helped to develop certain phases of the program. The superintendent made plans for experiences during the summer that would help with his problems, and the list of these experiences at the end of the workshop period contained the following items:

1. Considerable reading to gain familiarity with the better current school practices
2. Conferences with experienced superintendents to give a practical viewpoint on certain problems
3. Conferences to learn about the help that is available from such county services such as the health department
4. The operation of a summer recreational program in the community to provide for the needs of the children and to stimulate community interest in the school
5. Visits to the curriculum laboratory and the state Department of Public Instruction at Lansing to determine what aids were available there
6. Regular meetings of the school board, as well as conferences with its individual members, to understand their problems and to guide their thinking about education
7. Participation in group activities dealing with the secondary school curriculum and with relationships between the school and community.
8. If possible, some experience in the leadership of groups in the workshop, so that staff members could analyze the participant's leadership techniques and make suggestions for their improvement.
9. The drafting of a list of possible changes to be made in the school and its program
10. Other experiences to be planned in terms of specific needs that might arise

This superintendent was enthusiastic about his program and worked hard at every part of it. His trip to Lansing was particularly helpful, and the success of the summer recreational program was gratifying to him. He saw little value in keeping a daily diary of his activities and progress, but discussed them freely and often with the staff members. By the last week of the workshop period he and his adviser were able to compile the following list of suggestions for the improvement of his school and its program during the next few years.

### A. *Buildings and Grounds*

1. Continue urging the board of education to improve the conditions of sanitation (with help from the health department).

2. Continue working for better lighting and the redecoration of some rooms each year.

3. Encourage some group of older pupils to discuss and initiate an inexpensive plan for landscaping the school grounds and improving play facilities (with help from the nearby state college).

4. Establish a school garden—for both flowers and vegetables—in the near future, for values especially in relation to science teaching, agriculture, home economics, and the hot lunch program.

### B. *Instruction*

1. Entertain the senior class before school opens, explain the general school situation to them, and invite them to take the lead in helping the faculty and the community to plan and conduct a successful school year.

2. Investigate the possibility of securing practice teachers from Hillsdale College in music, art, home economics, and athletics (if their services could be secured on the usual practice-teaching basis, it might be possible to pay them a small amount for part-time assistance during the other semester).

3. Turn the north basement room into a general shop (perhaps boys could be interested in doing this) and develop a program of arts and crafts under the leadership of the principal.

4. Seek to direct the attention of the school and the community to agriculture and home economics, without providing specific courses of instruction in these fields by (*a*) emphasis in American history, English, and science classes; (*b*) having evening lectures in the school by the county agent, qualified local farmers, home bureau leaders, teachers from Hillsdale College in economics; and (*c*) special on graduation night.

### C. *General Administration*

1. Make a study of recent graduates and drop-outs to discover especially the kinds of occupations now pursued and the amount of later dispersal from the community now served by the school.

2. Make a map of the location and age of children who might be drawn into the school in case of later consolidation.

3. Make more friendly contact with the teachers and pupils in outlying districts. Invite a group in for an afternoon film showing. Take the school band out for short programs in the district schools.

4. Study the possibility of replacing the individual purchase plan of textbooks with a rental program.

5. Keep people in the community informed of developments in the school. Ask individuals and groups for advice and draw them into school projects. Have frequent meetings and film showings in the school. Have "open house" occasionally for inspection of the grounds, the shop, and displays or demonstrations of pupil work.

6. Make use of *General School Laws, Structure and Administration of Education, Schools in Small Communities.*

## ACTIVITIES OF THE CHILD DEVELOPMENT GROUP

The small group of participants interested in child development worked primarily on an individual basis. In each case they concentrated on the analysis of the problems of specific children.

*Background for Understanding the Child.*—To gain help in matters concerned with understanding the child, members of the group reviewed books on child psychology and child development, sought new data in recent periodical literature, and learned about the organismic theory of the whole child. They considered means of analyzing the specific problems or maladjustments of children, techniques of case study of environmental influences, devices for measuring child progress, and remedial programs of action.

This group made unusually good use of workshop resources, choosing advantageous times for observation, conferences with laboratory school teachers, and planning with their staff advisers. While each of them had selected child development as a minor interest, their studies and activities were closely related to the other workshop problems.

*Investigation of Problems.*—Procedure followed in studying problems of children may be illustrated by reference to the reports of members of the group. A member studying the case of a nine-year-old boy indicated that:

1. Her reading notes included quotations and interpretations from ten sources dealing with the growth and development of the child, the relationships of the child within the home, the concept of the organism as a whole, and special problems dealing with reading and other classroom subjects.

2. She made an analysis of this child in terms of his home conditions, his left-handedness associated with reading retardation, his social acceptance by the school group and needed adjustments, his habits of withdrawal characterized by

thumb-sucking and day-dreaming, his status within the community (which involved problems of possible community resentment against the position of his entire family) and his condition of health.

3. She made a subjective analysis of certain of his attitudes, traits, and work habits, together with a statement of problems she thinks he will face as he matures.

4. She prepared a report of a number of conferences held with various staff members on her problem.

She was particularly gratified with the contributions made by the laboratory school teachers to the analysis of the problem. She expected to work out a program for use during the next year, including:

1. The adjustment of the boy's daily program to the indicated need for more rest.

2. Provisions for observing and remedying withdrawal tendencies indicated by thumb-sucking and day-dreaming.

3. Concrete plans for helping the boy become a more stable member of the school group.

4. A systematic objective analysis of the child's program from data collected through the use of various tests and of anecdotal behavior records.

5. A program of work, involving the home and family as well as with the community, to increase the security of the boy in his environmental relationships outside of school.

This study, incidentally, bore a direct relationship to the teacher's own problem of personality adjustment. She had difficulty in analyzing some of her own tensions, and her adviser used indirect approaches to develop an appreciation of the similarity between the problems of this boy and those of the teacher's own child. In a demonstration of the Stanford-Binet intelligence test, this teacher's daughter served as the subject. It was apparent that the desire to understand the needs of the boy was due partly to her anxiety over her own child. By developing an understanding of desirable patterns for working on the problems of the boy, she gained knowledge that was able to apply to her own problems. Her reports show little recognition of this transfer, but her oral comments from time to time gave her adviser cues as to methods by which the two phases of her problem could be coordinated. In the final conference she said, "It has been a good summer. I feel that I can go back and help my school a great deal. And, you know, I feel better about my daughter. I didn't realize it, but I have been using some of the things I had planned for school in my work with her, and I find that they are helping her."

Another member of the group worked with a child in the laboratory school whose background, characteristics, and problems were almost identical with those of a maladjusted child in her school. She made an intensive study of the available records·on the child in the laboratory school, arranged for an interview with his parents, observed the child at work in his school program, held a series of conferences with his teacher, and entered into a number of his activities in school and out. She made two weekend trips to her own school locality to visit the boy in whom she was primarily interested, and his family, to consider the applicability of her workshop program of study to her school situation. She also studied various testing and measurement devices so that she would be able to use them with her school group.

### ACTIVITIES IN THE LABORATORY SCHOOL

*Organization.*—The laboratory school group was divided into three sections on the basis of age and interest groupings. The lower age group consisted of children who would normally have been in the first three grades, the intermediate group those in the next three, and the junior high school group the boys and girls who would have been in grades seven to nine. A few children, however, were placed in the next older or younger group on the basis of social age or strong interests.

The program conformed approximately to the time schedule followed in the regular school year: the group met at 8:30, used the period from 10:00 to 10:30 for playground activities, and were dismissed at 11:30. On a few occasions the group stayed until afternoon or reconvened in the afternoon for special interest activities. The laboratory school was in session from June 26 to August 1.

Attention has already been called to the fact that the program was so planned that boys and girls could participate in it even though they had originally planned other summer educational experiences. The application blanks sent to parents provided space for listing the summer plans for the child, his special interests, topics his parents wished to discuss with the laboratory school teachers at the parent interviews, and specific gains his parents would like to have him make during the summer. There was no charge for children enrolled in the laboratory school. Some children chose to bring their own crayons, pencils, puzzles, books, and the like, but it was recommended by the planning committee that no fee be charged or contributions exacted for such items in any case, because of the low economic status of many of the families involved.

*Parent Interviews.*—In staff planning for the operation of the laboratory school, provisions were made for an interview with the parent or parents of each child seeking enrollment. In these interviews care was taken to have parents understand that the summer school was not a "remedial" project, but that it should be a broadly planned program which would serve the child's best interests during the summer months. Emphasis was placed on a general understanding of the child's needs and a program planned to meet those needs rather than on advantages in participation in one phase of the list of activities. Notifications to the parents were accompanied by appointments for interviews, thus avoiding impatience and loss of time. The topics discussed in the parent interviews were intended to help the teacher decide what services the laboratory school might render to the child and his parents. Some of the subjects discussed in these interviews were:

1. The kind of help or training the parent desired the child to get in the summer school
2. Particular school problems the child had had
3. Special problems the child had had in the home
4. The condition of the child's health
5. The child's special hobbies, interests, and talents

The wide range of the parents' interests for their children is illustrated by the list compiled for children in the early elementary group. It was hoped that they would receive help in:

1. Developing self-dependence
2. Adjusting to other children
3. Learning to plan
4. Developing perseverance
5. Acquiring habits of orderliness
6. Using opportunities for free reading
7. Acquiring habits of concentration and dependability in following directions.
8. Learning to appreciate money values
9. Overcoming tendencies to take things that belong to other people
10. Learning to relax and to overcome nervous tension
11. Learning to "stand on their own feet"
12. Finding opportunities to express themselves in arts and crafts
13. Writing, with stress on the formation of letters
14. Overcoming neurotic tendencies
15. Ascertaining the cause for reading difficulties

This list of desired helps expressed by the parents of children in one group gave promise of opportunities for parent education, in addition to the other outcomes of the laboratory school program.

*Early-Elementary School Group.*—Twenty-two children partici- pated in the early-elementary school group at the beginning of the session. The room had been set up with a number of interest centers, and the children were allowed to engage themselves in whatever

*Attractive displays of books drew the attention of both children and teachers.
A child's landscape made an interesting background, and flowers
provided still another item of appeal.*

appealed to them. The following three quotations from the teacher's diary indicate the approach:

Each child (the first day) was given an opportunity to introduce himself and tell what he hoped to do in summer school. Some of the things enumerated were making boats and airplanes, painting pictures, putting on a play, reading stories, playing games on the playground, working with clay, coloring pictures and telling about places they had seen. Mention was made of sharing the build- ing with teachers who were also going to school. The children were given an op- portunity to explore materials in the room, following which they came together again to ask questions and discuss what they had seen. Several were interested in having a story read to them. They agreed on "Wee Gillis" by Leaf and Lawson. We discussed Scotch costumes and bagpipes. The children then chose individual activities such as painting, drawing, and looking at books. From 10:00 to 10:30 all were on the playground. They partook in shuffle board, swings, catch, and dodge ball. At 10:30 twelve children reported back to the room. Several painted and drew pictures. One child copied our plans from the blackboard. Another child looked through books and took notes on *The Flannigans' Pigs' Soup,* in preparation for a play. The children came together for the last few minutes to enumerate things they would do on Friday. They were dismissed at 11:30.

This morning I introduced new articles into the room. The introduction was not formal. I merely placed the things on various desks and tables. These included a printing set, a box of wooden letters, a tom-tom, a book entitled *Willingly to School* which is intended for teachers but is being enjoyed by these children, and several new pictures. My principal purposes for introducing these new materials are: (1) To see how children react to new articles; (2) To see what uses they make of them; (3) To stimulate new interests.

Shortly before 9:00 a girl from the later elementary group came in and asked if I could tell her anything about Indians. I took her over to the Indian exhibit in our showcase, took the various objects out one at a time, and explained how they were made and how they were used. Without any sign from me all of the children drifted over to the showcase and stood about in a group while I told stories of the Indians of the Southwest.

Other interests developed when children returned from camp and told of things that had occurred there. The various workshop resources, such as the arts and crafts department, were used to develop these interests for all the children of the group. Another major center of interest developed out of the exhibit of flowers made by a group of workshop members. The record of the group says,

At the conclusion of the story I told them that I had seen an exhibit of flowers down near the library. I also told them that the flowers had been brought in by members of the workshop and of the garden club. The group went down the hall to view the exhibit. Mrs. B. was there and helped them to identify a number of the flowers. We returned to the room and came together in a circle to see how many names of flowers we could recall. These names were limited to the flowers we had seen in the exhibit. I also showed the children a book of flowers that we had in our room, and they were interested in looking at the pictures and identifying the various kinds.

The children gave a great deal of attention to Indians and exhibits of their paraphernalia, but probably the most persistent interest developed around the story of "Jack and the Bean Stalk." On June 27 one of the boys brought a bean stalk and the story, suggesting that it might be used for a play. This interest continued with varying intensities until it culminated, July 21, in a play for which the children wrote the script and designed the stage setting and the costumes.  One youngster then decided to write a story about what happened to Jack after he chopped down the bean stalk.

In summarizing the progress made by this group of children their teacher made the following outline:

*Independence in planning activities.*  Many of the children were quite inexperienced in planning their own activities when they first came into the laboratory school.  By the end of the fifth week, every child in the group was capable of planning his time with little or no help from the teacher.

*Ability to use a variety of tools and media.*  The boys were especially interested in learning to use woodworking tools such as saws, hammers, planes, files, etc. Apparently most of them had never had instruction in handling tools of this kind and it was a completely new experience for them.  Few of the children had used water colors before and, though most of them had worked with tempera paint and crayons, most of their art work had been done as part of a specific project, not purely as a means of artistic expression and experience.

*Ability to take part in a group discussion either by contributing interesting statements or by listening attentively.*  When we first began our group discussion few of the children participated.  Gradually more and more of them were able to contribute.  Other problems were those of taking turns in talking and of preventing the monopolization of discussions by a few people.  By the end of the fifth week, marked improvement was noted in all phases of discussion techniques.

*Sharing items of interest with others.*  The first items to be shared were those brought by the teacher.  The children did not really begin to make their contributions until the fourth and fifth weeks.  Some of them were hesitant about bringing things and a little boy who brought a turtle seemed especially surprised that I should be interested.  Eventually we reached the point where we had a special sharing day.  Not only did the children agree to share objects of interest but also activities such as dancing, playing a harmonica, and telling a story. During the course of the session the following items were brought in by children for the enjoyment of others: a set of Indian books, Indian rugs, post cards, several volumes of "The Book House," miscellaneous library books, jigsaw puzzles, toy boats, paints, crayons, lantern slides, live turtle, candy, souvenirs, flowers, maps, etc.

*Orderliness, as in cleaning up after painting and putting the room in order at the close of the daily session.*  Special consideration had been given to the set-up of the room before the children arrived.  Their attention was called to this fact and their help solicited in maintaining high standards of orderliness. The majority of the children responded well to suggestions and it was never difficult to keep the room in order.

*The Later-Elementary School Group.*—The general organization and the plan of the later-elementary school group was similar to that of the early-elementary school group.  The average enrollment was about fifteen although at times there were as many as twenty-two boys and girls in attendance.  During the first two days the children discussed things they would be interested in studying.  The list under consideration included (1) living together in the modern world, (2) the living and the building of America, (3) the present war situation, (4) the future of America, and (5) transportation. After the discussion they decided on the general theme "The Living and the Building of America." Individual interests expressed as possible parts of the study of the central theme were: homes and buildings, transportation, clothing, stores, geography, recreation, history, people, animals, money, resources, health, and inventions. Naturally it was not

*The children learned to leave their work materials ready for the next person's use. Cleaning up and putting things in order were habitual ways of helping others.*

possible to make a thorough study of all these topics, but the subgroups followed various leads. One of the major interests of a group of boys developed around a farm unit. A group of girls worked on a model home unit. Another group studied Indians and developed an Indian pueblo unit. A group of boys worked on an airplane project. There were other, less prominent, short-lived activities.

Toward the end of the workshop period a play, "The Sleepy King," was adapted from a book and staged. In planning for this group it was decided to stress certain phases of record keeping with the workshop participants.  A cumulative folder, kept by the teacher, contained height and weight records, parent interview records, records of reading, results from Stanford Achievement Tests, cards listing the children's major interests, anecdotal records by the teacher, and samples of the child's work.  In addition, each child kept his own cumulative folder containing any materials he wished to keep, the teacher kept a daily diary of the activities of the group, some of the children kept individual daily diaries, and one child recorded a class diary for the group.

*The arrangement of these buildings and the plan for the farm layout were part of the work done by boys interested in the farm unit.  Two girls helped them by planning and painting the background mural.*

This group was also stimulated to an interest in their general school program, so that they welcomed taking tests to determine the areas in which they needed special help.  The laboratory-school teacher of the early-elementary group established rapport with the children and administered the tests.  After the tests were scored, each child was able to discuss his performance with the teacher.  The results were studied, also, by the group as a whole, to see what group activities might be most helpful.

The group was keenly interested in handwork, in the arts and crafts program, and spent much of their time in that work. They were also the most consistent and active group in the playground program.

*The Junior High School Group.*—The smallest of the three groups, with an average enrollment of about twelve, was the junior high school group. In the parent interviews for this group, instead of having the parents come to the school, the laboratory-school teacher visited each home and thus obtained a better understanding of the needs of the children than he could have gotten from interviews at school. This variation of procedure enabled the workshop participants to familiarize themselves with still another technique that could be used in studying the problems of children.

The major interests of the junior high school group related to social studies. In deciding what they wished to do, at the end of the second day of school, they listed the following places they wished to visit: tool and die factory, water works, bottling company, baking company, Spicer steel plant, Richard Brothers steel plant, and Stock's flour mill. In addition, they listed as a topic for study, ways of living and working; and made an analysis of the ways in which water can be helpful and the ways in which it can be harmful.

They developed good techniques of analysis and became particularly adept in planning for the things they wished to investigate when they made trips to the various industries and civic enterprises. Their questions showed a penetrating interest in mechanics. Another phase of their planning included ways in which they could acquaint other people with the things they discovered; for example, in planning the trip to the city water works they decided to take pictures, write a short story or report, make cut-away diagrams to show processes, make charts, and make pictures of things that interested them. The change in their thinking and in their appraisal of the importance of things is illustrated by this notation in the group diary.

In all of this discussion there seemed to be a growing sense of a community interest and a recognition of values in terms of importance to groups rather than to just individuals. For instance, the bottling works, which had been on the list of proposed trips since the first day, was disposed of because it was of minor importance to the community as a whole and not representative of something belonging to the whole community. There was considerable discussion of the relative importance of the Richard Brothers plant and Stock's mill. This was not in terms of importance to individuals but in terms of importance to the community. It was pointed out by several children that these two institutions were important not only to their own community but to the country as a whole. At the end of the discussion a vote was taken as to what the next trip would be. With only one dissenting vote it was decided that we should attempt to arrange a visit to the Richard Brothers plant.

The kinds of information these boys and girls obtained on their visits is illustrated by the following list, which they compiled after a trip to one of the plants:

### WHAT WE FOUND OUT AT THE RICHARD BROTHERS PLANT

They employed 375 men all together.
A year and a half ago they employed only 75 men.
Work is done to a very accurate dimension (2/10 of 1,000th of an inch).
All products are highly polished.
White "cutting oil" is used in some machines.
Seventy-five percent of their products are war materials. They make only parts which are sent to other factories.
All parts are cut and shaped to avoid weight.
Wages start at $26 a week. This goes up to two or three times as much.
Only three men at the plant know how to operate the threading machines. One of these works in each of the three different shifts.
Raw materials are shipped in from the steel mills.
Products are shipped out.

#### Problems

1. What will happen to this industry after the war?
2. Would that make any difference to Hillsdale and the people in Hillsdale?

Along with this listing of information there was also a good deal of graphic presentation of the ideas they had gained.

This group was used for a demonstration of discussion techniques, for which a sound moving picture, *The Plow*, supplied background. Preparation for the film had not been thorough, because it did not fit into any immediate major interest of the group; but the children demonstrated that they were interested in films of this type and that they were able to analyze it for many of its implications.

Another interest which developed spontaneously for the group was centered in the construction of a new office building in the city. A group of boys spent considerable time in observing the process and acquired a variety of interests which led to some comparatively eager study in the classroom.

*Participation by Parents.*—The responsiveness of parents in the initial interviews was matched by their continued interest throughout the laboratory school period. The parents of children in the elementary school groups were perhaps most active. They visited the school, conferred with the teachers, made telephone calls concerning specific problems, brought or sent materials of interest to the children, contributed useful supplies and equipment, and participated in a final meeting in which they discussed their reactions to the laboratory school program.

*Participation by Teachers.*—All observation of the laboratory school program and participation in it by the teachers in the workshop was voluntary. No staff member urged the participants to use the laboratory as a resource, except when individual conferences brought to his attention specific needs which could be met by observation of certain processes in the laboratory school program. The following help was given to those participants who were interested in using the laboratory schools as a resource:

1. At one of the early general meetings of the participants, there was a discussion of an agenda for workshop members wishing to observe in the laboratory school.

2. Each laboratory school group had a daily schedule of its activities.

3. Each laboratory school group placed on file in the library a copy of its daily diary report.

4. Mimeographed sheets listing "things to observe in the laboratory school" were made available to anybody wishing them.

5. The various staff members freely suggested types of observation and participation which could help individual teachers with their problems.

6. Laboratory school teachers were always ready and willing to plan conferences with individual participants, both before and after their observations.

The number of teachers who availed themselves of the laboratory school resources under this program was comparatively high, and the reports of both the participants and laboratory school teachers showed the wide variety of helps they received. A number of these appeared in the records of individual participants presented elsewhere in this chapter.

A number of the workshop participants had their own children enrolled in the laboratory school; and others brought children from the schools in which they taught, so that they might have an opportunity to observe them under the laboratory school circumstances.

### ACTIVITIES OF SPECIAL GROUPS AND COMMITTEES

*Noon Meals.*—Plans for the noon meals were made by a committee selected by the workshop group. The administration had arranged to have kitchen and cafeteria resources available, and had identified

personnel which could be engaged to prepare the meals; but to conclude the arrangements for the noon meal program, if there was to
be one, was the function of this committee.

The workshop group felt that it would be helpful to have the noon
meal together, and instructed the committee to make the necessary
provisions. The first arrangement they made was one in which the
entire cost for lunch was twenty-five cents a person. Because of
increasing costs of food, this program did not prove satisfactory, and

*Picnics furnished opportunities for outdoor recreation. They were the
scene of many informal conferences and discussions held under the trees.*

arrangements were then made to pay the costs for service out of
general workshop funds, leaving the charge paid by the participants
applicable entirely to the purchase of food. This transfer of costs
made it possible to provide more attractive and adequate luncheons,
and to plan for a number of well-attended noon-day picnics. Attendance at these luncheons was optional, and menus were posted a day
or two in advance; participants indicated days on which they expected to attend.

*General Recreation.*—The general recreational program of the workshop was planned to meet the convenience of those who drove long
distances as well as of those who found it necessary to maintain

their homes while they attended the workshop. The major activities, therefore, were planned either for the period directly after lunch or for some other time before 4:30. The period after lunch was used largely for group singing, instrumental music, ping pong, arts and crafts, shuffle board, a few organized games, and general conversation.

Picnics were held from time to time at the various city parks. The Hillsdale chamber of commerce gave a dinner for the workshop participants at the country club, where there were facilities for swimming, baseball, golf, dancing, and ping pong. A recreational evening was provided when the staff gave a picnic supper for the group. Near the end of the workshop program an evening party was built around the "Gay Nineties" theme, and held in the gymnasium. This party featured square dancing, amusing skits by workshop participants, games, and special music provided by an old-time fiddler.

In addition to these general recreational activities, smaller groups planned for their own recreation. One group had a picnic and steak roast at Pokagaon State Park near Angola, Indiana, attended by about half the workshop participants. Members took part in the general city recreational program on invitation from its various directors.

*Arts and Crafts.*—The arts and crafts program was organized so as to provide adequate leadership for any teacher who wanted to participate. It also provided opportunities for the children in the laboratory school to use its facilities. It assisted teachers by demonstrating teaching materials and techniques in arts and crafts, giving teachers an opportunity to learn to work with a variety of materials which they could later use in their own teaching situations, providing an opportunity for the relaxing experiences of working with arts and crafts materials, and providing an opportunity for teachers to observe and to work with children by participating with them in arts and crafts activities.

No definite time was set aside during which teachers were expected to work in the crafts shop. They were free to use its facilities whenever they desired and to work with whatever materials they preferred. The staff member in charge of the work gave freely of his time and instructional helps in filling the needs of each individual teacher. The possibilities of work in the crafts shop were discussed in general meetings; a master sheet of possible activities was posted on the bulletin board, and workshop participants chose those they desired. Staff members frequently invited participants to work with them or to hold conferences while the staff members were working at some craft. The interest value of the arts and crafts program to the workshop group was demonstrated by the increased use of its facilities as the workshop progressed. The first week found a small group beginning work there. Each succeeding week saw not only an increase in the size of the group, but also an increase in the amount of time that the individual members spent in craft work. The materials most used were wood, metal, leather, and craft strip. Most of the work with them was on the basis of things which the individual participant might do for herself. A few, however, used the shop to make articles for furnishing or decorating their school rooms. Occasionaly doubts were raised as to the advisability of having the children and the adults use the shop together, but many teachers reported that they had been able to gain considerable knowledge by working with the children and to make friends with the children on an easy social basis.

*Integration of the Program.*—Because the workshop program was organized around special interest groups, a committee was chosen whose function it would be to plan for an over-all integration of the program. This committee was composed of representatives from each of the special interest groups and of the faculty. They met periodically to coordinate the plans of the groups, and to harmonize their responsibilities for disseminating information.

*The School Improvement Group.*—Much has been said of the progress of certain individuals and certain groups of workshop participants in the solution of their problems under the discussions of the activities of the groups in which these people found their major interests. Attention should be directed to the progress of a group of rural teachers who were interested in improving their schools. Most of the teachers in this group were enrolled in sociology and in education, and they worked together throughout the summer in attempting to devise ways by which a program of arousing the public could be put into effect. At first their interest was spasmodic, and certain staff members used various techniques to keep it alive and to increase their confidence in their ability to attack and solve the problem. It was not until the last two weeks of the workshop that they gained enough confidence to plan a course of action; and it was not until the last two days of the workshop that they began calling upon other resource people to assist in their planning; but those last two days were busy ones. They held conferences with the county school commissioner, the chairman of the county service council, and the director of the county health department to discuss the possibility of obtaining assistance from the W. K. Kellogg Foundation if such a program of school improvement were started. They were able to formulate a set of plans for the ensuing months which they hoped would culminate in the improvement of the rural schools of Hillsdale County. Their program included plans for a visit to the W. K. Kellogg Foundation offices in Battle Creek; for the organization of a countywide committee composed of teachers, superintendents of schools, and citizens who would be willing to help in fostering such a program of school improvement; and for an active program of informing and educating the people of the county concerning the values to be derived by making the rural schools "better homes for the boys and girls."

### INTRAWORKSHOP RELATIONS

*General Meetings of Participants.*—The general meetings of the workshop group had three functions: interpretation, socialization, and information.

1. Some meetings were planned to help the participants understand the workshop program. Most of these meetings came early in the summer and were concerned with explanation of the philosophy of the workshop, its necessary organization and planning, and similar matters that were expected to improve the participants' orientation.

2. Other meetings evoked cooperation in planning the organization of the workshop and in solving the problems that arose from time to time. Committees reported progress, and the group suggested further work for them to do. Such meetings seemed to contribute most to the development of an integrated social group.

3. A number of meetings were held to present information. At one, a group of citizens gave information about community organization and resources. At another, a teacher in the local college offered an analysis of war conditions. At a third meeting, a visiting lecturer told of the work her school was doing in child development and guidance. A sociologist, at another general meeting, described an index of social understanding. At still another meeting, representatives of textbook companies, librarians, and the county school commissioner discussed the selection of school encyclopedias.

Another means of stimulating intraworkshop relations consisted of having staff members and community associates present various materials to the major interest groups.　For example, each staff member spent at least one period, by invitation, with the group whose major interest was in English expression; the laboratory-school teachers were frequently invited to participate in the planning and discussions of certain major interest groups; the visual education materials and movies were available to all groups; rural teachers from Hillsdale County invited the county school commissioner to meet

*Wild flowers from the countryside, books from the library, placards by participants, and an identification contest stimulated interest in the flower display. Group discussions brought to light other ways of arousing interest in nature study in rural school communities.*

with them to discuss the textbooks and study outlines he recommended for use in the county; various staff members worked with individual children from the laboratory school; special materials dealing with bookmobiles, a unit on Guatamala, and exhibits of historical, arts and crafts, and photographic materials were shown to the entire group; and a demonstration of the use of movies with the junior high school group was attended by many workshop participants.

These activities gave teachers many opportunities to envision richer and more varied uses of materials in stimulating interest and in setting advantageous learning conditions. One such occurrence followed the display of a group of native wild flowers. The library was searched for means of botanical identification of the flowers and for related books, stories, and poems to be included in the display. The children in the laboratory school became interested, and the early-elementary school group decided to have its own flower display. Parents' comments noted the children's increased interest in flowers, in cultivating them, and in sharing them.

*Staff Planning.*—The staff met frequently to discuss problems of the workshop and to plan for their solution. Much of the time was spent in planning activities by which each participant could increase his skills in gaining and expressing ideas, in working with others, in identifying, analyzing, and solving his problems, and in evaluating his progress.

A review of the records of the staff meetings shows the progress made in planning. In the early meetings planning was done mostly in terms of individual conferences and the use of each participant's folder of records by the staff member responsible for advising him. At later meetings they planned to leave the record folders at a central point where all staff members might use them, and began planning "cross-reference" conferences to make the assistance of more staff members available to the participants. Still later, staff meetings were concerned with the understanding of the problems and progress of each workshop participant, and with devisings ways to help individual participants.

*Visits to the Homes of Participants.*—Understanding between staff members and workshop participants was promoted by visits to the homes of participants. At least six participants invited groups of staff members to their homes for meals or for social calls. One staff member wrote, "It certainly was enlightening to visit Mrs. C. in her home and to see the conditions under which her daily work progresses. I can appreciate her hard work and effort even more after driving twenty-five miles to her home, having seen the lack of facilities in it, and having observed her doing her share of the farm work after she has returned from the workshop."

### DEVICES AND TECHNIQUES FOR EVALUATION

Evaluation of the progress of participants was continuous. Impressions that contributed to evaluation were gained in the participants' conferences with staff members, in their summaries of daily work and of completed portions of their programs, in their informal conferences, and in their diary reports.

*The Evaluation Questionnaire.*—In addition to these evidences, the committee charged with integrating the workshop program decided to secure reports on a uniform blank from all participants. The proposed blank was discussed with the group, and it was agreed that filling out the blank should be optional and anonymous.

The committee distributed an instruction sheet with the questionnaire, stressing the helpfulness of evaluating experiences and calling attention to various techniques of evaluation. It suggested that each participant review the questionnaire carefully, that small groups might want to discuss it together, that it could be used in the various class groups, and that finally it would be helpful if each member would fill out his copy and return it to the committee. All did so.

The questionnaire was divided into four sections:

1. *Physical resources of the workshop.* The participants were asked to check the various physical resources of the workshop in terms of adequacy or inadequacy, and to suggest specific ways in which the resources might have been improved.

2. *Participation in workshop activities.* A tabular form was provided, with a list of activities accompanied by spaces for indicating the number of activities, hours spent in each, and whether the opportunities provided were excessive, about right, or inadequate. The major headings in the list were: individual activities, discussion and committee activities, individual conferences, community activities, observation and participation, social and recreational experiences, and the sharing of personal resources. Each of these headings was divided into a number of subheadings dealing with the specific activities represented.

3. *Acquisition of knowledge and changes in thinking.* A tabular form was set up, with instructions to "check in the proper space to indicate the amount of growth you believe you have made this summer in each of the areas listed." Columns were provided with headings "a great deal," "some or average," "very little." The areas listed were knowledge of subject matter, personal abilities, understanding children, improvement of teaching, and other areas of growth. Each of these areas was subdivided into specific items, as was the preceding list.

4. *Solution of problems and changing of ideas and attitudes.* The participant was requested to give subjective evidence of his problem as he thought of it when he came into the workshop, changes which occurred in his thinking and planning, definite problems he felt he had solved, and problems with which he had not received help.

### SUMMARY OF EVALUATION BY PARTICIPANTS

*Physical Resources of the Workshop.*—The group was unanimous in the opinion that rooms for meetings, classrooms, places for conferences, room for arts and craft work, library books and pamphlets, places for reading, and bibliographies were adequate for the need of the workshop. A few of the teachers felt that there was some inadequacy in the supplies for arts and crafts, the amount of observation room in the laboratory school rooms, and in the facilities for recreation. Two suggestions were made for the improvement in the physical facilities: a number of people said that the furniture was not satisfactory for the workshop group, and a few expressed the wish that an air-conditioning system could be provided.

*Informal conferences between participants and staff members were frequent.*
*Here Miss Livsey (center) has called on Mr. Bullock for help*
*in considering a participant's problem.*

*Individual Workshop Activities.*—In reporting their individual activities the workshop participants expressed surprise at the amount of reading they had been able to do. Their notations indicated that many of them had done more reading than they usually did in other summer school experiences. They expressed satisfaction with the unusually large amount of time they had been able to give to planning their individual work. Few of them had kept diaries, but those who had done so expressed the opinion that these records had been very effective in helping them analyze the progress they had made.

*Discussions and Conferences.*—All the participants felt that they had gained a great deal from their participation in discussion groups and committee activities. The greatest amount of value was thought to have been derived from informal discussions. Most participants emphasized gains from the opportunities to talk over their problems with small groups of fellow members. The participants were almost unanimous in expressing satisfaction with the helpfulness of conferences with staff members. The diaries of the staff members indicated an unusually large number of such conferences; and an examination of the progress reports of both staff members and participants indicates that these conferences probably contributed more to the growth of workshop members than any other activity.

*Community Activities.*—A large number of participants reported satisfaction with their activities in their own communities. They were especially pleased with the helps they had received by taking staff members and other workshop participants into their own schools and communities for help in analyzing their problems and for suggested solutions. Many participants stated that their visits to other schools and communities had given them more confidence in attacking their own problems.

*Laboratory School Observation.*—The amount of observation and participation in laboratory school activities was comparatively small. A number of teachers expressed the wish that they could have devoted more time to such observation. The principal reason for this lack of opportunity was the fact that some interest groups planned fixed schedules of group meetings and activities which took all their time during the laboratory school session. This feeling of need for more opportunity to observe and participate in laboratory school practices was evinced by a number of suggestions that different time schedules be arranged in future workshops. Participants who observed in the laboratory school were highly satisfied. One participant wrote:

> I have gained much in my ability to understand children and in knowledge of ways in which I can work with them more successfuly. I was able to observe the things that they did as well as the ways in which the laboratory teachers helped them to improve their work habits and skills. In addition to this I was able to get help in planning things I could do, and then I had the opportunity to actually put my plans in practice. I know that my work with children next year will be much better because of the experiences I had with them this summer.

*Social and Recreational Experiences.*—The main socializing experiences, in addition to social opportunities of the working day, were provided by the noon lunches at the workshop and the picnics. Those who participated regularly in these activities felt that they had gained many benefits from them. They were pleased with their freedom in discussing problems with staff members under the informal circumstances of a lunch or picnic. One teacher wrote, "I do not think that I would have been able to get as much help from my conferences with staff members if I hadn't already become acquainted with them during our lunch hours and picnics."

*The Sharing of Personal Resources.*—Participants reported that they received a great deal of help from others through a sharing of time, skills, ideas, and materials. More than a hundred different conferences were listed in which one participant requested and received specific kinds of help from his fellow members. Some of these conferences were suggested by staff members who recognized the contributions that certain participants could make to others. Many more were suggested by members who had already received help from individuals concerned. This program of exchanging ideas and of planning cooperatively was a potent influence in unifying the teachers of Hillsdale county. A number of groups planned to continue the sharing of ideas and experiences during the coming school year.

*Gains of Knowledge and Changes in Thinking.*—Responses to the section of the questionnaire dealing with gains and changes in thinking indicated considerable similarity for the same major interest groups. The group interested in library science recorded satisfaction with their gains in ability to organize and administer libraries, and with their increased ability to find and use resources and resource people, and to discover, clarify, and solve their own problems. They felt that they had learned much about special means of motivation and about the organization of materials for the teaching of reading. They thought they had changed little in their abilities in recreational activities and in understanding children's problems.

The group interested in sociology expressed satisfaction with the progress they had made in knowledge of sociology materials, in using resource people and materials, and in independent thinking. They cited numerous gains in the understanding of the individual differences in children and in the treatment of children's difficulties with school work. They reported improvement in dealing with reading techniques, arrangement of the schoolroom, program planning, and the organization of materials for teaching.

The group primarily interested in English reported increased ability in formal English expression and in organizing materials, planning work, thinking independently, and using community resource people. They felt that they had gained much in organizing materials for teaching and in the improvement of their techniques in the teaching of reading.

The groups interested in curriculum planning and in child development and adjustment reported gains in discovering and solving their own problems, in planning their work, and in organizing their materials. They indicated progress in developing general teaching techniques, in arrangement of the classroom, in program planning, in recognizing the developmental problems of children, and in specific techniques in teaching social studies and reading.

*Progress in Solving Problems.*—The reactions of the workshop participants to the progress they made in solving their own problem may be typified by excerpts from their reports. Speaking of the work on her problem of English, one teacher wrote, "For the first time in my life I feel sure that I can write correctly." Another member of the group reporting her experience said,

I have been sending school news for years but this is the first time I have really talked to the editor of the paper. He has helped me a lot. I can send him better materials now, and I know how interested he is in having the children do good writing.

A teacher interested in library work reported that,

Opening my school as a summer library is helping the community a great deal. It is surprising how many people come in to read a while and to take books home with them. A number of them walk from the farther parts of the district. My visits to the homes got them interested in books and it has helped me to know the people better. We are already planning on things to do next fall.

Another teacher wrote,

I never realized how little my community offered its people. There is very little social life except when the people go to free movies at W. The knowledge I have gained of the needs of the community will certainly help me in planning more activities for them this fall.

A group of teachers working together reported,

Our visits to homes and our interviews with mothers have enabled us to secure much better understandings of the problems of the children in our school.

One teacher reporting his work in guidance said,

It has been most interesting and helpful. Almost every graduate that I interviewed was serious and anxious to tell of his experiences so that I could help others. My superintendent and I both feel that the information will be very valuable in helping teachers plan for better guidance of high school students.

The superintendent who was planning a program for his school wrote,

I realize that there are many problems I haven't planned for and that many of the things I have planned for will take a long time to accomplish, but I have gained much knowledge of my job and I have much more confidence in my ability to do the things necessary to make it a success. I have a pretty definite program in mind, and I believe I can "make a go of it." I don't know what I would have done if I hadn't had the help of the workshop.

A teacher who was working on special problems of child adjustment said,

I feel that I can go back to my classroom and give J. the help he needs. I also feel much more capable of talking with his father and mother, and planning with them for the kind of a program which will help him most.

The chairman of the committee planning for rural school improvement wrote,

It has taken us a long time to gain confidence in ourselves. We felt that there was no use trying because the odds were too great. Now we are beginning to see that by working together and by using all our resources we can accomplish what we really want to do.

*General Evaluation.*—Typical comments on general evaluation, taken from the questionnaires filled out by participants are the following:

We have had a grand staff. My contacts with them have been very profitable.

I think I could get more out of another workshop. It took me nearly three weeks to find out how to go about things.

I am sorry I did not keep a diary. I can now see how much diaries have helped some other participants.

The workshop had a fine laboratory school but I just couldn't find enough time to really see it.

The workshop was too slow in starting. Many people were unprepared for such freedom.

I feel that much has been "taken in" but not assimilated. It will all come back and be valuable to me as I meet new situations.

From observations made and many experiences in the workshop I am sure that the schools of this area need a skilled librarian to provide practical suggestions and assistance in the care of school libraries.

I feel confident that I can now go ahead and enjoy my task of organizing a library.

The workshop has been very profitable, at least to me this year. It was just what I wanted but feared that I could not get.

A number of the workshop participants suggested that it might be desirable to consider future workshops on an eight-week basis. This suggestion was accompanied by a plan to allow the first five weeks for work in the special course areas, and the last three weeks for concentration on the integration of work and planning, and on the solution of the problems still needing solution.

### EVALUATION BY THE STAFF

The evaluation of the workshop made by the staff members was informal. The various staff members made comments and suggestions from time to time, and at the end of the workshop period each staff member wrote a report of his observations and suggestions. These reports contained a wide variety of information and materials dealing with the organization and physical setting of the workshop, the progress of workshop participants, the adequacy and effectiveness of the workshop program, the functioning of the staff as a group, the value of the laboratory school program, and suggested changes for future workshop. These reports are summarized in the following paragraphs.

There was general agreement that the physical setting of the workshop was adequate except in the matter of furniture. It was suggested that it might be possible to utilize a site that would stimulate more out-of-door activities.

Much evidence was submitted to show the high level of performance of the workshop participants. A number of the staff members expressed surprise not only at the amount of work individual participants did, but also at the progress many of them made in analyzing and solving their problems.

The general effectiveness of the workshop program was felt to have been high, but suggestions were made fr the improvement in specific areas. . Some staff members felt that more meetings of the entire workshop group would have helped to unify the program and to develop an esprit de corps. Others felt that the individual needs of participants were more readily identified in small groups. It was suggested by several that the arts and crafts department would have been more satisfactory if a full-time staff member had been provided for that work. There was agreement that the community resources were utilized fairly adequately.

The entire staff felt that its individual members were highly co-operative and worked together sincerely and earnestly for the best interests of the workshop. They recognized differences in viewpoints, but felt that they had achieved closer fundamental unity of view-point on many problems with which they dealt. They expressed satisfaction with the effectiveness of the staff meetings held to dis-cuss the problems of individual participants, and with the contribu-tion of these meetings to their individual work with participants.

Most staff members reported that the laboratory school program had much to contribute to teachers, and all agreed that the labora-tory-school teachers served a valuable function in helping the par-ticipants with individual and group problems. The opinion was ex-pressed that observation in the laboratory school might have been more effective if it had been organized more highly, although it was agreed that those who did observe, after planning with their advisers, utilized their opportunities very well. Many staff members were surprised at the number of participants who commented on labora-tory school activities in their diaries, but had not observed the laboratory school program.

There were some suggestions for changes in the daily program of the laboratory school. The laboratory-school teachers thought the program would have been more effective if it had not been adjusted to accommodate the children who had planned other educational experiences for the summer. They felt that very irregular attend-ance was a distinct handicap. They agreed, however, that the children had gained much, both individually and as a group, from their ex-periences, and in a number of cases they called attention to stimula-tion which had come with the return of children who had been away.

The staff considered the participation of parents and community members in the workshop very helpful, citing numerous instances to support the judgment. They were also in agreement as to the broad values derived from being able to work with the participants on problems in their own communities.

The major suggestions for future workshops dealt with integration. It was suggested that staff members should have more opportunities to become acquainted with the area before the opening of the work-shop, that the staff might well spend a longer period together in planning for the workshop, and that more devices were needed for integrating the members of the workshop.

One staff member analyzed the unique contribution of this workshop as follows:

1. The workshop was organized on the basis of principles determined by in-service teacher committees, and in light of the needs and wishes of the teachers to be served.

2. It was held in the area where teachers' problems exist and where easy contact was possible between the workshop and the local school and community.

3. It was an integral part of the year-round education of teachers, children, and parents.

*The parents of the children in the laboratory school met with the staff members to help evaluate the laboratory school program and to compile suggestions for future modifications.*

4. It was characterized by the coordination of efforts of the people in the community, the University of Michigan, the University of Chicago, and the W. K. Kellogg Foundation. The opportunity for such concerted efforts in the solution of problems where they exist is a most valuable educational innovation.

### EVALUATION BY THE COMMUNITY

Various community members expressed their judgments of the workshop in terms of their special interests. The members of the teacher education committee who had the major responsibility of organizing and planning for the workshop were unanimous in their agreement that the values which the teachers derived from their experiences were well worth while, and in their report on the workshop they endorsed the request of the teachers that another workshop be considered for the summer of 1942. The superintendent of schools, while not a member of the workshop, visited it frequently, and praised its values. He brought members of his school board to observe with him, and at the close of the workshop said, "I believe that the summer school has been a good thing for the children. If conditions warrant it, I think we should consider having one next year whether there is a workshop or not." Two members of the board expressed the same opinion. The principal of the building in which the workshop was held said, "It has certainly helped some of the children who needed just this kind of an experience." The interest of parents was demonstrated by their activities in connection with the laboratory school. In addition to the casual everyday contacts, many parents planned conferences with the laboratory-school teachers. The following comments noted in these individual conferences with various parents typify their reactions:

> I know that this has been the best kind of a school experience F has had yet.
> The school has done much for M. She needed just this experience.
> V was very happy in the summer school. She has learned many useful things.
> G feels that you took such a personal interest in him.
> I have definitely seen a change for the better in C's personality since the summer school began.

During the last week of the summer school all the parents were invited to attend a meeting to discuss their reactions to the summer school program. At this meeting the following questions were raised:

> 1. Do you feel that you child has benefited by his experience in the laboratory school?
> 2. What was your reaction to the initial parent interview?
> 3. Would you be interested in having your child attend another laboratory school session next year?
> 4. What things could another laboratory school do for your child that you feel were not attempted or developed this year?
> 5. Have you noticed any changes in your child's attitudes or habits due to his laboratory school experience.

Fifteen parents attended the meeting. All of them felt that the individual children had benefited by the laboratory school experience, and many of them made statements similar to those listed above. Most parents felt that the initial interviews had been valuable to them, and a number said that they would like to have a final interview with the laboratory school teachers before the workshop closed. They requested that the teachers review with them, at this meeting, the notes taken at the initial parent interview, and that the parents be given assistance and suggestions in ways of continuing the work that the laboratory school had started with the children. About twelve parents availed themselves of this opportunity.

The parents were unanimous in their desire for other summer school experiences for their children. Most of them felt that the next experience would be even more valuable than the first. There were also numerous suggestions that the parents should have more help in understanding the laboratory-school program before it started. One mother said, "Few parents knew anything about the laboratory school. I think that another year there should be more educating of the community before the workshop begins to operate." A father said, "If parents were interviewed as early as January, many of them would be interested in having their children in the laboratory school and would be willing to help plan a program for a more thorough study of the community." The only suggestion for emphasis in the laboratory school program was that more attention be given to music.

The reports indicated that the Hillsdale Community Workshop was a valuable experience for participants, children, parents, community members, and staff. It contributed to the development of all of its members, and it aided in the solution of many of the problems which they faced, both as individuals and as groups. The progress made gave every indication of continuing beyond the end of the workshop.

CHAPTER VI

# GENERALIZATIONS FROM EXPERIENCE[1]

In order that others may benefit most from the experience in the Michigan Community Health Project with community workshops for teachers, it seemed advisable to conclude this volume with a brief summary of the generalizations which two years of experimentation have suggested. Throughout this period of exploration there was never any thought of pitting one type of course against another, one type of workshop against another, or of proving that the community workshop was better than or not as good as certain other methods of in-service or pre-service education of teachers. The project moved forward on the hypothesis that the community workshop had certain unique contributions to make as one phase or segment of a broad program of teacher education. The first problem, then, was to identify as well as possible these peculiar values of a community workshop. This was done in Chapter I. The second problem was one of planning and managing the community workshop in such a way as to bring these values to fruition.

The primary function of this monograph is to describe how this planning was done and to give a detailed description of what actually took place in the four community workshops conducted during the summer of 1941. Out of this experience we have learned certain lessons which might be helpful to others who see merit in the community workshop and who wish to experiment with it. These lessons are summarized in this chapter.

### MEMBERSHIP

The four community workshops of 1941 were planned to meet the needs of teachers of a seven-county area. The types of problems to be stressed in each workshop were different so as to give a broader range of selection by individual teachers. Analysis of the registration in each workshop revealed that by far the majority of those in attendance came from the county in which the workshop was located.

[1] This chapter was prepared by Dr. Henry J. Otto, who was Consultant in Education to the W. K. Kellogg Foundation from 1935 to 1942. Dr. Otto resigned his position to accept a Graduate professorship in the School of Education at the University of Texas with duties beginning in February, 1942.